Warwick University Ca

Behind the Planter's Back

Lower class responses to marginality in
Bequia Island, St Vincent

Neil Price

MACMILLAN CARIBBEAN

© Neil Price, 1988

All rights reserved. No reproduction, copy or transmission
of this publication may be made without written permission.
No paragraph of this publication may be reproduced, copied
or transmitted save with written permission or in accordance
with the provisions of the Copyright Act 1956 (as amended).
Any person who does any unauthorised act in relation to
this publication may be liable to criminal prosecution and
civil claims for damages.

First published 1988

Published by *Macmillan Publishers Ltd*
London and Basingstoke
*Associated companies and representatives in Accra,
Auckland, Delhi, Dublin, Gaborone, Hamburg, Harare,
Hong Kong, Kuala Lumpur, Lagos, Manzini, Melbourne,
Mexico City, Nairobi, New York, Singapore, Tokyo*

ISBN 0-333-47460-0

Printed in Hong Kong

British Library Cataloguing in Publication Data
Price, Neil
 Behind the planter's back: lower class
 responses to marginality in Bequia Island,
 St. Vincent. — (Warwick University
 Caribbean Studies).
 1. St. Vincent and the Grenadines.
 Bequia Island. Black
 persons. Social conditions.
 I. Title   II. Series
 305.8′96′0729844

ISBN 0-333-47460-0

Cover based on a painting by Aubrey Williams
presented to the Centre for Caribbean Studies, University of Warwick

Series preface

The Centre for Caribbean Studies at the University of Warwick was founded in 1984 in order to stimulate academic interest and research in a region which, in spite of its creative vitality and geopolitical importance, has not received the academic recognition it deserves in its own right. In the past, the Caribbean has tended to be subsumed under either Commonwealth or Latin American Studies. The purpose of the Centre is to teach and research on the region (which includes those circum-Caribbean areas sharing similar traits with the islands) from a comparative, cross-cultural and inter-disciplinary perspective. It is intended that this Pan-Caribbean approach will be reflected in the publication each year of papers from the Centre's annual symposium as well as in other volumes.

Each year it is planned to include among these a study of a small community as the Caribbean cannot be fully understood without considering its many micro societies. This is the second of such studies published in this series. Based on extensive fieldwork it gives useful insights into conducting research in a small community which has a healthy distrust of outsiders. Set within a broad discussion of forms of dependency it shows the interpenetration and interaction of market forces today with residual pre-capitalist forms of production. The analysis moves from the plantation mode to its replacement after Emancipation by sharecropping and then to fishing. The final contemporary period deals with the impact of tourism and real estate development, arguably the most destructive form of dependence to which the islanders have been subjected. This study raises crucial questions faced by all Caribbean societies but especially those of the smaller islands, and is a valuable contribution to the often ignored responses of the marginalised.

Prof. Alistair Hennessy
Series Editor

Warwick University Caribbean Studies

Andrew Sanders
The Powerless People – The Amerindians of the Corentyne River

Editors: Jean Besson and Janet Momsen
Land and Development in the Caribbean

Kelvin Singh
The Bloodstained Tombs – The Muharram Massacre in Trinidad 1884

David Nicholls
From Dessalines to Duvalier – Race, Colour and National Independence

Editors: Malcolm Cross and Gad Heuman
Labour in the Caribbean – From Emancipation to Independence

Harry Goulbourne
Teachers, Education and Politics in Jamaica, 1892–1972

Neil Price
Behind the Planter's Back – Lower Class Responses to Marginality in Bequia Island, St Vincent

Douglas Hall
In Miserable Slavery – Thomas Thistlewood in Jamaica, 1750–86

Acknowledgements

Fieldwork for this study was undertaken on a UK Social Science Research Council research studentship (79/20991/SSA) between March 1980 and June 1981 and subsequently formed the basis of, in 1984, a Ph.D. thesis at the University of Bristol.

I would like to thank first and foremost the kind people of Lower Bay, Bequia (pronounced 'Beckway') without whose patience and tolerance none of this would have been possible. I wish to acknowledge particularly the courage and resolution shown by the community in the face of Hurricane Allen in August 1980, when many homesteads, crops, boats and nets were damaged or lost.

Encouragement for writing this book came from a number of colleagues and friends. I would like to thank in particular Professor Alistair Hennessy, Professor Robin Cohen, Professor Chris Harris and Professor Meghnad Desai. Support and advice on the formulation of the text came from a great many – but I am forever grateful to Dr Rohit Barot, Dr Mick Lineton, Dr Philip Harding and Mr Roy Dellow.

This book is dedicated to my parents Peggy and Elwyn and to Caroline.

Contents

	Series preface	iii
	Maps	viii
	Preface	xii
	Introduction	1
CHAPTER 1	The changing patterns of dependence: modes and forms of production in Bequia from pre-European settlement to 1959	6
CHAPTER 2	Contemporary forms of dependence and interdependence in Bequia	27
CHAPTER 3	The Lower Bay economy	50
CHAPTER 4	Household and family in Lower Bay	102
CHAPTER 5	Kinship and friendship networks: extra-domestic relationships in Lower Bay	139
CHAPTER 6	Lower Bay lower class culture	160
CHAPTER 7	Tourism and real estate: forces of change in Lower Bay	206
	Conclusion	245
	Appendices	251
	Bibliography	264
	Index	269

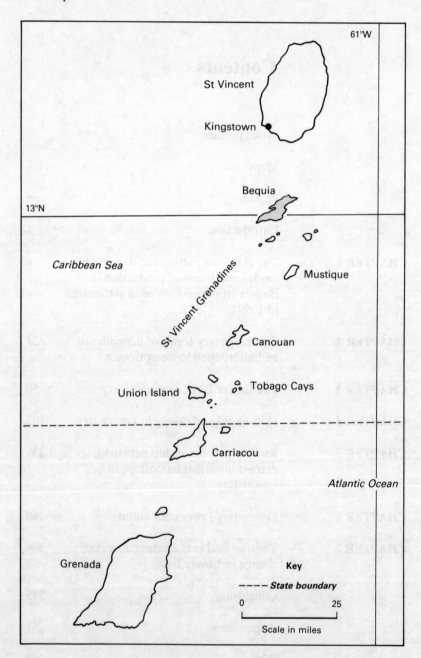

Map 1 St Vincent and Grenada

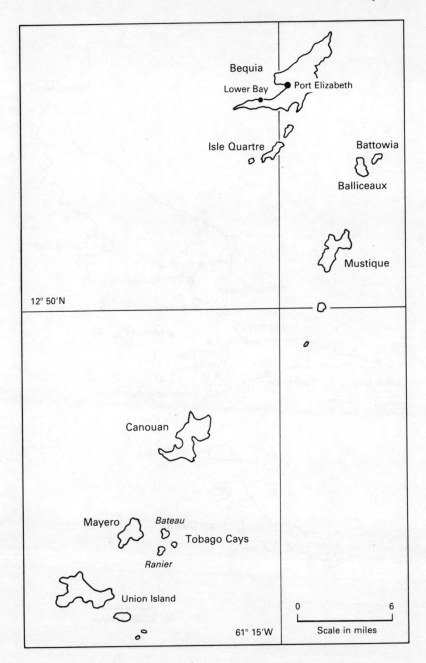

Map 2 St Vincent Grenadines

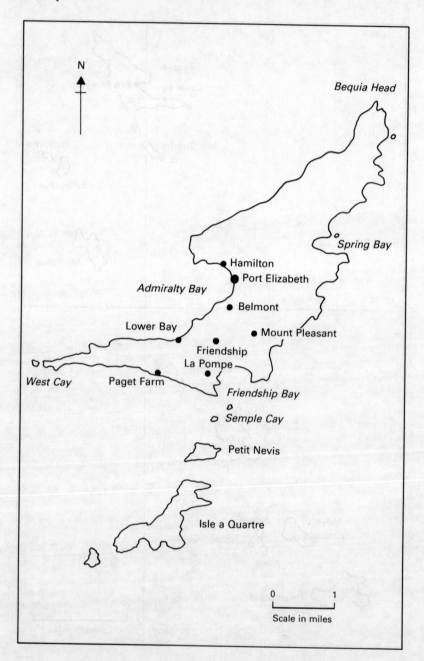

Map 3 Bequia

Maps xi

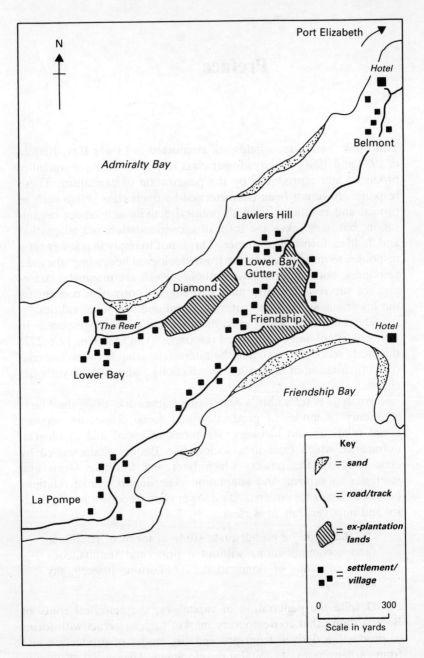

Map 4 Lower Bay

Preface

This book, based upon fieldwork conducted in Lower Bay, Bequia in 1980 and 1981, explores lower class responses to the marginality produced and reproduced by the penetration of capitalism. These responses have not been characterised by overt class action such as protest and resistance through political activity and labour organisation, but have taken the form of accommodation and adaptation and 'hidden' forms of resistance. This is not to imply that lower class responses to marginality derive from ideological hegemony: they are responses, both material and symbolic, which are pragmatic strategies for survival. It is not meant to suggest normative consent by the lower classes to their material, social and symbolic realities.

By considering lower class material and symbolic responses in terms of 'silent and unorganised responses' (van Onselen, 1976:277) this study sets out to examine the interrelationship between material (the organisation of labour and production) and cultural (symbolic) change.

Analysis is set within a materialist framework, using the Marxist theory of modes of production and social classes to examine social relations and ideology. Relations of social and ideological dominance which exist in a society like Bequia characterised by classes, reveal the powers which limit and facilitate forms and strategies of survival and adaptation. The importance of relations between classes for understanding lower class responses to marginality and impoverishment is clear:

> ... there can be no adequate study of forms of resistance (and accommodation) without a prior and simultaneous study of forms of domination ... (Turton, 1986:39, my brackets).

Despite the penetration of capitalism, the empirical study of Bequia shows that contemporary market forces interact with forms of production derived from precapitalist modes of production and from earlier phases of capitalist development. The crucial distinction between modes and forms of production lies in the notion of a totality: a mode of production is a totality of social relations (ideological, political and economic) in which the mode of appropriation of surplus labour and the specific way in which the means of production are socially distributed, the relations of production, are dominant (see Hindess and Hirst, 1975:10). Forms of production refer to the economic sphere only, and as such are not autonomous categories: in their contemporary format they are influenced by the earlier modes of production and stages of capitalist development from which they are derived. The capitalist mode of production (CMP) is dominant in the Bequia social formation. Only by subordinating other modes and forms and by appropriating their labour power and means of labour can the capitalist mode reproduce itself.

The dominant position of the capitalist mode means that Bequia is characterised by the existence of classes. A dichotomy of classes is evident: an exploiting class (the owners and controllers of the means of production; the ex-planter and merchant class who are politically and ideologically dominant) and an exploited class (the non-owners of means of production in the CMP i.e. the bulk of the population of the island who are politically and ideologically dominated). But, as Poulantzas (1973:71) stresses:

> In the theoretical examination of a 'pure' mode of production ... we see that its effects on the supports is reflected in a distinction between two classes ... However, a social formation consists of an overlapping of several modes of production, one of which holds the dominant role, and it therefore presents more classes than the 'pure' mode of production. This extension of the number of classes ... is strictly related to (a) the modes of production in this formation, and (b) the concrete forms taken on by their combination.

Although in Bequia the dominant characteristics of class relations are capitalist, the residual characteristics of derived forms of production are persistent: communal, peasant, sharecropping and petty-commodity production. The hierarchy of *actual* classes in the island is not simply those of owners of means of production – non-owners, but one in which a dominant (ex-planter/merchant) class owns and controls the productive means and markets of non-capitalist as well as capitalist production, and in which classes such as peasant producers, sharecroppers, petty-commodity fishermen, artisans and small entrepreneurs are dependent upon, and thus exploited by, this small powerful class.

The concept of class is that prescribed by Poulantzas (1975). Social classes are not the sum of the individuals of which they are composed; i.e. classes are not necessarily exclusive categories of people, for classes are determined by social relations. In this sense a lower class person in Bequia is periodically a peasant producer (production for consumption), a sharecropper, a commodity fisherman, an entrepreneur, and a wage labourer. The co-existence of the CMP with residual forms of production and the precarious position of marginality experienced by the subordinate classes means that the CMP periodically draws labour from other forms of production for its maintenance and reproduction.

The analysis is further concerned with the symbolic sphere through which lower class Bequarians make sense of their social world. Although the symbolic sphere is rooted in the material order, it takes on what Parkin (1971:26) has termed '... an existential quality and so in turn reacts upon this (material) order' (my brackets). The dominant ex-planter class maintains its position of power and privilege by not only controlling the means of production of wealth but also through control of the means of production of discourse. The lower classes are unable to generalise and articulate their life experiences, so their culture (the totality of beliefs, values, norms and practices: the lower-class symbolic meaning system) is expressed in terms derived from the culture of the ex-planter class (the dominant meaning system).

In analysing the relationship between lower class culture and the material order, ideology is a crucial concept. Ideology in this respect refers to a system of ideas derived from the existing structures of power and as such is not an autonomous category. Ideology is a partial and systematically distorted account of the world, capable of generating high commitment and serving to justify and generate values, norms, ideas and practices. The ideologies contained in the dominant meaning system of the ex-planter class contain moral orders clearly at odds with the reality of lower class life experiences. My concern is specifically with the ways in which lower class culture, which exists as a product of the symbolic (moral) order derived partially from earlier modes of material production, promotes accommodative responses and 'hidden' resistance to inequality, powerlessness and low status.

Introduction

Bequia island

Bequia is an irregularly-shaped, seven square mile island in the former British colonial state of St Vincent and the Grenadines in the Caribbean (see Map 1). Lying ten miles south of Kingstown, the commercial and administrative capital of the state, Bequia is the largest and northern-most of the St Vincent Grenadine islands, supporting a population of approximately 5,000 people living in scattered hillside settlements. It is an island of sharply rising hills, few flat lands, poor soil quality (with the exception of the foreign-owned land to the north), dense cedar forests and sporadic rainfall: factors that contribute to the low level of agricultural activity and lack of crop variation and animal husbandry. Maritime activities, including boat building, fishing and seamanship, seasonal and/or temporary employment with foreign-owned and controlled enterprises, emigrant remittances and entrepreneurship constitute the means of livelihood for most lower class Bequarian households.

The peripheral position of the Bequia economy in the world capitalist system and the consequent fluctuation in wage labour opportunities for the majority of the lower classes makes economic activity in the residual forms of pre-capitalist production, such as small-scale peasant production, sharecropping and fishing, essential. It is in this context that 'community' as a legacy of earlier modes of production remains a significant category for the lower classes.

Lower Bay community

Lower Bay community encompasses the village of Lower Bay, the scattered hillside settlement at Lawler's Hill, and the north-western section of Friendship, known locally as Lower Bay Gutter, to where many kinsfolk of Lower Bay village families migrated in the 1960s under pressure of land shortage and overpopulation (see Map 4). Lower Bay community demonstrates internal characteristics, in the form of interdependent relationships of an enduring quality and structure, together with a conscious recognition of membership by the inhabitants of the three settlements, which are quite distinct from relationships and identifications with the social and economic world outside the community. Several economic activities within residual forms of production entail a division of labour organised around interdependent and adaptive relationships between members of kinship and friendship networks distributed between all three settlements, e.g.:

(i) petty-commodity fishing, where crews are drawn from the three settlements. The marketing and distribution of catches further reflect the interrelations between groups from the village, Lawler's Hill and Lower Bay Gutter (see pp. 76–89);

(ii) sharecropping, which is characterised by the apportioning of labour and resources between women from the three settlements (see pp. 89–95);

(iii) communal activities in construction and maintenance of houses, fishing equipment, boats, etc. which are based on reciprocal labour-exchange relationships between members of friendship networks drawn from the three settlements, although such labour exchange is on the decline (see pp. 95–98).

Subject to the capitalist division of labour and international market forces, Bequarians in the three settlements retain a distinctive character as a community in relation to work activities in the residual forms of production.

Individuals from the three settlements further express a strong sense of affiliation to the local community. 'Lower Bay' is a term used nominally and contextually by inhabitants of the three settlements, and by outsiders, to denote membership of the community. Categorically, it refers to a sense of belonging: a perception of 'we' by members of the settlements. The frame of reference for informal group membership/affilation within which individuals in Bequia operate cognitively is a complex and contextual one, and this is discussed in more detail in Chapters 2 and 6 below. But in general, the expression 'she come from Lowbay' refers to a person living in the *community* of Lower Bay.

Community members, engaged in mutually interdependent work activities and sharing a common sense of belonging, further express and demonstrate their affinity through community practices such as kinship and friendship networks, Friendly Societies, Church activities and sport and leisure activities which are referred to in subsequent chapters.

The opening chapter is an historical analysis of changes in modes of production in Bequia since settlement in the nineteenth century. It demonstrates that the position of marginality and dependence experienced by the lower class population is a consequence of historical inequalities as they developed locally. The transitions in the Bequia social formation which have heightened its dependence on international capital have created a number of co-existent forms of production which present themselves as an 'economic palimpsest' currently subordinated to the capitalist mode of production (CMP), which relies upon such forms for its continued existence and reproduction.

Having located the island system of production structurally and historically, the remainder of the book concentrates on the responses, social, economic and symbolic, of the lower classes in Lower Bay to inequality, exploitation and suffering, by asking the question: what are the outcomes of changes in production relations and how do the lower classes respond to the harsh realities which they face in their social life as a result of such changes? The analysis is organised into the following chapters.

Chapter 2 discusses the mutually dependent and interdependent nature of production within and between island settlements, providing illustrative material on the dominance of international capital. The chapter begins with a sociological profile of the island documenting the differential access to employment opportunities, markets and means of production experienced by localised island settlements. Inherent in the chapter is the relationship between class and state, specifically the position of the dominant classes in Bequia and of expatriate entrepreneurs and speculators in state politics.

Chapter 3 is a detailed account of the political-economy of Lower Bay, locating it within the island economy and the global division of labour. It makes use of the case study method to demonstrate that capitalist relations of production are combined with forms of economic activity embedded in the traditional division of labour to cause marginality, dependence, impoverishment and inequality amongst the lower classes. In documenting lower class resistance and other responses to poverty, attention is paid to population movements – specifically migration out of Lower Bay – caused by recent land shortages. Access to land remains important for the marginal lower classes as a means of subsistence in the residual economic forms, as does the household and kin/friendship networks.

Chapter 4 concentrates on household organisation in the context of changes in production relations and also relies on case study material. The intrahousehold shifts in power from men to women in periods of economic transition form the basis of the chapter: household form being directly related to material factors. Matrifocality, which includes child-shifting and parental role replacement, as an accommodative response to impoverishment and marginality, is seen as a manifestation of limited lower class access to means of production and wage labour.

Chapter 5 extends the analysis of lower class resistance and responses to political-economic marginality and dependence, analysing extra-domestic social and economic exchange relationships through patterns of kinship and friendship networks. Fixed kinship groups engaged in corporate activity are absent in Bequia and formal kinship bonds are lacking. Consequently, personal alliances between kin and non-kin in the form of networks provide flexible and adaptive responses to resources of a shifting and impermanent nature. Networks of dyadic relations link the household to external economic and political centres in the absence of effective state bureaucracies.

Lower class practices discussed up to this point include work, household form, mating patterns, mutual aid and reciprocity. Such practices are often at odds with the notions of properness and worthfulness contained in the dominant ideology of the ex-planter class. Chapter 6 examines the ways in which lower class culture carefully orders ideas to make living experience meaningful for the plebeians. An essential concept in this analysis is suppression of discourse, by which the dominant class inhibits the articulation of lower class experience into an objectivated system. As such lower class culture expresses itself as a negotiated or 'stretched' version of the dominant meaning system (Parkin, 1971), reflecting the powerlessness of the lower classes.

Chapter 7 analyses the nature of foreign investment in Bequia and the consequences of the international division of labour for plebeian life chances in Lower Bay, as expressed through tourism and expatriate residency. The continued presence of representatives of metropolitan capital, such as property speculators, involved in capital investment in tourist and real estate enterprises, heightens feelings of resentment, dissatisfaction and inequality amongst the lower classes. The chapter documents the contexts in which such perceptions are expressed, and the potential of lower class actions for influencing structural change.

I conclude with a brief chapter which pulls together the main theoretical threads, and attempts to articulate the dynamic interaction between production relations and ideology in Lower Bay.

Introduction 5

Notes

Throughout the script I use pseudonyms and initials to protect the identity of islanders past and present. I have chosen to express informants' dialogue in the creole. I am unaware of any written Bequia creole and so I have relied upon phonetic representation of the vernacular.

CHAPTER 1

The changing patterns of dependence: modes and forms of production in Bequia from pre-European settlement to 1959

Modes of production, social formation and classes

This chapter traces the history of Bequia up to 1959, using mode of production and class relations as a basis to explain the transition that the system of production has undergone in the course of two hundred years.

A mode of production consists of the relationship between primary producers and those who own and/or control the means of production, and as such is an articulated combination of relations and forces of production structured by the paramounce of the relations of production (Hindess and Hirst, 1975:9). By considering the interrelationships between forms and modes of production (in the context of the development of the CMP) the chapter is concerned with the crucial role played by international capital, as a form of external control and influence, in the development of the island. As such, the relationship between Bequia and other social formations is pertinent and requires analysis of the class relations at specific moments in the history of the island.

Poulantzas (1975) stresses that the classes in any social formation only exist in the context of the relations of the formation with other formations. In the case of Bequia it is the supremacy of the capitalist mode of production at the international level which describes and maintains the form and character of the CMP and the residual forms of production that exist within Bequia society:

> 'Uneven development is produced by the articulation within the social formation between the capitalist mode of production, as it reproduces itself, and these other modes and forms of production' (Poulantzas, 1975:43).

The relations of dominance which bind Bequia to the European and North American economies are reproduced within the Bequia system of production. In this respect, as will be shown in this chapter, the forms of domination that characterise the classes in power in these dominant social formations express themselves in a specific manner within the organisation of class relationships within Bequia society:

> 'This domination corresponds to forms of exploitation ... in which the popular masses of the dominated formations are exploited by the classes in power in the dominant formations: an exploitation linked to that which they experience from their own ruling classes' (Poulantzas, ibid.:44).

Applied to Bequia, relationships of domination and exploitation are determined by and expressed through ownership and control of the means of production by multinationals and by the island-based ex-planter/merchant class. It is the global position of Bequia, situated in a relationship of dependence on, and domination by, these external powers (at the level of international capital) that requires a discussion of external control in the context of transitions in the system of production at island level.

European expansion and domination

1 Plantation sugar production: the slavery mode

Before 1720 Bequia was uninhabited, used by Carib Indians from St Vincent as a source of timber for canoe construction, the gathering of wild fruits and vegetables, and as a camp site for fishing expeditions (see Young, 1795). The period 1720-1762 saw the establishment of French plantations on the island of St Vincent and the first small holdings on Bequia. French settlement was the direct result of the Carib Wars of 1719, in St Vincent.[1] After the war a treaty signed between the French and the victorious Black Caribs of southern St Vincent gave the French rights to land on the east and west coasts of the island; and French colonisers arrived from Grenada (which had been under French control since 1674).

In 1762 St Vincent was captured by the English and grants of land were made available for British settlement in St Vincent, Bequia and other Grenadine islands. Planters came from Barbados,

Antigua and Nevis where plantation-production based on slavery was well established.

Slavery, although incorporated into international capitalist exchange and, as such, a stage in the development of capitalism in the region, existed as a pre-capitalist mode of production:

> ... based upon a particular combination of capital, land and labour power. The basic contradiction in slavery was not that of capitalism, between social production and private appropriation of the product, but the fact that the slave combined in person both labour power and fixed capital (Post, 1979:22-23).

The expropriation of capital from British West Indian islands under slavery was necessary for the development and consolidation of a new industrial capitalist mode of production in Britain. The islands' fundamental contradiction during slavery was their role as producers of raw materials, a role directly created by the colonial power, and the control that power had over the disposal of the plantation products on the world market. Slave-based sugar production in the West Indies, and the southern United States, appeared as a function of the demand for consumption items by the European metropolitan countries. Plantations were the effect of the international division of labour created by the needs of capitalist industry and the growth of the world market.

The wars between European colonial power during the sixteenth to eighteenth centuries need to be seen as the consquences of expansionist policies, the search for foreign produce, aimed at establishing and consolidating the unilateral transfers of capital, used primarily for the furthering of European industrial development. Britain, having gained a further raw material producer in St Vincent, concentrated its war efforts on Grenada, which was captured and placed under Crown control later in 1762 when the Grenadines were divided between St Vincent and Grenada, a division that has remained politically intact to this day.

By 1776 there were four sugar cane plantations in Bequia, worked by African slaves, and 22 small holdings cultivating cotton which had been introduced from Carriacou in the Granada Grenadines (see Anon Report, 1776). Valentine Morris, the then Governor of the state of St Vincent and the Grenadines, in his published *Memoirs* (1776) provides information on the development of plantations in Bequia. The first of these plantations was owned by the Warner family[2] although a French settler by the name of Lafayette, who had remained on Bequia after the defeat by the English, was granted land by the Crown and established a large estate in the south known as Derrick or Paget Farm estate (see Shephard, 1831, Appendix VI).

Despite wars, insurrections and changes in colonial control in St Vincent over the next thirty years,[3] by the early 1800s the plantation system was well established, and St Vincent was producing over 32 million pounds of sugar a year. Although production was reaching full levels on St Vincent, Bequia's planters were experiencing hardship. By 1828 the island's plantations numbered nine, and recorded their highest annual production figures of just 907,300 lbs (Shephard, 1831, Appendix VI). The forces of production within the slave-plantation economy meant that the plantation was never a stable or viable institution in Bequia[4] because:

(i) all but two of the estates were absentee-owned, run by overseers with little or no interest in the welfare of the slaves or the conditions of the estates;
(ii) there were continuous market variations and price fluctuations for sugar cane; and
(iii) there were serious environmental restrictions such as lack of rainfall,[5] shortage of gently sloping or flat lands, and soil erosion resulting from planter deforestation (Adams, 1976:11).

Despite some agricultural diversification in the early colonial period, when small holdings were producing and exporting cotton, indigo and cacao as well as sugar, by 1831 the only exports from the island were plantation products of rum, molasses and sugar cane (St Vincent Blue Books, 1831). A small number of sheep and goats was recorded as being sold in the St Vincent slave market.

Monopolisation of fertile land by the planters saw small-scale production and diversification of crops give way to plantation dominance in Bequia during the later eighteenth century. Despite the non-viability of many of the estates in Bequia during slavery, the slave mode of production appeared characteristic of plantation production throughout the British Caribbean: sugar production having been transformed from a domestic consumption crop (one of many) to a single export crop, through the polarisation of society into a small ruling class with control over not only production but also the aesthetic, moral, social and religious lives of the slaves. However, unlike slavery in the larger islands, which developed in response to a labour-demand following the eradication of indigenous Indian populations, Bequia planters had no such indigenous population with which to contend when they gained access to land at a time when the slave trade was well organised and firmly established. Initially the planters worked the slaves that had accompanied them from Barbados, Nevis and Antigua; it was only when production increased and monopolisation of land became effective that planters became directly involved in the 'triangular' trade, importing slaves from Africa.

Hindess and Hirst (1975:157) discuss the development of slave production in North America and the Caribbean in three phases, an analysis that seems particularly valuable for understanding the development in Bequia. Phase 1, characterised by non-capitalist settlement, involved slaves merely supplementing the labour of the settlers in the cultivation of farms and estates on which production was primarily for subsistence; only a small surplus entering the international market. During the early period of settlement in Bequia small-holdings were predominant, little or no surplus left the island, and crop diversification was practised and encouraged.

Phase 2 (Hindess and Hirst, *ibid.*) refers to the large scale production of sugar for sale on European markets by means of plantations worked by slaves, with slave labour purchasable as a commodity. This was characteristic of early nineteenth century production in Bequia. Due to late settlement this phase was considerably shorter than elsewhere in the Caribbean. Cotton production, to supply the demands for raw materials for European capitalist industrial production (Hindess and Hirst's Phase 3) was a phase that Bequia entered into long after Emancipation, and was, as we shall see below, unviable and shortlived.

2 Post-Emancipation peasant and sharecropping production

Unsurprisingly, then, the plantation system failed to survive the effects of Emancipation in 1838, as Bequia's planters were faced with acute labour shortages and a decline in the markets and prices for sugar. Ex-slaves left the estates, some to squat in the non-plantation lands between Friendship and Paget Farm Estates where they represented the first post-slavery peasant production in Bequia. However, the majority emigrated to Trinidad, whose planters offered free passage, rent-free chattel houses, gardens for growing provisions, and daily rations of food as well as basic 'wages'. The extent of the exodus from Bequia and other Grenadine islands is illustrated by the total population of the St Vincent Grenadines declining from 3,000 in 1835 (St Vincent Blue Book, 1835) to 1,933 in 1851 (St Vincent Blue Book, 1851). Frank (1976) lists the slave population of Bequia in 1831 as 1,237 and the *total* population of the island as only 969 in 1871.[6]

The lifting of preferential duties on West Indian sugar by the British government in 1848 and 1854 meant that Bequia planters could no longer compete with the low priced sugar produced elsewhere.[7] Production fell in 1854 to 206,838 lbs (St Vincent Blue Book, 1854), just 22 per cent of the 1828 level. (By 1931 there were only five acres of land under sugar production in Bequia [Abstracts of the Census of St Vincent, 1931]).

Monopolisation of land by the planter class continued during the immediate post-Emancipation period: peasant squatters on marginal and non-productive lands remained dependent on the estates for their livelihood, despite their engagement in household and communal production. Although the fleeing from plantations can be seen as resistance to plantation policies (see Scott, 1986:2), household and communal production left the squatters on the margins of the productive system and vulnerable to exploitation. The result was that by 1871, all but 15 per cent of the island's working population (see below) were forced back onto the estates to work as sharecroppers whilst tending small gardens and raising limited numbers of livestock.

The system of production at this stage was dominated by sharecropping: the two classes present being the planter (exploiting) class and the sharecropper (exploited) class. A class of peasant-producers also existed: peasant production being subordinated to and articulated with the sharecropping form of production through the appropriation of labour power and means of labour from the peasant sector. The marginality of land meant that all classes, except the planter and other land-owning classes, were dependent upon access to land through sharecropping for their means of livelihood.

Sharecropping in Bequia at this time represented a form of production at a specific stage in the development of capitalism. It could be classified during this period as a 'significant' form of production because it subordinated other co-existent (and hence 'less significant') forms, such as peasant and communal production. But the political and ideological relations that dominated the formation were those of metropolitan capitalism, the relations of production in sharecropping, however, remaining pre-capitalist in nature. The appropriation of surplus labour did not take place directly through commodity exchange, although some purchase of necessary items like clothing would have been undertaken by the direct producers.

In the production of cash-crops such as sugar cane, copra and cotton, the planters exercised full ownership and control over the means of production (the land and the provision of seeds, equipment, etc.) and retained half the total crop produced (the surplus product), with the producers receiving the remaining half. Through export of this surplus product, the planters maintained their economic superiority: their profits being represented by the total revenue from the export of cash crops less the maintenance, seeds/equipment and export costs.

In the production of 'subsistence' crops (peas, maize, cassava) which planters also allowed their sharecropper tenants to cultivate on estates, the seeds and equipment were provided by the producers themselves, the planters appropriating only one third of the crop, the sharecroppers retaining the remainder. There was thus no capital expenditure by the planters who, nevertheless, profited by allowing primary producers to provide their own subsistence, as for instance migrant labourers do when they return to their homelands in South Africa. Some wage labour was available to sharecroppers in the form of copra-husking and construction/maintenance of planters' houses, but the ex-slave population was only marginally a part of the money economy, their livelihood being essentially one of subsistence, through production for use.

Throughout the years immediately following Emancipation, planters placed obstacles in the way of widespread independent land settlement by ex-slaves. The planter-dominated Legislative Council in St Vincent in 1842, as in many other states in the region at the time

> ... refused to initiate surveys of Crown Land as a preliminary to smallhold settlement, and they adopted strict legislation against squatting on Crown Land. The planters either refused to sell surplus and marginal estate land, or they charged high, even exorbitant, prices for small portions of it (Marshall, 1968:255).

Hillside squatting in the early post-Emancipation period had produced settlements where the villages of Belmont, Lower Bay, La Pomp and Paget Farm stand today, and these grew in size in the years after 1850 when small-scale land acquisition became possible for freedmen and ex-slaves. Planters anxious to draw labour back to their estates sold agriculturally marginal land to their ex-slaves in the hope of securing an advantage in the labour market for sharecropping; and some planters, chronically in debt, welcomed the cash returns from disposal of marginal lands. Restrictions on the sale of

Crown Lands were also relaxed during this period.

Most of the arable land, however, remained in large land holdings; all estates still exceeded 50 acres. In 1888 (see 'St Vincent Government Gazette: Land and House Tax Rolls', 1888, as quoted in Adams J, 1976:17) six individuals owned 75 per cent of Bequia's total land area. It was only following the division of the smaller estates of Belmont, Mount Pleasant, Paget Farm and Diamond (Lower Bay) in the late 1880s and early 1890s, through sale or bequest that such monopolisation was eased.

While the planters retained control of productive land in Bequia, their political power and position was ensured. The larger estates remained intact during the latter decades of the nineteenth century, but the decline in mono-crop agricultural production that had continued throughout the post-Emancipation period led to a further drain on the planters' money supply, a drain that began with the abolition of the slave mode of production. Adams (1971b, 1976) has provided further details on the failure of sharecropping to improve the economic position of the planter class through the destruction of vegetation cover together with soil erosion.

The fragmentation of some of the smaller estates, together with the decline in sugar production, meant that the lower classes in Bequia were less dependent upon the planters for access to land and cultivated peas, maize and cassava for domestic consumption on their own household gardens. Many did, however, continue to work as sharecroppers on the remaining estates (notably Friendship and Spring) but it was to maritime forms of production that they turned during this period of commercial agricultural decline.

3 Maritime production

Fishing by slaves during the slavery period was limited by planters in order to maintain the slaves' dependence on the estate and hence protect and maintain the exploitative relationship that existed between the planter and slave. Price (1966) suggests that in all Caribbean plantation islands fishing was a form of production on the periphery of the slave mode: '... a unique and self-perpetuating fishing subculture sprang up within the plantation system' (Price, 1966:1371).

Not only did fishing contribute to the sustenance of the slave population, but it satisfied the requirements of the planter:

... producing fish mainly for the pleasure of the master and his guests ... these fishermen played a role that was perhaps more social than economic (Price, *ibid.*:1370).

Small-scale fishing, primarily for household consumption, continued in Bequia during the period when sharecropping was a signficant form of production. Ownership of large nets, such as the seine and fillet (see Chapter 4), remained in the hands of the planters and, as there was no commercial outlet for fish during this period, they were used essentially for satisfying local consumption needs. However, as sharecropping declined and markets became available, fishing activities increased and diversified and fish became an exchangeable commodity.

The relations of production in fishing were those of a petty-commodity form; the direct producer, although owning his means of labour (boat, equipment, etc.) had limited access to the means of subsistence. The decline in agricultural production and dependence on outside commodities meant that households could not meet their maintenance requirements, and so fishermen began to exchange their catches on the available markets.

With the decline in commercial agriculture towards the end of the nineteenth century, i.e. when sharecropping was no longer the most significant form of production, fishing replaced agricultural work for many lower class men: peasant production and sharecropping becoming essentially the work of women. As men turned away from agriculture, the planter class sought to exert its influence and control over the developing maritime economy, viz. boatbuilding, inter-island trading, whaling and fishing, in an attempt to re-establish its political as well as economic power in the island. From 1850 most schooners constructed in Bequia were used to transport general cargo in the Southern Caribbean, generating income for the planter classes, who used the profits to invest in the building of other vessels. As a result a new schooner aristocracy was established, drawn from and affiliated to the planter class. The success of this schooner aristocracy was due to its ability to draw labour from the residual peasant, sharecropping, and developing small-scale fishing forms of production. As schooner construction and maritime trade grew in the 1870s, the number of seamen in the Grenadines (drawn largely from Bequia) rose from 15 per cent of the male labour force (i.e. 73) in 1871 to 30.5 per cent (157) in 1881 (Adams, 1970:131).[8]

The transition from sharecropping to a new economic activity based on maritime trade and fishing can only be understood in the context of the development of the whaling industry in Bequia. Whaling was the single most influential maritime industry from which the acquisition of the skills and technology of boat building, fishing and sailing sprang. It was, in effect, to serve as the material base for the appropriation of surplus product and labour by the planter class, and for the proliferation of alternative maritime activities and skills, which contribute significantly to the livelihood of almost every household in Bequia today.

The whaling industry in Bequia was founded in 1875 by William T. Jameson, the son of a Scottish planter who owned Friendship Estate.[9] The whaling concerns that developed and operated in Bequia[10] up to the 1930s were owned and controlled by powerful ex-planter families, notably the Jamesons and the Lafayettes (owners of Paget Farm Estate).

Whaling was a form of petty-commodity production: ownership of the means of production (the whale boats, lances, harpoons and oil processing equipment) was concentrated in the hands of a small class of ex-planters, and distribution of the whale meat was according to a simple share system – wage labour being totally absent. The men who worked the whale boats were unable to sell their labour power: the relations of production in whaling, as in the forms of fishing production that developed out of it, meant that the producers (crewmen and assistants) became increasingly reliant on the market. Production for consumption, which had characterised peasant and sharecropping activities was replaced by production for exchange as the dominant form of production relations in Bequia.

Whale meat was, and is, when a whale is occasionally caught today, shared on the basis of one-third to the owners of the whaling concern, one-third to the captain and harpooners (and the owner if he served as captain or harpooner) and one-third to all other crewmen and workers. The meat appears to have been consumed and exchanged within the settlements from which labour for the concern was drawn, a portion being salted and set aside for future consumption. The owners shipped meat to Kingstown, St Vincent for sale at the fish market. The export of whale oil out of Bequia was owned and controlled by the schooner aristocracy, who often also owned, or had shares in, the whaling concerns. Expenses for the export and maintenance of the whaling concerns were taken out of the remittances from the sale of the oil before the cash was shared out, on the same basis as meat-sharing, i.e. one-third each to owner, captain/harpooner, and crew. As the owners of the whaling concern often acted as captains on the whaling boats, and had shares in the trading schooners, the level of appropriation of the product from the concerns was far higher than the share system, *per se*, suggests.

The whaling industry continued to grow in the late nineteenth and early twentieth centuries, reaching its peak of activities in 1910 when 100 men were engaged in regular employment in Bequia. After 1925 the industry went into decline and has been of little economic significance since.[11] By the turn of the century the main exports from Bequia were fish, whale oil and some small amounts of copra and livestock. Sugar production was now limited to one hundred acres (St Vincent Blue Books). This reflects the dominance of maritime production over agricultural production during this period. Although fishing appears to have been an integral part of the post-slavery peasant-sharecropping economy, it was only with the advent of whaling and maritime trade that it became of commercial significance to the lower classes in Bequia. The development of the smaller and slightly modified version of the whale boat (a double-bow, open sail boat modelled on the Nantucket whale boats aboard which Jameson had worked), which replaced the traditional dug-out canoes and square-sterned fishing boats, was instrumental in this change. The durability, stability and speed of the new boats, and the sailing skills acquired through whaling, provided the Bequia fishermen with the ability to reach fishing grounds and markets formerly inaccessible.

Bequia fishermen marketed their catches in Kingstown, St Vincent and as far south as St George's in Grenada: transport and marketing being outside the control of the planter-merchant class. Fishing became commercialised during the first half of the twentieth century, mainly through seine enterprises owned by the planter-merchants; the powerful classes controlling the transportation of large catches to markets. Some small fishing enterprises still relied on their own forms of transport for reaching markets. After World War II French traders from Martinique came to St Lucian and Vincentian waters to poach and purchase fish from Grenadine fishermen; French capitalists developed icing and storage facilities in Canouan and Union islands and a light aircraft trade route to Martinique. By the 1960s Bequia ex-planters had begun converting inter-island trading vessels to ice-storage fish transporters and effectively cut out the Martinique middlemen. The French traders in Union and Canouan, however, continued to prosper, despite Bequia traders' incursions into the Southern Grenadines.

Whaling was further responsible for supplying the skills and techniques which gave Bequia seamen the reputation of being the finest and most experienced in the West Indies. This allowed many men access to employment aboard inter-island trading vessels and merchant shipping vessels. Employment for seamen reached a peak in Bequia during Work War II, and produced a temporary decline in commercial fishing, as for the first time a demand arose for unskilled labour in the Caribbean. The war brought military bases to the area, inter-island trade increased many-fold and employment on schooners rose, and many Bequian men between the ages of 18 and 40 emigrated to the islands of Curaçao and Aruba to work in the oil refinery construction industry.

The growth in inter-island trade further improved the economic and political strength of the planter class. In the 1940s Bequia's ex-planters represented an aristocratic class whose power derived from ownership and control of the means of trade, consolidated by international and regional capitalist companies. During the period 1921–1965 65 schooners and large sloops were built by merchants and ex-planters in Admiralty Bay and Friendship, although since the early 1950s schooner trade has been in decline in the region, leading to the reduction in shipbuilding in the Grenadines. (The recent rise in tourism has, however, boosted inter-island trade and three schooners were under construction in 1981).

As maritime trade declined labour migration to other Caribbean islands, and emigration, increased. Men and women left for neighbouring islands which offered employment in the developing manufacturing and tourist industries. By the early 1950s the flow of families to the USA and UK was well established under the immigration schemes of those countries. At the international level, the capitalist-dominated social formations of the north, and the developing capitalist economies of the Caribbean, were drawing labour from the subordinated and dependent system of production in Bequia. The high levels of unemployment and under-employment within the capitalist mode of production in Bequia ensured a reserve army of labour, essential within the requirements of an international capitalist division of labour – labour power becoming subsumed by the capitalist relations and the metropolises.

With increased commerce and production in the Caribbean in the 1950s came European and US owned merchant shipping companies transporting ore, oil and other raw materials to markets in the north. These merchant shipping companies provided wage labour opportunities for Bequia men. The US owned National Bulk Carriers (NBC) was by far the largest employer of Bequia labour. In 1959 an agent was sent to St Vincent to recruit seaman labour from Bequia, and by 1964 64 Bequia seamen were in full employment with NBC alone, the majority of these having been recruited from the harbour region of the island (see pp. 38–45 below for the political significance of this). By 1974 it was estimated that 25 per cent of the working male population of Bequia was serving aboard local and foreign vessels ... and their earnings represent(ed) the most important source of income for the island' (C. Frank, 1976:38).

The advent of a merchant shipping labour market, together with increased commercial activity in the inter-island trading sector and the fish exporting industry, the latter both owned and controlled by the planter/merchant class and a small number of French capitalists, were to have far-reaching effects on social relations in Bequia. The post-war changes represented a phase of intensification of capitalist forces at a number of levels. The remaining chapters deal with many of these effects in detail, through focusing on Lower Bay. To conclude this chapter, however, I wish to look briefly at the rise in foreign capital investment in Bequia associated with a recent decline in merchant shipping jobs and the export of fish.

4 Tourism and expatriate housing: the rise in foreign investment

Employment with NBC, which was largely for men in and around the harbour settlements, and with companies such as Caribbean Steamships and Barbados (International) Shipping for men in other settlements in Bequia, meant that many lower class households became less dependent upon fishing and agriculture for their means of livelihood: labour being drawn from the residual forms of production at an unprecedented rate during the 1960s and early 1970s.

Emigrant remittances and seamen wages gave the lower classes increased purchasing power. The planter class response to this was to seize control of the developing commodity markets and outlets in and around Bequia, importing and retailing food stuffs, clothing, building materials, etc. With the rise in tourism and the development of an expatriate and resident non-national housing construction industry in the early 1960s, planters sold the fertile estates in the north of the island (Spring, Park, Industry) and parts of Friendship in the south to US and Canadian multinational property developers. Land prices in Bequia rose dramatically (see, for example, Chapter 7).

Despite fragmentation of some estates at the turn of the century, large landholdings continued during the first 50 years of this century (as Table 1a shows).

Table 1a: Landholdings, Bequia, 1899–1973

Year	No. of properties between 1–5 acres	Percentage of land area in holdings over 100 acres
1899	19	80%
1911	40	N/A
1921	68	68%
1931	91	N/A
1943	127	58%
1950	144	N/A
1963	176	37%
1973	199	22%

(N/A = not available)
(adapted from Adams, J, 1976:18)
Note: most lower class landholdings in Bequia are less than 1 acre.

The existence of middle sized (1–5 acre) properties owned by descendants of the planter class, resident non-nationals and the middle classes, resulted from the failure of the planter class to consolidate its position of power within agriculture during the period 1920–1960. Sea Island cotton was introduced in the early 1920s but its lack of success as an export crop can be contributed to weak forces of production within sharecropping. Maritime production had taken labour out of the agricultural sector and the planters experienced difficulties in attracting labour back onto the estates on a sharecropping basis. Price and market fluctuations dogged the cotton industry and erratic rainfall, together with continued soil erosion on gently sloping estates, presented severe physical and climatic restrictions to plantation agriculture. The period 1957–59, when rainfall was so scarce that it became known as the 'Bequia drought' saw the total collapse of cotton production.

The sale of arable lands to resident non-nationals and multinational companies indicates the extent to which the planter class had lost its power base in agriculture. (These lands remain under-utilised agriculturally, serving only the developing tourist sector). However, with the construction of hotels and expatriate houses, control of the service industries went into the hands of the ex-landowners, through investment of capital from land sales. These ex-landowners also maintained control of inter-island trade and, in association with French capitalists, the fish export industry.

The rise in foreign, and multinational, economic activity has not effected any degree of capital reinvestment in Bequia. Much of the capital generated by the tourist industry is exported. The ex-planter/merchant class owns and controls the businesses that service the tourist industry; tourist enterprises such as charter yachts services, car rental, etc. are operated by resident non-nationals; and the lower classes have little access to the means of production in these sectors of the CMP.

Unemployment and under-employment in the CMP has resulted from the demise of the merchant shipping labour market since the mid-1970s and the recent decline in the construction industry as hotel complexes are completed (see p.45ff.). A decrease in wage labour opportunities, together with changing market and environmental factors affecting the fishing industry, such as exploitation of fishing waters by US and Martiniquan fishing boats poaching and destroying the coral reef using wire mesh drag nets, and inflation which has restricted boat building, have contributed to a recent return to production for use and a greater degree of dependence on residual forms of production. Most lower class households are experiencing poverty as they are forced to rely on emigrant remittances and seasonal/temporary wage labour in the tourist sectors of neighbouring Caribbean islands for the cash required to purchase essential commodities and for household expenses such as electricity, ground rent, etc. Much of the surplus from fishing production is now consumed and few fishermen are able to realise a profit after marketing their catch. Under conditions of marginality and declining resources most lower class households are faced with the technological[12] problem of how to keep output at a level which allows for maintenance of the domestic unit with limited monetary investment (credit is unavailable for most and 'savings' are minimal). This system of production contrasts dramatically with the postwar period when market forces had penetrated the system and fish stocks were plentiful around Bequia.

To sum up: since the abolition of slavery there have been three stages in the development of Bequia: the sharecropping stage, during which peasant and communal production were subordinated to the plantation economy; a stage in which maritime activities, based around petty-commodity fishing, whaling and inter-island trade, replaced sharecropping as the dominant form of production; and a final stage characterised by fluctuating opportunities for wage labour. The recent demise of merchant shipping has severely restricted the earning power of the lower classes. Tourism and foreign housing programmes have failed to replace adequately the jobs lost in shipping.

Transformation in the system of production

This chapter has considered the local and international conditions under which transitions in the system of production in Bequia have taken place. The analysis has concentrated on the period from settlement to 1959, establishing the overall effects of changes on the social formation, and locating the structure of Bequia historically. Although some of the post-1959 developments have already been introduced these are dealt with in detail in the remainder of the text which examines how recent movements of international capital have affected social, economic and cultural life in the community of Lower Bay.

The changing patterns of dependence in Bequia have produced a number of co-existent forms of production subordinated to the CMP, viz. sharecropping, small-holding (peasant) production, communal production and petty-commodity production, which today exist as a palimpsest. Hindess and Hirst (1975:263ff.) stress that any determinate transformation from one mode of production to another must involve the non-reproduction of the political, economic and ideological conditions of existence of the dominant mode of production in the social formation during the transition phase. To conclude this chapter, I have outlined the conditions under which transitions have been effected, indicating the context within which residual forms, notably sharecropping, have remained despite their displacement from positions of significance within the social formation.

The mode of production of the Caribs based upon fishing and gathering/gardening was structured by a limited development of the forces of production and a simple division of labour that required no permanent agricultural base. The exploitation of the natural resources on and around the coast of Bequia during expeditions from coastal settlements in St Vincent ceased during plantation slavery. During the mid-eighteenth century small-holding production by French settlers in Bequia co-existed with the simple mode of production of the Caribs, no restrictions being placed on the Indians visiting the island. With the consolidation of mono-crop, export-oriented production under plantation-based slavery, which was effected under conditions of little or no resistance from the settlers in pre-plantation production, the planters used force and legislation to prevent the Caribs from exploiting the island's resources. The colonial power, Britain, further assisted, both politically and economically, plantation production with the effect that small-holding production became subsumed under, and dominated by, slavery.

From its inception, the plantation system that grew out of early settlement, was geared towards the unilateral transfer of capital to Britain and, despite the low levels of productivity of many of the estates, preferential duties and protectionism sustained the mode of production until Emancipation.

The abolition of slavery, through legislature, clearly prevented the political, economic and ideological reproduction of the slave mode of production after 1838; and absenteeism and the climatic restrictions that had contributed to the low productivity of many of the estates further contributed to the post-Emancipation decline in plantation production. Unlike in the major sugar producing islands of Barbados, Jamaica, Trinidad, etc. where a tied wage labour system was introduced following abolition of slavery, Bequia's planters faced acute shortages of capital and labour as slaves left the plantations to squat locally or to work in Trinidadian estates. The introduction of sharecropping was an attempt to pull labour back to the estates and to re-establish economic and political control, with minimal capital investment in the plantations.

Peasant and communal production by ex-slaves in communities that grew up on the marginal non-plantation lands took place during the years immediately following the collapse of slavery. These forms of production continued during the period when sharecropping was the significant form in the Bequia economy. Further erosion of vegetation and soil cover, the lifting of preferential duties on sugar in the metropolis, fluctuating world markets for sugar and its by-products, and fragmentation of some of the smaller estates represented weakened forces of production. As a result plantation share-cropping production declined dramatically in the latter half of the nineteenth century and established the conditions for a transition to maritime economic activities based upon whaling, schooner construction, inter-island trade and commercial fishing.

Through ownership and control of the whaling industry, the planters in Bequia translated their economic and political strength, derived from land, into a maritime-based economic form. The whaling industry allowed ex-planters the material base for proliferation and diversification into schooner construction and inter-island trade and commercial fishing.

During the slave mode of production slaves were allowed to fish to reduce the need for planters to sustain their work force. With the abolition of slavery and the reduced legislative control of the population by planters, the ex-slaves increased their involvement in fishing activities. Fish became an exchangeable product, although limited access to technology and markets restricted production to household consumption and local exchange. The skills and knowledge acquired by lower class men engaged in whaling, plus the importation of seine nets from Europe by planters, led to increased production in fishing, replacing agricultural work for lower class men in Bequia. Although the planter/merchant class was unable legally to monopolise the objects of labour (fish) in fishing as they had in monocrop production (land), they monopolised the most productive means of labour (e.g. the seine) and, later, controlled markets and trade. Petty-commodity fishing became subordinated to, and dependent upon, planter/merchant controlled production and markets.

Lower class Bequarians have remained dependent upon access to plantation land as sharecroppers to meet their household needs, despite fragmentation of estates and irregular wage labour opportunities since the late nineteenth century. The transition to a maritime capitalist mode of production effected a change in the sexual division of labour, transferring agricultural work on plantations from men to women. Commercial fishing remained under-developed during this transition: the planter/merchant class consolidated its position through schooner construction, whaling and inter-island trade, periodically drawing labour from residual, co-existent forms of production. By granting limited access to sharecropping to lower class women, and ensuring the low level of production in fishing through control of technology, the powerful classes established and secured the position of the lower classes as a reserve army of labour. Fishing and agriculture produced little surplus in the subordinate forms of production and barely met the household needs of the lower classes.

The conversion of small inter-island trading vessels into fish-transporters gave the powerful classes control over markets, in association with French capitalists in the neighbouring Grenadine islands of Canouan and Union and was an effective expression of the power of these classes. The position of marginality and dependence experienced by the lower classes worsened under increased control and influence from outside forces aligned with the local dominant classes.

A change in the sexual division of labour in agricultural production further reduced sugar production on the estates, sharecropping becoming a domestic form of production (see p.89ff.) both conceptually, as defined in plebeian culture, and materially, in supporting household dietary subsistence requirements. Planter/merchant control over fertile lands continued through the twentieth century despite the low level of production on the estates. The planter/merchant class, through ownership and control of land and maritime trade, with direct and indirect support from international markets and capitalist-controlled financial institutions, created and maintained the subordinate position of all other forms of production and their dependence upon the capitalist mode of production. As a result of limited access to productive land of their own, to share-cropping and to wage labour opportunities, and of fluctuating markets for fish, lower class households were dependent upon extra-community sources of income. Peasant and petty-commodity producers who turned to the planter/merchant class for an income to supplement their household needs, on estates, whaling enterprises and trading schooners, were periodically expelled from the capitalist sector to return to community-based fishing and agriculture, or chose the limited opportunities that existed in small enterprise, and/or emigration.

The continued existence of peasant and petty-commodity production was, and still is, an absolute requirement for the local community, who still serve as a reserve labour force, just as it was, and remains, an absolute essential for the effective operation and functioning of the capitalist mode of production, which was and is, neither able nor willing fully to support or employ its labour force.

During the twentieth century the peasant, sharecropping, petty-commodity and small entrepreneurial forms of production have remained subordinate to, and dependent on, island-based capitalism and to movements of international capital. Island trading schooners, migration and emigration to wage labour opportunities, merchant shipping and, lately, tourism, have all relied upon the lower classes to down tools and leave the household-community when called on, just as the lower classes have waited for, and depended on, the capitalist, whether Bequia planter/merchant, American shipping company, or other multinational or expatriate hotel owner, to provide access to means of production and wage labour in order to supplement their incomes because community production has been unable to sustain levels sufficient to support their households.

Changes in modes and forms of production in Bequia represent the historical crystallisation of inequality, marginality and dependence for the lower classes. This chapter has shown that international capitalism, mediated by the dominant Bequia classes, has unfolded class relations that reproduce inequality, impoverishment and suffering amongst the lower classes. The following chapter looks at the contemporary form of lower class dependence on international capital set in the context of a discussion of relationships between and within island settlements.

Notes

1. In 1675 when a slave vessel bound for Barbados sank off the Bequia coast (see Edwards 1807, Vol 1:412) the surviving slaves took refuge on Bequia. Historians dispute the nature of the relations between the Caribs they encountered on Bequia. Shephard (1831) and Young (1971:6) have suggested that the Africans were captured by the Caribs, whilst Duncan (1941) maintains that the two groups intermixed socially and intermarried. Whichever the case, the result was the establishment of a 'Black Carib' community on the southern coast of St Vincent by the early eighteenth century. Enmity between the Black Caribs and those that did not mix with the African slaves led initially to many blacks fleeing to the north-eastern woodlands of St Vincent (see Beckles, 1986:89–90) where they joined many other negroes from neighbouring islands, who had also intermixed with Caribs and formed a 'nation of Black Caribs' (Young, *op. cit.*:8). By 1700, says Young, the Blacks had sufficient numbers and strength to return to the fertile lands of the south and capture 'pure' Carib lands. The Red Caribs fled to the north-west of the island where they established a distinct community. Enmity between the two groups resulted by 1719 in war, in which the Black Caribs defeated their northern neighbours who were attempting to re-establish themselves in the south. The significance, historically, of the war was that it brought the French navy from Martinique to St Vincent, summoned by the northern Caribs. Although the war was over by the time they arrived, the French remained on the island with the aim of establishing settlements because of its rich and fertile soil.
2. The Warner family were granted 483 acres of land in 1763, and the resulting estate became known as Friendship. The owner, Charles John Warner, was murdered in 1797 by two of his slaves (Shephard, 1831:214) and in 1828 his daughter, the devisee, sold the estate to the Police Magistrate for the Grenadines, William Thomas Jameson, who had acted as manager for the estate while the family were in England. Following the return of the daughter, Sarah Ann Warner, Jameson married her. The Jameson family were to become one of the most powerful and historically significant on Bequia, as they introduced whaling and the associated industries in the late nineteenth century.
3. Events on St Vincent during this period are, briefly: in 1772 a Carib insurrection against land seizure by the English colonists was subdued by colonial forces from America, the Caribs being forced to settle in the north of the island. In 1779 the island was again captured by the French, but returned to the English in 1783 under the Treaty of Versailles. Intensive production of sugar cane was started at this time. In 1795 war broke out between the Caribs, and French, and the English. On 26 October 1796 the Caribs and French were defeated and 5,080 Carib men, women and children were exiled to Bequia, and later shipped to Ruattan in the Bay of Honduras. Those who were allowed to stay were granted land in Sandy Bay and Morne Ronde villages in the north of St Vincent where they remain today. They were forbidden from growing sugar cane by the colonial government.
4. Ideally a West Indian sugar plantation had to produce a minimum of

200,000 lbs of sugar a year to remain economically viable. In Bequia only one estate – Spring, in the north of the island – had an annual average production of around 200,000 lbs. The other eight estates fell well below the minimum and four had production levels of less than 50,000 lbs annual average (Adams, 1976:14).

5   Bequia averages less than 60 ins. of rainfall a year, and records show years of 40 ins. and less.
6   This figure is significantly low – as during the 1860s (see J. Sheppard, 1974:86) 'poor whites' from Barbados had settled on the flat lands of Mount Pleasant in Bequia.
7   Notably Barbados and Jamaica, and European beet sugar.
8   Before Emancipation less than 4 per cent of the working population of St Vincent and the Grenadines had been seamen (Adams, 1970:130)
9   Taken from the diary of William T. Jameson, now in the possession of his elderly granddaughter who lives in Friendship, Bequia.
10 For a full account of whaling operations in Bequia see Adams (1971a).
11 The overkilling of whales by large northern companies had a disastrous effect on the Bequia whaling industry which remained in a state of low level capitalisation. Whaling concerns in the Grenadines went bankrupt in the 1920s and 1930s, with the exception of the one in Friendship, which was jointly owned and controlled by the Jameson and Lafayette planter families. They reinvested in it in 1961, by building a whale oil processing plant and landing slope on the island of Petit Nevis which was owned by the Lafayette family as part of Paget Farm Estate. In 1965 only 1,000 gallons of oil was exported and the industry has been largely unproductive since.
12 By technology I am referring to the material implements and production activities (equipment, maintenance of equipment and the fishing process).

CHAPTER 2
Contemporary forms of dependence and interdependence in Bequia

This chapter opens with a sociological profile of Bequia, situating the island settlements according to their position in the system of production as well as geographically. It shows that despite a strong localised sense of identity and self-reliance within each settlement or group of settlements, there exists an important and necessary degree of interdependence as a consequence of restricted access to limited resources. In the general discussion of differences between settlements, the reader is introduced to the nature of stratification in Bequia, which is based upon age, sex and skin colour, as well as class. The sociological profile is thematic and ethnographic, using case study material and specific examples where such material is available.[1] It introduces the heterogeneous nature of Bequia society whilst retaining an analytical focus on the nature of inequality and dependence.

The chapter moves on to provide illustrative data on the nature of work activities in Bequia. It analyses the ways in which dependency, as a product of a global division of labour, is experienced locally and determines and restricts lower class access to employment opportunities and means of production, influences population movements and entrepreneurial activity and results in competition for declining resources and markets. As details of the structures of power emerge it will become evident that, despite an implicit awareness of the relationship between class and state, the account is not concerned with the relationship in the wider context of St Vincent and the Grenadines, but with the position of the dominant Bequia classes (ex-planter/merchant) and of expatriate capitalist entrepreneurs in state politics.

A sociological profile of the island

Bequia (see Map 3) has eight settlements or villages which are spread throughout the island and confined, by physical factors and differential access to land, to specific population concentrations. In addition there are a number of small clusters of households scattered over the island's hillsides.

Port Elizabeth (the 'harbour') is the centre of administration and commercial activities associated with trade and tourism, and is the site of the island's clinic, bank, high school, cemetery, police station, post office, customs office, District Council offices, Magistrates' Court, tourist office, vegetable and fish market, and a number of shops, businesses and churches. The recent growth in tourist and expatriate activity in the harbour has led to the construction of restaurants, bars, a supermarket, guest houses and apartments owned and operated predominantly by members of the ex-planter class and foreign entrepreneurs. Enterprises servicing yachts-tourism have grown up in this part of Bequia as ex-landowners from throughout the island have set up businesses on and around the wharf. A member of the powerful ex-planter family, the Walters, has recently opened a sail-making and repair workshop. He previously worked for the whaling enterprise in the south of the island, but as whaling declined he transferred his skills to private enterprise. This illustrates the sort of shifts in production that have taken place since the development of new economic activities in Bequia, the harbour being the obvious site for the establishment of businesses geared towards tourists. Because of the costs of leasing or purchasing sea-front premises it is the powerful landowners (or ex-landowners) in association with external capital, who have exercised most influence in this new sphere of activity. An English entrepreneur runs a boat supplies shop, an ex-planter family has set up an engine repair service, in conjunction with a Danish engineer, and a Californian shipwright has recently leased a large tract of land at the eastern end of the main street in the harbour for the construction of 'Bequia dinghies' for export, and traditional schooners for rich foreigners (in 1980 he completed a schooner for the American singer, Bob Dylan). Foreign yacht owners anchor their yachts in the harbour, offering charter services from a hotel in Belmont.

These changes have provided increased opportunities for lower class economic activity in the CMP. As well as drawing seasonal and temporary labour from residual forms of production, the tourist sector, and its offshoot industries such as construction, maintenance, etc., stimulates entrepreneurial activities, especially amongst the unemployed or under-employed youth who are currently involved in hawking, busking, etc.

To the west, and merging with the backstreets of Port Elizabeth, is the village of **Hamilton**. The men of Hamilton and Port Elizabeth were the first to be employed as seamen with National Bulk Carriers (see below) and continued to constitute the majority of the Bequia labour force employed with the company during the

1960s and 1970s. Wattle and daub houses are a thing of the past in these settlements, and only a small number of 'board' houses (wooden dwellings raised from the ground on stilts or on stone bases) which typify most of the other settlements, remain; remittances from seamen and emigrants having gone to build stone, or 'block', houses. Domestic agricultural production declined in the 1970s to the extent that many kitchen gardens and provision grounds were left idle or rarely worked.

Amongst other Bequarians these two settlements are sometimes referred to by the common title of 'harbour'[2] although within the respective groups a strong sense of being either 'harbour folk' (Port Elizabeth) or 'Hamilton folk' prevails. The inhabitants of both Port Elizabeth and Hamilton tend to be blacker than other Bequarians due essentially to the location and size of estates. The southern estates were smaller than those of the north, notably Reform and Spring, and hence the degree of miscegenation between planter and slave was greater in the south. The decline in plantation agriculture led to squatting and settlement in the south, but many of the slaves from the northern estates found settlement impossible because of the dense forestation around Spring and Industry estates. The result was a concentration of ex-slaves, of considerably darker colour than their southern counterparts, along the shores of Admiralty Bay, where the harbour and Hamilton stand today. Hamilton initially sprang up as an ex-slave settlement from the estate at Reform and grew, along with Port Elizabeth, after the exodus from Union, Spring and Industry estates in the north. I introduce this phenomenon here because, as will be shown later, skin colour is socially significant in Bequia and one of the categories by which Bequarians classify themselves within the island, and hence a factor in social stratification.

Hamilton, unlike Port Elizabeth, has experienced no boom in private enterprise, despite its proximity to the harbour. The high population concentration in this settlement, and the absence of a beach-front means few tourists visit the area and work activities are limited to seamanship and fishing. Fishing is a residual form of production into which many men have been forced to return as a direct result of fluctuating and declining employment opportunities aboard merchant ships. This decline, especially affecting young men with no experience of merchant shipping, has forced many lower class women to open up their kitchen gardens as more and more of their men folk rely upon traditional work patterns for their means of livelihood. Younger men, with no means of fishing production and no skills, spend much of their time in the harbour looking for tourist-related employment, or hawking around the bars and restaurants.

About a quarter of a mile south of Port Elizabeth is **Belmont**, a settlement populated largely by non-nationals and tourist operators. To the north of the settlement is the Frangipani Hotel, owned by the present prime minister of St Vincent and the Grenadines. Belmont is the site of one of the smaller of Bequia's former estates within the grounds of which stands the Sunny Caribbee Hotel complex built around the former plantation house. Belmont is today dominated by foreign capital: local small land owners have sold up to take advantage of escalating land prices and a number of beach front bars, restaurants and shops have opened during the 1970s. The recent success of the Sunny Caribbee complex with its time share cabanas has pushed the price of land up in Belmont faster than anywhere in Bequia and very little land bordering the beach is now owned by Bequarians.

The three settlements of Port Elizabeth, Hamilton and Belmont have experienced rapid change in the past fifteen years, far in excess of anywhere else in the island. As one Lower Bay man put it: 'Some day when I walk in de harbour dere more foreign face dan dere is Bequarian'.

On the southern shores of Admiralty Bay is the village of **Lower Bay**, one of the three settlements that make up the community of Lower Bay. Lower Bay (and unless otherwise stated I shall refer to the settlements of Lawler's Hill, Lower Bay Gutter and Lower Bay by the common name of Lower Bay – see Map 4) differs considerably from the settlements of Port Elizabeth, Hamilton and Belmont. There is a far higher proportion of light-skinned members living there, because of the miscegenation resulting from a small estate, and Lower Bay lower classes have remained more dependent upon customary work activities in residual forms of production because of limited access to employment in the 'modern' sphere.

As the remainder of the book is concerned with the sociology of Lower Bay, I shall present only a brief picture of the community to maintain continuity and to provide comparative material. In 1981 only 18 per cent of adult males in the community were employed in full time wage labour (as seamen – see Table 3e p.66). Despite limited access to wage labour, Lower Bay remains dependent upon external monetary sources. Emigrant remittances, migration and seasonal and temporary employment in the capitalist mode are essential means of livelihood for the lower classes, who remain dependent upon the ex-planter families in the community for access to the means of production in the traditional spheres such as subsistence and petty-commodity fishing, household agriculture, and sharecropping. Four individuals, descended from planters of estates within and beyond the community remain the major owners and controllers of productive means, namely land, seine boats, seine nets, and other fishing technology, and cassava mills.

Fishermen are dependent, not only on members of the ex-planter class for access to the more productive fishing technology, but also upon the availability of markets, determined largely today by the foreign-owned tourist industry. Local markets for fish are limited to community sales and to island hotels and restaurants, and fishermen find themselves dependent upon Bequarian and Martiniquan fish traders who service the tourist industry, fix fish prices and control the market for fish. Storage facilities are absent from the community and fishermen are forced to sell to traders whose vessels are equipped with icing facilities for export to the French islands of Martinique and Guadaloupe where fish prices are three to four times those paid to Bequia fishermen.

Tourism is still marginal in the community; a small number of houses are rented to visitors, and a bar and restaurant was built in 1975 geared essentially to the needs of tourists. But tourism is becoming increasingly important for the livelihood of the lower classes as wage labour opportunities in merchant shipping decrease and emigration becomes increasingly difficult.

Lower class people in Lower Bay exhibit a strong sense of community identity and self-reliance. Despite stratification within the lower classes, based upon material wealth and skin colour, they express solidarity in relation to other island settlements. They do, however, remain dependent on many of the groups from whom they dissociate themselves. Apart from dependence upon island and foreign capitalists for wage labour, as fishermen they require fishing supplies from foreign entrepreneurs and, as boat building has died out in the community, they rely on shipwrights in La Pompe and Paget Farm for new fishing boats. As one fisherman told me:

> 'Southsiders (from Paget Farm) real good shipwright true. All de old heads in Lower Bay who done build dem schooner and boat, dey all dead today, and none of we is carrying on de skill. So we have for rely on others ...'

Unlike Lower Bay Gutter (north-west Friendship), the remainder of **Friendship** is populated mainly by migrants from Port Elizabeth and Hamilton who have purchased land on the road leading down to the 'Friendship Bay' hotel, with savings from merchant sailing. A small number of non-national residents have also purchased land and settled in this area and holiday-let houses are being built by descendants of planters and other powerful groups in the island, viz. government officials and expatriates. On the southwest road are a few scattered households, where the descendants of the Jameson planter family still live. According to Bingham Jameson, the only remaining whale boat shipwright in Bequia, his and his sister's house were the only ones in Friendship before 1960:

> 'Before that family of mine done sell up the land you could look out of my window and see nothing but pea fields and trees. Now it getting like they moved a city here ...'

The Jameson family sold the land to the east of Friendship Gap, and above the road to the hotel in the 1960s, leading to non-national settlement and migration from the harbour. The estate land is still sharecropped and, although fragmented, much remains in the hands of descendants of the Jameson family, some having been sold to smallholders. Some of the women of Lower Bay and Lower Bay Gutter work as sharecroppers here (see p.89ff.).

South of Friendship and overlooking Friendship Bay is the village of **La Pompe**, a settlement of approximately 75 households occupied predominantly by the descendants of the planter families, Lafayette and Jameson, and of the ex-slaves who squatted on the lands after Emancipation. La Pompe has the highest percentage of light and brown-skinned inhabitants of all the ex-plantation settlements in Bequia, a characteristic often cited by other Bequarians when they wish to provide explanations for particular instances of deviation by persons from La Pompe from cultural norms.

Although little more than 50 yards of road separate Friendship from La Pompe and despite intermarriage between the Lafayettes and Jamesons, there is yet again a strong identity with the village of residence. Like Lower Bay, only a small percentage of the adult men in La Pompe derive their incomes from merchant sailing. Many are fishermen spending long periods diving in the southern Grenadines for lobster and conch. Boat building, once a major employer of men, is now limited to small fishing boat construction for local sale. A few men of ex-planter descent still operate and own, or have shares in, wooden schooners engaged in inter-island trade (in the tourist season) and the export of fish to the French island of Martinique. Subsistence agriculture on home provision grounds is still predominant amongst the women and a few engage in sharecropping on the ex-plantations of Friendship and Paget Farm. Some of the richer families own 'holiday-let' homes but again, as in Lower

Bay, tourism remains marginal, although the activities of La Pompe-owned schooners and sloops depends very much upon tourist demands in Bequia and other islands.

On the southwestern-most shores of the island, and separated from La Pompe by about three-quarters of a mile of road and wooded hillside is the village of **Paget Farm**. Amongst other islanders, La Pompe and Paget Farm are sometimes together referred to as 'South Side' – although the term predominantly applies to Paget Farm itself. At the peak of the whaling industry's activities whale boat crews were drawn from Lower Friendship, La Pompe and Paget, the industry being jointly owned and operated by the Lafayettes and the Jamesons. Today whaling is of little economic significance for the villages, but represents one of the very few activities in which men from La Pompe and Paget Farm work together. The distinctive character of the two villages is shown in their fishing trips: in the lobster and conch season divers from both villages sail or motor down to the Tobago Cays (see Map 2) but set up camp on separate uninhabited islands, La Pompe fishermen on Bateau, Paget men on Ranier, and search for their own markets. This highlights the inapplicability of sociological accounts that consider these two settlements constitute a 'community' (e.g. Gibson 1981, Lowenthal 1972). Such accounts base their categorisation on skin colour and continued dependence on maritime production, but fail to take into account the distinctive systems of production and the identification with settlement of residence by the respective villagers.

Like La Pompe, however, lower class households in Paget Farm are dependent upon external sources of income from emigrants and wage labour in the capitalist mode; but forms of production derived from earlier modes persist, like sharecropping and household agriculture, fishing and boat building. Shipwrights from La Pompe and Paget have a virtual monopoly over the fishing boat market in Bequia for, with the exception of one man in Mount Pleasant and a family in Hamilton, there are no other indigenous shipwrights building fishing boats in Bequia today.

Stratification by social class is less marked in Paget Farm than anywhere else on the island. Means of production are more evenly distributed amongst the villagers, but do tend towards ownership and control by the few members of the ex-planter and merchant classes, the Lafayette, James and Brown families, who still live in the village. As will be explained below, Paget men have little experience of merchant shipping, although recently a few younger men have found temporary employment as crew on foreign-owned yachts and island-trading schooners, the latter through family connections with La Pompe-owned enterprises.

There are no tourist-oriented businesses in Paget Farm, nor are there any non-national residences or purpose-built holiday-let accommodation, although in 1980 and 1981, with the increased numbers of drifter tourists in Bequia (see Chapter 7 below) some households were offering rooms to rent. Continued dependence on traditional work activities in the residual forms of production by Paget lower classes is reflected in their perception of 'community' with regards to outsiders. Paget people are renowned throughout Bequia as being hostile to all non-Paget people, especially to tourists and foreign journalists and writers. This latter phenomenon can be partly understood as the result of several articles that have appeared in American sailing magazines, tourist/travel journals and the National Geographic, which present Paget Farm people and their culture as a sort of quaint community of primitive whaling and fisher people. I was unaware of the resentment of this sort of media coverage and of the coverage itself, when I first arrived in Bequia. During my first month in the island I rented a holiday house in Friendship whilst I conducted a cursory study of the island settlements prior to selection of one locus. The case below, extracted verbatim from my field notes, illustrates the suspicion that Paget Farm people have towards white outsiders, of my ignorance of such attitudes, and its consequences.

**Case 2a   An early encounter with Paget Farm fishermen:
                11 May 1980**
My practice for the past three weeks has been to visit Paget Farm each Sunday when the fishermen have returned from their day's fishing and are in the rum shops, having arranged for the marketing of their catch. My approach, during these visits has been one of a 'curious outsider' making no reference to my academic purpose. Most of the men I have spoken to have been distant but amicably polite, and the nearest I have ever got to talking about fishing was a seemingly disinterested enquiry into the success of the day's activities. This morning I arrived early in the hope of finding the men relaxed and in an informative mood. After walking around the village for about an hour, observing people come and go from church, I stopped at the 'Conch Shell' rum shop, where a group of about seven or eight fishermen were sitting looking as if they had already well celebrated their Sunday catch. They beckoned me over and a young, intoxicated, man asked: 'What your mission is, man?' I replied that I was a research student interested in local fishing.

What followed can only be described as unexpected in the light of previous experiences with other fishermen. Many questions were thrown at me, like 'So you done interest in fish, hey?' and 'We hear you been askin' questions ...' It was clear that they were well aware of my 'investigations' probably from a man I had been talking to the previous night in a rum shop in La Pompe.

Trying to remain calm and collected in an encounter which had a definite air of hostility to it, I attempted to answer their questions. Whilst doing so, an older man of about 40 with a bucket of fish and a tramil net pulled a fish from the bucket and asked me if I knew what kind of fish it was. I shrugged my shoulders, to which he replied, 'dis is an American Fucking Fish, very dangerous, it done alway arrive for the whalin' season'. It was obvious that a joke was being had at my expense, and there was little I could do about it. I felt helpless. I couldn't begin to explain my research, but to walk away would be to admit defeat, and perhaps mean I could never seriously expect them to confide in me in the future. So I tried to show an interest in the fish and its habits. More mythical stories relating to the techniques of catching them were given until the man who had initially beckoned me over stood up and said: 'Hey, Mr White-man, it time you done make movement outa Paget Farm'. The situation had worsened and I now felt decidedly uneasy about the whole affair. I was just about to depart when the man with the fish asked me my name. I replied 'Neil' thinking that informality might help reduce the tension: 'Mr Nail, I Mr Hammer. Now fuck off!'

As I was walking away I felt disappointed and upset, and yet at the same time could appreciate their attitudes. I had been labouring under the delusion that I could be accepted into a community which is, by Bequia's standards, poor and obviously suspicious of outsiders' intentions. As an outsider minding his own business I had been treated with superficial deference, but once my intentions, even if they were misunderstood, had been discovered, they felt threatened and abused. Such hostility was never repeated to this extreme throughout the remainder of my fieldwork, for once I had become identified with Lower Bay, my motives came to be seen as less threatening by Paget people. Towards the end of my stay in Bequia I was invited to a 'farewell drink' with some of the younger men in Paget Farm, with whom two of the younger fishermen from Lower Bay had been working.

Although Paget Farm, as a community, demonstrated solidarity and a sense of independence, in relation to outsiders and other island groups, there nevertheless existed a growing dependence on island-based capitalist enterprises and other settlements for markets. **Mount Pleasant**, on the island's central plateau could, however, be said to constitute a socio-economically and culturally distinct and insular community, descended from the 'poor whites' of Barbados.

The poor whites arrived in Barbados in the seventeenth century from a diversity of political and socio-economic backgrounds: Scots prisoners captured and transported by Cromwell; Irish deportees from the same period of political unrest in the UK; 'regular indentured servants emigrating in order to seek better opportunities in the New World...' (Sheppard, 1974:73); and youths and deported criminals. Following their periods of indentureship, which ranged from three to seven years, many were given small plots of land. By the early eighteenth century, with the growth in the slave trade and a decline in the indentureship practice, the poor whites had become a marginal class of peasant agriculturalists and fishermen and an under-employed labour force. Emancipation in 1838 brought a considerable change for the worse for the poor whites: the release of slaves onto the labour market meant the end of whatever employment opportunities existed for the poor whites, and the disbanding of the white Militia, in which many served in return for a two-acre plot of land, took away much employment. The Barbados government, concerned for the welfare (sic) of the poor whites unable to compete with the skills acquired by the freed slaves, chose to resettle four hundred poor whites in Doresetshire Hill, St Vincent.

The records are unclear as to whether the whites of Mount Pleasant in Bequia originated from the Dorsetshire community, or whether they came directly through the resettlement scheme. Gibson (1981:57) suggests that Mount Pleasant planters sold plots of land to some of the settlers at Dorsetshire Hill, but whichever the case a settlement of 'poor whites' from Barbados had established themselves in Bequia by 1870 (Sheppard, *ibid.*:86). Mount Pleasant is now a community of approximately 130 whites living in 28 households dispersed over the sparse, dry central upland of the island. Agricultural activity is limited to maize, pigeon peas and cassava production for the home, with a small number of gardens growing tomatoes, ground nuts and ochra for sale. The flatness of the land allows for limited livestock grazing of cattle, sheep, goats and a few horses. Like other Bequarians, many Mount Pleasant men have turned to the sea for their livelihood.

Prior to the St Vincent Lobster Protection Ordinance of 1954, Mount Pleasant fishermen were engaged in small-scale lobster fishing operations, using small sailing craft to reach the fishing grounds and selling to the Martinique middle-men, whose schooners, equipped with cold storage facilities, visited the Grenadines once a month.[4] As lobster numbers decreased, closed seasons were introduced and the Martinique fish trade ceased in 1959.[5] Mount Pleasant fishermen ventured further south to fish and market their catches in Grenada. They built two motorised sloops for this purpose and made four or five trips during the lobster season of October to April. The industry was economically successful during the 1960s but the sloops were sold off in 1971 as a result of overexploitation of the species, decreased landings and the highly capitalised nature of the industry. Many fishermen still work in the Lower Grenadines, diving for lobster, conch and red fish for sale to French traders and tourist outlets in Union and Canouan islands.

With savings from the 1960s lobster concerns and remunerations from shares in the sloops sold, Mount Pleasant villagers have invested in tourist entrepreneurial activities. A few families run small boutiques in the harbour, four men operate taxis, and some women offer laundry services to yachts people. Unlike their Bequarian neighbours, no Mount Pleasant men work aboard National Bulk or other US-owned merchant shipping lines. A small number have found employment with the Geest Banana Line operating from the Windward Islands to Barry in South Wales, while others work on family-owned, inter-island trading schooners and fish exporters.

During its 110 years of existence, Mount Pleasant has remained isolated and endogamous. Until very recently Afro-Caribbeans were physically restrained from entering the village, being subjected to stone-throwing, aggressive dogs and verbal abuse if they chose to do so. With the advent of tourism in the 1970s some of the younger men and women of the village have begun to denounce the separatist ideology and are now seen on the beaches in shorts and bikinis mixing with tourists. Most Bequarians remain suspicious of Mount Pleasant folk. Their adherence to the Seventh Day Adventist Church, which was introduced in the late nineteenth century by planters who resented the freed slaves attending Anglican services, and is today predominantly attended by planter and Mount Pleasant families, their strange physical and mental appearance, due to continuous intermarriage, and their reputation for violence when drunk, does little to enhance the chances, even of the younger members of the community, of breaking down the self-image of racial and cultural superiority that they have created and maintained since their arrival in Bequia.

To sum up: the island's settlements display considerable diversity in terms of their economic activities and dependence on outside forces. The harbour communities have experienced far greater involvement in the foreign-owned and controlled sector of the economy, viz. merchant shipping and tourism. Southside settlements remain more dependent upon traditional work activities in the maritime economy, notably boat-building, fishing and inter-island trade. In terms of production Lower Bay lies between these two: customary work activities remaining essential despite recent developments in the tourist sector. Mount Pleasant, however, stands apart from the rest of Bequia's settlements, representing an inward-looking and relatively self-reliant community.

The extended case study below, on National Bulk Carriers, highlights the differential dependence of Bequia's settlements on international market forces.

The dominance of international capital: structures of power and access to wage labour in Bequia

1 National Bulk Carriers

The relative weakness of Bequia to provide employment opportunities for the bulk of its population has meant that the lower classes of most of the island's settlements and communities have been, and remain, dependent upon outside sources of money supply, viz. emigrant remittances, labour migration, and work with international companies, for their livelihood. The exception has been Mount Pleasant which has developed essentially through enterprise in response to externally stimulated change, e.g. lobster fisheries and island-based tourism. Labour migration and emigration have been relatively low amongst Mount Pleasant folk in comparison with the rest of Bequia, although in the years immediately following World War II some Mount Pleasant men, notes Adams (1970:134):

> ... found work in the USA mainly in shipyards and foundries. After working in the USA for several years most returned to their home island and invested their American-earned savings in the construction of schooners.

For the remainder of the island's lower classes, international capital has played a paramount and historically necessary role in providing their means of livelihood. The case of National Bulk Carriers highlights this dependency excellently and illustrates the role that the island power structure plays in determining access to work in the CMP. Gibson (*op. cit.*:65) notes during her fieldwork in 1975:

> The advent of National Bulk Carriers and other [merchant shipping] companies has probably had the most far-reaching effect of all economic changes since slavery ... it provided Bequians with an income which is on average greater than they could have hoped to have enjoyed in most other available occupations ...

When the recruiting agent for National Bulk (NBC) arrived in St Vincent in 1959, some Bequia men had already gained experience of merchant sailing with the US-owned Harrison Line. The reputation of Bequia men as excellent sailors stemmed from their history of whaling, inter-island schooner trading and fishing from open-sailed boats and sloops, so it was predominantly to Bequia that NBC turned their attention rather than to St Vincent. Many experienced fishermen and schooner sailors found employment with the company which, in 1960, had 30 ships operating with crews that included Bequia labour. Despite opportunities for seamen jobs with other merchant shipping companies, NBC was by far the single biggest employer of Bequia seamen during the 1960s. The Company continued to expand its operations during this period and in 1967 introduced a training scheme, whereby men with no experience of sailing were offered two-year apprenticeships with the company. Although the wages for apprentices were low, they exceeded local schooner wage rates and all the training posts were filled, predominantly by young men. When NBC reached the peak of its activities in 1975, they were operating over 50 vessels and employed approximately 300 Bequia men: 25 per cent of the adult male population of the island.

Employment with NBC led not only to increased standards of living for many lower class households but effected a radical change in the island's age-related earning structure. The majority of men employed with the company were aged between 17 and 40 and, as we shall see in Chapter 4, this had far-reaching effects on household structure, marriage rates and land distribution and prices. Many young men from the lower classes never acquired the skills or the means of production for work in the traditional sector, such as fishing and house construction, so that when the company went into decline in 1977, unemployment had serious consequences for this sector of the population.

There were a number of factors behind the decline in job opportunities with NBC, amongst which were the introduction of capital intensive technology in the mid-1970s, and reduced crew sizes to compete with Russian-bloc vessels trading out of European ports (notably Antwerp). By 1976 job losses were in evidence. As one seaman told me:

> Man, dem companies (NBC and other US-operated) making we for work for de same money we done get ten year afore. And dey espek we for do two man work. All de time dey trying for reduce de size of crew on dey ship. True a man can make $1600–$1700 EC ($640–$680 US) a month wid overtime but it was getting real hard for keep job. Man, I could see in dose days (1976) dat it ain't gonna get no easier wid National Bulk. And if you ain't got work den you ain't for getting nutting coming in for feed de house. Dem men who done work wid ships outa Barbados at least dem get money ($40 EC a week) from de Barbados Seamen's Union, as long as dey done put dey name down to say dey looking for sailing work, and so long as dey done pay dey union money when dey sailing. But NBC dey ain't hafi nutting like dat at all ... Man, we haf plenty problem for find work in dese times.

In 1977 the number of vessels operated by NBC declined sharply. NBC's owner, the US industrialist Daniel Ludwick, began investment in the Amazon Paper project that year. Many NBC vessels in need of maintenance and repair were sold to Taiwan for scrap. Others, fully operational at the time, were sold or leased to other companies, many of which drew their labour from outside the region. An exception to this was Navius, another US-owned company, which bought and leased NBC vessels and in 1978 sent a recruiting agent to St Vincent resulting in some redundant Bequia seamen securing employment. By 1981 NBC operated only cleven vessels.

A 50-year-old man from Lower Bay with 25 years of sailing experience recalls the effects of this decline and the reasons why some settlements experienced differential access to employment with NBC:

> Man, when NBC done come to St Vincent we in Bequia done be struggling for find jobs. Dere ain't much opportunity for men to work in dose days and plenty people done move outa de island for find work. But in de 1960s things were real good for many families. De money was much more dan many of we had ever had before. True some folks done waste a lot buying hi-fi and things, but

most people done build good house for de first time. But it still harder for we in Lower Bay and especially for Southside, for find work with National Bulk. It all depend on where you done live in Bequia and how you done vote. While dem men around de harbour just sit around waiting for job, we in Lower Bay and Southside would be fishing down de Cays. If we done aks for work wid de agent he just turn round and tell we dat if we wanna get job we gotta be available. But we ain't prepared for just sit around. And anyway dey prefer for give de work to harbour men.

Employment with NBC did indeed go predominantly to men from Hamilton and Port Elizabeth. The disproportionate opportunities for harbour men to gain employment with NBC highlights the relationship between local politics and dependence: the exercise of power to 'buy votes' by 'selling jobs'. This statement can only be fully appreciated by considering the positions of power and influence occupied by the Taylor family and their involvement in state politics.

The agent for National Bulk after they commenced operations in St Vincent was Clive Taylor, a member of a powerful Bequia family who, at that time, was the elected Representative for the Grenadines in the St Vincent House of Assembly. His father, Yando Taylor, was one of the few indigenous black large landowners in Bequia to have acquired his land through purchase rather than inheritance. His purchase of Cinammon Gardens, a part of the Spring Estate which is still sharecropped and leased to Hamilton and harbour folk today, with money earned through labour migration to Aruba and Curaçao, and the subsequent construction and operation of two schooners and a retailing business in the late 1950s and 1960s made the Taylor family one of the most powerful and affluent families in Bequia.

In 1980 Clive Taylor became the leader of the People's Political Party (PPP), the then official opposition party in St Vincent, and although he resides on the mainland, he owns land and part-shares in the family's businesses in Bequia. His two brothers, who still live and work in Bequia, today between them own and run the island's cinema, a rum shop, a building supplies store and a trucking company. Their sister owns a clothes shop in Hamilton.

The translation of wealth into political power by the Taylor family can only be understood by locating Bequia politics in the formal political structure of the state of St Vincent and the Grenadines. Since the introduction of suffrage in the state in 1951 the House of Assembly has been made up of 13 seats: 12 elected from the mainland of St Vincent and one from the Grenadines. From 1952 until 1966 Clive Taylor, a member of the People's Political Party, represented the Grenadines in the House of Assembly, the PPP having formed the government in the state from 1957 to 1966. The Party was founded in 1952 by a Trinidadian school teacher, Joshua, who aligned his party to the main unions on St Vincent and derived support from the working classes. In opposition during the period of PPP rule was the St Vincent Labour Party (SVLP), under Milton Cato, who were backed by the middle classes and gathered increasing support in the rural areas of St Vincent.

Up until 1966, Clive Taylor retained his seat in the Grenadines with ease, facing little serious opposition from the SVLP. Much of his support in Bequia came from Port Elizabeth and Hamilton, where the greatest concentration of the electorate lived at the time (see Table 2a). Gibson (*op.cit.*:80) reports that, during Clive Taylor's term as Grenadines Representative, his father, Yando:

> ... used to distribute free flour and sugar to the 'poor people' of Hamilton and presumably built up a considerable system of patronage.

Households in Hamilton and Port Elizabeth had been leased provision grounds, many women working Taylor lands on a sharecropping basis. Many of their men folk found employment on Taylor-owned inter-island schooners. With the arrival of National Bulk Carriers, this patronage was extended to employment on merchant freighters.

Although Taylor was popular amongst the electorate in and around the 'harbour' he was by no means held in such esteem by members of Mount Pleasant and Southside communities. I was repeatedly told during my fieldwork that whilst Taylor was in power he had '... only look after "his people" (of Hamilton and Port Elizabeth) because dey plenty enough to win he through ...'

In 1965, however, there was for the first time in Bequia a serious challenge to Taylor's dominance in local politics. 'Kid' Andrews, whose family had originated as planters from Canouan, returned from England where he had been educated as an agronomist. He stood as an Independent candidate against Taylor, for the Representative of the Grenadines seat in the 1966 Election. Andrews gained many votes from Mount Pleasant, Southside and Lower Bay in Bequia and became the new Representative of the Grenadines. The political split that occurred in the Bequia electorate – Taylor gathering support predominantly from the harbour and Andrews from the remainder of the island – was, suggests Gibson (*ibid.*) mirrored by a skin colour split. Andrews, light-skinned because of his planter ancestry, being supported by the

Table 2a: Population by electoral constituency, Bequia, 1970

Constituency	Population	No. of Households
Hamilton A	573	103
Hamilton B	568	112
Reform		
Cinammon Gdns		
East Port Elizabeth		
West Port Elizabeth	585	143
Union Vale		
Spring/Park		
Hope		
	1726	
	(45%)	
Belmont		
Mount Pleasant	328	74
Lower Bay		
Friendship		
Lawlers Hill	386	74
Ambois		
	714	
	(18.5%)	
Friendship Bay		
La Pompe	589	103
Paget Farm		
Derrick	805	151
Gelliceau		
	1394	
	(36.5%)	
Totals	3,834 (100%)	760

Details obtained from Census Officer of St Vincent and the Grenadines, 23/5/80)

planters, Mount Pleasant people and the lighter skinned lower classes, whilst Taylor (black) was favoured by the blacker skinned lower classes around the harbour. Skin colour separation in voting was, and remains a popular image in Bequia lower class culture, although increasingly more black people now support Andrews than they did in the 1960s.

Whatever the importance of skin colour separation, of more importance at the time of Andrews' success was the issue of employment with NBC. The system of patronage and its resultant political affiliation and divisions since the early 1960s meant that few men from Mount Pleasant and Southside secured employment with National Bulk. Andrews represented a challenge to this patronage. In Lower Bay, political affiliations were divided during this period, some men finding their support for the government instrumental in securing jobs or places on apprentice schemes with National Bulk. One such man in Lower Bay, who had inherited part of Diamond Estate from his mother, Joyce Powell, was reputedly forced to sell some of this land to a government minister in 1962 in order to secure employment with NBC. The land has remained idle since the sale and is today used by Lower Bay people as a 'village green'.

Other men from Lower Bay, with experience on Harrison Line vessels trading in and around the Caribbean, were forced to look further afield, and through kinship and network ties were able to find limited employment with Barbados Shipping Co., International Seafoods (Barbados) Ltd., and inter-island trading companies and charter/cruise liners. Some Lower Bay seamen eventually settled in the larger islands in the Caribbean and on the north-east coast of South America (see p.54 below and Appendix I). But like the Southside communities, fishing has remained a significant residual form of production for the lower classes in Lower Bay.

The economic and social effects of labour demand by National Bulk have not, however, been limited to changes in production associated with the exploitation of marine resources. The influence of National Bulk on agricultural production and consumption patterns further illustrates the dominance of international capitalism and the relationship between different modes, and forms, of economic activity in Bequia. Whilst the Southside villagers, Mount Pleasant and Lower Bay communities continued to work subsistence provision grounds and engaged in limited sharecropping, many of the women in Hamilton and Port Elizabeth sold or leased their provision grounds and suspended sharecropping during the 1960s when regular flows of cash from their 'Bulkmen' meant that they were able to purchase imported foodstuffs.[6] The introduction of import controls in 1972 and increasing inflation forced some of these women back to their grounds; but the post-1976 decline in merchant shipping labour recruitment in the West Indies has meant that the problems of food supplies for some of these 'harbour' families has been more severe than in other villages. Some men in Hamilton and Port Elizabeth have returned to fishing but for many of the young men, fishing skills and techniques have never been acquired as they took to 'seamanship' in their early teens.

Most young men seek work in hotels and bars or as crew on foreign-owned charter yachts. The influence of tourism on employment aspirations, forms of production and social and economic life in general has not been limited to the 'harbour', although it has been more rapid and structurally evident there. As I shall be devoting a chapter (Chapter 7) to the impact of tourism and the activities of expatriates in the island, I shall deal here only with the major effects on island economic and social exchange.

2 Tourism and expatriate housing projects

St Vincent government policies since the early 1960s reflect the perceived importance of the development of the tourist industry on the mainland and in the Grenadines. The introduction of 'pioneer status' in 1960 gave a minimum ten year exemption from customs import duties, profit taxation, etc., to local entrepreneurs or foreign businessmen prepared to invest in projects seen as likely to benefit economic and infrastructural development in the state (see Chapter 7). The sale and 30-year leasing of parts and sometimes whole islands in the Grenadines and the unconditional sale of lands by individuals and the government in Bequia to North Americans and Europeans, has meant that land prices have risen dramatically since the late 1960s; much of the capital generated in the tourist and housing industries is exported; prices of basic food, clothing and building materials have been inflated; and much of the employment in the tourist housing sector is taken by foreigners.

The sale of a large part of Spring Estate, the largest and most fertile ex-plantation, in 1962, to a US hotel development agency is a case that serves to illustrate some of the points made above. When work began on the construction of Spring Hotel and luxury houses in 1964 many 'harbour' men were employed in the initial clearing of grounds and early construction. As they left to go to sea they were replaced by Vincentian labour (see Chapter 3 below). Total employment has declined rapidly since the completion of the hotel and many of the luxury houses, but demand from North America and Europe means that a number of houses are still under construction, even at a cost of up to $100,000 US each. In 1975, says Gibson (*op.cit.*:67): 'The project still employs 60–100 men of which six are from Bequia'. By 1981 this number had reduced again, although five Bequia men were regularly employed during my fieldwork.

The initial work at Spring produced a number of 'freelance' masons, carpenters, plumbers, electricians and painters in Bequia, who still supplement incomes from fishing and sailing by working on construction of foreign, and some local, houses. Whilst the remaining plantation lands at Spring produce fruit and vegetables for the hotel, and limited production of copra continues, it is recognised throughout Bequia that these fertile lands are under-utilised in terms of food production at a time when many Bequarians depend to a large extent on expensive imported foodstuffs.

3 The role of Vincentians in the Bequia economy

No discussion, however general, of dependency and power relations in Bequia would be complete without reference to the role of Vincentian labour and entrepreneurs in the island economy. Vincentians are in competition with Bequarians for jobs, especially semi-skilled and unskilled manual work, in businesses and, lately, within small scale entrepreneurial activities like hawking.

Vincentian labourers and craftsmen have been regularly visiting Bequia since the boom in construction in the early 1960s. Gibson (*ibid.*:68) suggests that Bequarian men are averse to gang work of any type, and agricultural labour: 'Bequians (Bequarians) attach a stigma to manual labour on the land and so Vincentians are despised for their willingness to do what Bequians will not'. While there is clear evidence of Bequarian dislike and distrust of Vincentians, there is little to validate the claim that this stems from the fact that Vincentians are prepared to engage in types of work that Bequia folk despise. The case of Spring contruction shows that at its outset it was predominantly Bequia labour that was employed in land clearance, and it was only following the increased availability of employment with National Bulk that harbour men left the site to be replaced by Vincentian labourers. Later in the book (especially in Chapter 6) when I discuss lower class culture and ideology, I shall be presenting material which suggests that it is perceptions of political and economic exploitation by the St Vincent government that has been at the root of anti-Vincentian sentiments in the Grenadines, together with a strong sense of nationalism and self-sufficiency that pervades lower class culture.

The data I collected from Lower Bay show that many men, especially the young unemployed, are prepared to do any kind of paid work they can find. It would appear that Vincentians, like the harbour men with NBC, are played off against other potential workers in Bequia to secure the interests and positions of power of international capital and dominant classes. In 1973 the British Development Division in Barbados sponsored a road-reinstatement project in Bequia. The project, which lasted a year, employed predominantly Vincentians, who were recruited by the government, in the tarring and digging operations with Bequarians finding employment in clerical, overseeing, trucking and masonry posts.

Bequia people resent the role that Vincentians play in the economy of the island. Bequia's social and economic progress up to the 1970s is seen by the islanders as largely due to their own enterprise, diligence and ingenuity and they strongly resent the payment of taxes and the flow of tourist and yacht remittances to Kingstown (see Chapter 7 below). Vincentians that are overtly recognised as, and accused of, taking jobs from Bequarians are those in key administrative and professional posts, such as the police, revenue officers, clerks and the priests, all of these positions being currently filled by Vincentians. Vincentian men are employed by CDC (the electricity company) which is a further source of anti-Vincentian sentiments. Haulage and taxi services were first introduced into Bequia by Vincentians and a few shops and bars in the harbour are still owned and operated by Vincentians.

The competitive role of Vincentians in the Bequia economy has been further enhanced as a result of increased tourist activity locally. As Chapter 3 demonstrates, one of the responses to the marginality experienced by young men as a consequence of unemployment has been a shift into small scale enterprises based on hawking. There is a high degree of competitiveness between locals for markets for their artefacts; and the recent arrival of Vincentian hawkers, selling coral jewellery, macramé, etc., has caused tension and dissatisfaction amongst lower class Bequarians for whom hawking represents hope amongst the hopelessness of their impoverishment and dependence.

The return to subsistence: economic demise in Bequia

The first 75 years of the twentieth century witnessed a transition in the system of production in Bequia from subsistence-based agricultural and fishing activities to a cash economy, following the commercialisation of fishing, whaling and boat building and the creation of labour markets. Modes of economic activity based upon monetary exchange were well established in the island by the 1930s.

Between 1975 and 1981, because of declining labour markets and marine resources, and limited emigration and labour migration opportunities, there was a gradual return to subsistence activities within residual forms of production by many lower class households. Little, if any, surplus was produced during this period by the lower classes, who became increasingly dependent upon emigrant remittances and seasonal/temporary wage labour.

The lower classes in all the island's settlements have been dependent upon movements of international capital since settlement in the eighteenth century. The extent of this dependence and its manifestation in terms of access to wage labour and means of production during this century, has been examined here in the context of relationships within and between settlements.

Lower class Bequarians have been faced with systemic forces which have restricted their range of effective choices with regards to modes of economic activity, and which have further maintained the structures of inequality in the island. Co-existent modes and forms of production have become subordinated to, and dependent on, foreign-owned and controlled shipping companies and tourist enterprises, externally controlled markets for fish, and the ownership of productive land and fishing technology by powerful island-based groups. Through the creation of a reserve army of labour drawn from the lower classes, the interests of foreign capitalists and powerful classes in Bequia are secured by playing different groups of workers, or potential workers, off against each other (e.g. Vincentians against Bequarians, harbour men against Southsiders), thus controlling demands and institutionalising redundancies and employment insecurity. Profit maximisation by foreign and local capitalists determines the organisation of production in Bequia, forcing the recent return to subsistence production, and shapes the employment/under-employment/unemployment structure, a theme which is further explored in the next chapter. The tourist industry, despite the aspirations it has raised amongst many members of the lower classes, is characteristic of the above structure of social relations: profit maximisation, little reinvestment, creation and reliance on a reserve army of labour, job insecurity and low wages, and has done little to improve the livelihood of lower class Bequarians. As subsequent chapters will show, tourism has also had far-reaching and adverse effects on lower class culture and social practices.

Notes

1 The sociological data that I gathered on settlements outside Lower Bay was limited by fieldwork technique: the trenchant solidarity expressed towards the settlement/community of residence by indigenes made a general sociology of Bequia virtually impossible. Once I was accepted into the community of Lower Bay, my association and interaction with other island groups had to be tentative and qualified so as not to constitute a threat to my affiliation with Lower Bay and its members. This was at its most emphatic with regards to Mount Pleasant.
2 The term also includes the scattered homesteads at Reform and Union Vale, which lie to the north of Port Elizabeth along the main road to Spring.
3 For a fuller discussion of the Resettlement Scheme and the post-Emancipation conditions of 'poor whites' in Barbados see J. S. Handler (1974).
4 See Adams, 1971b.
5 Trade with Martinique has now restarted (see Chapter 3).
6 See Gibson (1981) for fuller details, as her fieldwork was based in Port Elizabeth. Most fresh vegetables are imported from St Vincent and non-perishables from Caricom countries, USA and Britain.

CHAPTER 3 | The Lower Bay economy

This chapter focuses on the current economic structure of the community of Lower Bay, as a representation of the different types of production relations into which Lower Bay people enter in the course of their economic activities. This requires more than the segregation of people into groups of similar economic status and activity, for production of the means of livelihood is social:

> ... the operation of an economy is the total manifestation of the *interrelationships of the people* in regard to the production of wealth in society. (Mukherjee, 1957:12 – my emphasis)

The inter-relationships between people in production bring them into co-operation and conflict, according to the place they occupy in a historically determined system of production. The different places that such groups occupy represent the classes in the social formation, determined by their relation to the means of production and:

> ... by their role in the social organisation of labour and, consequently, by the dimension and mode of acquiring the share of the social wealth of which they dispose. (Lenin, 1971:231)

Classes in Bequia have, as shown in Chapter 1, evolved in the context of the transition between related modes of production. Today, the classes present in their full determination within the capitalist mode are the exploiting *ex-planter/merchant class*, which is politically, economically and ideologically dominant, in alliance with foreign capital, through ownership of and control over the means of capital production i.e. land, technology, tourist/real estate enterprises and trade; and the *exploited lower class* of non-owners of means of production. Although the capitalist mode of production in Bequia is now dominant, in the sense of subordinating the functioning of other, and hence residual, forms derived from earlier modes of production, the CMP relies upon these residual forms for its reproduction through appropriation of labour power. Consequently the lower (exploited) classes in Bequia cannot be regarded as constituted by their individual members; for their position as a reserve pool of labour for the CMP, on the fringes of the modern capitalist economy, confines them to a sector cutting across the residual forms of production and the CMP. As such the class structure of Bequia is represented by the following hierarchy of classes, local perception reflecting this hierarchy:

(a) *lower classes*
  (i) *peasant producers:* characterised by production for use (no surplus), and ownership and control of their means of production; small-scale agricultural production on household gardens and fishing for household consumption. Peasant production is generally considered the 'lowest' form of production in plebeian culture;
  (ii) *sharecroppers;* again characterised by production for use, but non-owners, or partial owners, of their means of production, receiving a share of the agricultural produce of their labour. Small surpluses, after meeting the needs of the household, are sometimes exchanged;
  (iii) *petty-commodity producers:* owning or part owning their means of production; through limited access to the means of subsistence, production is essentially for exchange. The division of labour is, therefore, mediated by market forces. Fishing represents the major form of petty-commodity production but increased tourist and expatriate activity in Bequia has stimulated small entrepreneurial activity and hawking: the production/purchase and sale of commodities by individuals or households through a division of labour characterised by the absence of wage labour and mediated by the market;
  (iv) *wage labourers:* non-owners of the means of production, employed (largely temporarily and/or seasonally) in the 'modern' economy of island and international capitalist enterprises: tourist businesses, construction industries, merchant shipping, etc.;
(b) *middle classes*
  (i) *professionals and administrators* in the larger foreign-owned and indigenous capitalist enterprises, dominated by foreign labour;

(ii) *small businesses* employing wage labour, largely absent amongst Bequia indigenes because of the continued dominance of household/family labour in entrepreneurial activities, as a result of limited access to credit and resources for the lower classes;

(c) *capitalists*
owners of the island's means of production: inter-island trading, land, tourist enterprises and real estate companies; the ex-planter/merchant class and foreign capitalists.

The participation of the lower classes in the 'modern' economy is distinguished by marginality and dependence, a conditioning situation which determines the limits and possibilities of their production activities. The lower classes are forced to rely upon 'customary' work activities belonging to residual modes and forms of production. In this context the household remains significant for the lower classes and constitutes a sort of 'fall back' system: a mode of subsistence and security for the under- and unemployed. Customary work activities do not require the support structure of a complex social organisation, nor units larger than household or friendship (peer) groups. The needs of the household and certain non-resident family members (see Chapter 4) are the primary material concern of the lower classes. The lower class household cannot exist solely through production in the residual forms: access, albeit unstable and limited, to wage labour and/or emigrant remittances remaining essential for the lower class household to sustain the livelihood of its members. The household, then, is a crucial unit of production within the forms derived from earlier modes of production.

Production relations and engagement in productive activities leads to the empirical classification of community economic activities into: wage labour, fishing, agriculture, communal production and entrepreneurial activities. These activities can be hierarchised according to their material and symbolic importance for the lower classes (see below, p.53). The perceived importance of a particular work activity is, as will be shown more clearly in Chapter 6, assessed within the community in '... social, personal and economic terms and measured by moral and material criteria' (Wallman, 1979:7-8). Evaluation of work and perceptions of the importance and appropriateness of specific forms of work, depend in part upon lower class cultural values relating to sex and age as well as class, and upon the immediate material circumstances and experiences of the individual and his/her dependants. Customary work involves a plurality of activities in which work, leisure/recreation, family, religion, Friendly Society and community form a continuous and mutually inclusive set of activities congruent with a general perception of everyday life. Although the lower classes have been dependent upon external, and externally generated, sources of revenue for their livelihood since the post-Emancipation phase, this dependence has become more marked during recent years with increasing commercialisation and declining natural resources, e.g. falling fish stocks and soil erosion.

The diminishing status of customary work activities such as fishing and labour exchange (see Chapter 6) within lower class culture reflects the reality of the marginal position of most lower class members of the community and their increasing need for a regular money supply. The rejection of the centrality of non-salaried work in residual forms of production, especially communal production by the lower classes, has been accompanied by increasing importance being attached to wage labour and entrepreneurial activities. The hierarchised classification of work activities below is, therefore, based upon perceptions of social value within the lower classes: perceptions which reflect the reality of changing material conditions. Fishing, which traditionally embodied the work/community ethic and was considered the most appropriate work and social activity for a Lower Bay man (again, see Chapter 6, and Wadel, 1979) is valued only by the older members of the community and, by definition, the seine owners. The hierarchy of work activities is:

Increasing ↑	Wage labour
importance	Enterprise
for the	Fishing
lower	Agriculture
classes	Communal production
	(labour exchange)

This chapter, then, presents empirical material on work activities amongst the lower classes in Lower Bay, and attempts to locate the Lower Bay economy historically and structurally within the wider context of the island and international division of labour. By discussing each of the categories of work presented in the above hierarchy, I shall focus attention on social relations of production between and within classes, introducing the significance of age and sex categories in such relations. This will further necessitate a discussion of the relationships between forms of production and the influence of external factors on the evolution and reproduction of production relations.

Wage labour

Although wage labour opportunities existed during slavery, when freedmen were paid for maintenance work on planters' houses, these opportunities were very limited and access was restricted. Following Emancipation, limited opportunities for paid employment in Bequia continued, mostly in copra husking and building repairs and construction. By the turn of the century wage labour opportunities remained scarce despite the establishment of inter-island schooner trade: the planter/merchant class relying predominantly on family labour within the developing industry.

1 Labour migration

With the advent of the Second World War came the creation of a market for unskilled labour in the Caribbean Basin, through the construction of oil refineries in Aruba and Curaçao and military bases throughout the region. The virtual absence of wage labour in Bequia at the time meant many Bequia men left the island during the war. Appendix I documents some of these labour movements, based on oral history drawn from informants as no official records are available.

Labour migration was not a new development in Bequia's history as following Emancipation many ex-slaves left for Trinidad to work for a tied wage. There were, however, few movements out of Bequia between the initial post-Emancipation exodus and 1939. After 1939, periods of absence from Bequia, associated with the search for wage labour, varied considerably. The majority of those men successful in finding work in the construction and maintenance of military bases had returned by the end of the war, whereas those employed by the oil companies in Aruba and Curaçao found their contracts extended until the late 1940s and early 1950s as a result of increased exploration and drilling of oil off the Venezuelan coast. Migration during the 1939–52 period had a considerable and far-reaching effect on the stratification of the island population. This is excellently illustrated by the case of Len Lafayette.

As a descendant of one of the most powerful planter families in Bequia, Len Lafayette was assured of access to land through inheritance. However, being one of a large sibling group his potential share of the family's estate would have been relatively small. By 1939, at the age of 26, he had gained experience of inter-island trading schooner employment aboard his father's vessels and, with money he had saved from such work, he went to Curaçao to work on the contruction of oil refineries. When he returned to Bequia in 1951 he was, in the words of one of the older men in Lower Bay community:

> ... a rich man compared wid most people in de island. He done save plenty of he wage, and when he come back he done afford endless thing dat most of we together couldnah buy.

Amongst the material assets in which Lafayette invested his savings were land in Lower Bay, bordering land already owned by his family which he later inherited, a seine net and boat, a fillet net and boat, and a cassava mill. In 1952 he built a trading schooner using predominantly family labour, which operated successfully until 1962 when he sold it to another prominent island merchant to concentrate on seine fishing.

Lafayette became one of the most powerful members of Lower Bay community through his ownership of land, houses, and fishing and agricultural means of production. After selling his schooner, he built a holiday-let house on land bordering his own dwelling and in 1980 started work on construction of a second such house near the beach. His migration to Curaçao served to consolidate and enhance his already guaranteed position of prominence in the local system of production and exchange.

The increased material wealth, social mobility and, in some cases, power that was achieved by men who had secured wage labour employment during and immediately after World War II polarised the island community during the early 1950s and exaggerated the marginality of the majority of the lower classes who remained dependent on traditional economic activities, viz. fishing, agriculture and communal production. Feelings of deprivation and frustration amongst the poorest of the lower classes became enhanced during the period of returning migrants. The following extract from a conversation with an elderly Lower Bay woman highlights some of the factors and effects of such frustration:

> When ordinary people in Bequia start bettering deyselves wid money and belongings dat dey menfolk bring back from Aruba and dem places we poor folk start to thinking about things. In dem days we was used to seeing de rich people living decent lives but we ain't realise it so easy for a ordinary person for make deyself comfortable. Almost everyone in de village (Lower Bay) start talking about

trying for get work on dese other island. And when dey start building factories and hotels in Grenada and Barbados plenty people start for leave de island. Some of de men who working on schooner start for staying off in Guyana, Trinidad and de like ... Everyone want for leave Bequia and earn deyself a living ...

The 1950s witnessed the largest movement of people out of Bequia since the post-Emancipation exodus of freed slaves. Before the advent of a merchant shipping labour market in the late 1950s, industrialisation on neighbouring islands provided work for many lower class Bequarians. Seamen from inter-island trading schooners settled in Barbados, Trinidad and Guyana which represented the cornerstones of the local trading routes, and Lower Bay women found employment in the newly-built nutmeg factories in Grenada in the mid 1950s (see Appendix I). At the time there was an almost total absence of wage labour opportunities for women in Bequia, but flexible child-rearing arrangements and the matrifocal nature of lower class households (see Chapter 4) meant that women were able to migrate to St Georges (Grenada) and settle there with the option of sending for their children later.

The destinies of Lower Bay, and other Bequarian, migrants during the post-war period were not, however, limited to the Caribbean. There had been a steady, albeit small, flow of Bequarians to the USA since the end of the war which was curbed in 1952 by the US government's passing of the MaCarran-Walker Act aimed at restricting the entry of Afro-Caribbeans into the country. The UK Commonwealth Immigration Scheme, by which Afro-Caribbeans and Commonwealth members of the Asian subcontinent were actively encouraged to emigrate to Britain, attracted many Bequarians between 1955–61. Although no figures are available for the numbers of emigrants from Bequia, those relating to citizens of St Vincent and the Grenadines reflect the scale and nature of emigration to the UK during the 1950s.

The financing of emigration to the UK was difficult for many Bequarians. As Tables 3a and 3b, show it was predominantly men who left the islands to take up work, establishing themselves in London, Reading and the Midlands industrial cities. Although many of the emigrating males were single, there were a number of cases of married men emigrating initially alone and later sending savings to pay the fares of their dependants (again, see Appendix I for some examples).

Since the tightening up of the immigration laws of the US and

Table 3a: Emigration from St Vincent and the Grenadines to the UK, 1955–1960

Total population of St Vincent and Grenadines, 1960	80,705
Emigration figures to UK, 1955–60	4,285
Emigrants as percentage of total population	5.3%

(Adapted from Peach, 1968:15)

Table 3b: Males as percentage of West Indian emigrants from St Vincent and the Grenadines to the UK, 1957–1960

Year	Numbers of male emigrants	Male emigrants as percentage of total emigrants
1957	515	69.3
1958	304	54.3
1959	1,088	65.3
1960	858	73.5
Total number of male emigrants (1957–60)	2,765	Average yearly percentage of male emigrants 65.6

(Adapted from Peach [op.cit.])

Britain[1] there have been many cases of Bequarians effecting illegal entry to the USA. One method for gaining entry to the States, used by many Bequarians, is through short-stay visitor visas granted to persons taking a holiday. Once entry has been achieved the individual 'loses herself' in the large cities, relying upon seasonal or temporary employment in industries such as catering, hotels, construction and agriculture, and being paid well below the minimum wage by employers offering work to persons with no work permit or Social Security number. The case below draws out the experience of one Lower Bay woman who worked illegally in Dallas in the early 1970s.

Case 3a   A Lower Bay woman's experience of working illegally in the USA

Tania left Lower Bay in 1953 at the age of five with her unmarried mother and elder sister for Trinidad (see Appendix I). Her mother owned no land in Lower Bay at the time of her departure and was living in her parents' house working seasonally as a sharecropper on Friendship Estate. Shortly after arriving in Trinidad, Tania's mother found work in a clothing factory and in 1955 married a Trinidadian. When her mother died in 1971 Tania used the money she was left to pay for a flight to the USA. In her own words, this is a brief account of her stay in the States:

> When my mother die I decide for go visit two old school friends from Trinidad who working in Dallas. I manage for get a visitor visa for one month, and I flew out early in 1972. After I bin dere about two week, having a real nice time, I find most of my money gone so I took dis work in a small restaurant downtown – really it was just washing dishes and cleaning de kitchen. Well, I wasnah earning much cos de boss he know I ain't got no social security number or nutting but I getting enough for help pay some rent on de apartment of dose friend of mine. So I decide for stay on. After de restaurant I has plenty job: waitressing, bar work, cleaning for rich American families, but all de time I ain't haf social security number so de 'Man' he pay me what he like – alway less dan other people earning. But I enjoy de city life – plenty of thing for do. But after I bin dere about two year I start for get tired of being treated like shit by every boss I working for so I come back to Bequia. I ain't really see Trinidad as I home – I only haf a brother dere and he married – my family still in Lower Bay. I bin here now for nearly eight year and I start thinking for get back to de States, but it ain't easy. I ain't really haf no life here at all, and thing only seem for getting worse dese days.

Since returning from the USA, Tania has lived with her mother's mother, an elderly woman in her 70s, in Lower Bay. In 1978 she had a child by a man from Southside who gives her occasional financial support. Between 1980 and 1981 she ran a small rum shop for her brother who returned from Trinidad in 1976 to work with National Bulk Carriers. Her stay in the USA has made her far more critical of the inadequacy of Bequia to provide housing, employment and a reasonable welfare system for the lower classes. During long conversations in the rum shop she repeatedly told me of her desire to leave Bequia to provide a '... decent life for me and my child'.

This case illustrates a number of important factors and consequences of emigration and begins to show the significance of matrifocality for lower class women, a theme discussed more fully in Chapter 4. Tania's mother's emigration to Trinidad in 1963 was at a time when the larger Caribbean islands were undergoing significant economic changes associated with industrialisation and the development of tourism. In Bequia no such developments were taking place, the major source of wage labour being in the merchant seaman labour market. Wage labour opportunities for women were absent. Tania's mother was materially dependent upon her parents for accommodation and on limited access to sharecropping for her material support. Although Tania was only five at the time of her departure from Bequia she remembers her mother telling her '... how much a struggle life be in Lowbay in dese times'. Apparently her mother received no material support from the father of her children. The marginality and dependence of the lower classes was, and remains, a major 'push' factor behind emigration and labour migration from the community, and the island.

Tania's period of work in the USA is typical of that of many lower class Bequarians who have chosen to enter the country illegally and engage in work activities in those sectors of the economy exploiting the insecure position of such migrant labourers. While most members of the community who experienced short-stay employment in the USA relate their experiences with nostalgia, focusing predominantly on the leisure sector of North American society, when asked of their working conditions they invariably expressed feelings of exploitation and insecurity.

During the 1960s and 1970s illegal entry to the USA by lower class Afro-Caribbeans continued as did that of other migrants, especially Mexican Americans into California and Texas. One common method of Afro-Caribbeans effecting entry was for crews on trading vessels and yachts to obtain a short-stay visa on arrival at ports and to 'stay off' the vessels. By far the most common means of entering the USA and one which carried little risk of deportation up until 1970 was via the US Virgin Islands.

Between 1961 and 1969 there was a boom in the US Virgin Islands' tourist industry which created a demand for construction workers and tourist-sector staff, essentially in hotels and restaurants. In 1961 the US Immigration Service and Labour Department introduced the 'bonded alien labour' system, whereby an employer who was unable to find a native Virgin Islander to fill a specific post could have an 'alien' (immigrant worker) bonded to him. Under the system, an alien who lost his/her job was forbidden to take another and was deported within five days. Lukas (1971) describes the exploitation of bonded alien labour as complete: immigrant workers were paid below the minimum wage, many earning only 60c (US) an hour, and many employers registered skilled workers as manual and unskilled and paid them accordingly. The bonded alien system represented for employers: '... a perfect pool of defenceless, cheap labour' (Lukas, *ibid.*:103), with aliens forbidden from entitlement to benefits accorded to US Virgin citizens. Aliens were not permitted to send their children to state schools, did not qualify for public housing, and received no paid holidays, retirement benefits or health insurance. Employers often paid no social security or unemployment compensation to aliens, who were effectively 'non-persons' (Lukas, *op.cit.*) although essential to the island's economy at the time.

Many Bequarians, along with men and women from Antigua, Nevis, St Kitts, St Lucia, Tortola, Montserrat, Trinidad and St Vincent, found work as 'bonded aliens' in the US Virgin Islands during the 1960s. So great was the influx and the consequent exploitation of cheap labour that the Labour Department disbanded the system in 1970 in response to rising unemployment amongst the indigenous labour force and the decline in construction activity in the tourist sector. Aliens were given 60 days to find alternative employmet, failing which they were deported. The entry of further migrant labour was prevented, and the police conducted a purge on illegal aliens, knocking on doors day and night. Most of the Bequarian immigrants were forced to return home during 1971, although a few were granted social security numbers, the 'Green Card' denoting temporary US citizenship, and allowed to stay provided they had secured full time employment. Two brothers who left Lower Bay in 1967 (see Appendix I) both survived the clampdown on immigrant labour in the islands in 1970 and now work as a bar manager and a head waiter in large hotels. Another young man who entered St Thomas in 1966 as a 'bonded alien' secured work on the construction of a large hotel in the island. After the hotel was completed his employer gave him a junior management post in the catering section of the hotel complex. In 1970 he secured a Green Card and took up the post of bar manager in a hotel owned by the same company in Miami. Since then he has been granted US citizenship and lives in Miami, married to an American woman.

Population movements out of Bequia have declined dramatically since 1970. Of those cases of Lower Bay emigration since 1970, many have been dependants joining their families, illegal entrants to the USA, or those settling other Caribbean islands. This decline, however, does not reflect a comparable increase in wage labour opportunities locally, but a tightening up of immigration legislation throughout the Caribbean and North America. Aspirations to emigration remain high amongst the lower classes – for many, especially the young, it represents the only solution to their marginality. In the words of a Lower Bay man who spent three years in the USA in the 1960s:

> Man, it easy for see why people looking for leave Bequia. Land getting harder for come by all de time as prices go up and dere more mouth for feed; dere no real chance for getting good education here ... and work hard for get for most of we.

Indeed, as the population increases then land shortages, lack of educational opportunity and, above all, unemployment and underemployment mean that the lower classes are becoming increasingly marginalised; dependent upon kin and friendship networks for support, including emigrant remittances, and upon work within the residual forms of production. Access to wage labour remains unstable, as do sources of cash from emigrant kin. Internal migration, within the state, in a search for land and wage labour has also declined and as a result competition for seasonal and temporary employment in the public and private sectors has increased.

2 Public sector employment

The previous chapter introduced the dominance of Vincentian labour in the public sector in Bequia. Vincentians, in a similar class situation, compete for wage labour opportunities with Bequia lower classes. Limited opportunities for temporary, full time and part time work for Bequia men in the public services remain. As Table 3c shows, in January 1981 only two Lower Bay men were employed in the public sector, one full time as a 'scavenger' (road sweeper) on a temporary contract paid daily at $10 EC per day, and one part time with the electricity company. The latter (see Case 5a, p.141) lost his job in 1981 and left the island to work illegally, in the Virgin Islands. Other public service jobs available to Bequia men include refuse collection, administration and teaching, although no men

Table 3c: Male wage labour employment, Lower Bay community, 1981

	January 1981					May 1981				
	No.	%	FT	PT	Perm/temp	No.	%	FT	PT	Perm/temp
Seamen	20	19.42	20	0	0 20	19	18.63	19	0	0 19
Skilled manual (masons etc.)	5	4.86	1	4	0 5	6	5.88	1	5	0 6
Unskilled manual (labouring-construction)	3	2.91	1	2	0 3	3	2.94	0	3	0 3
Public sector	2	1.94	1	1	0 2	1	0.98	1	0	0 1
Tourist (barmen etc.)	8	7.77	5	4	1 7	1	0.98	1	0	0 1
Over 60 years of age	13	12.62	–	–	– –	13	12.78	–	–	– –
15–60 with no wage labour	52	50.48	–	–	– –	59	57.82	–	–	– –
Totals	103	100.00	28	10	1 37	102	100.00	22	8	0 30

FT = Full time
PT = Part time
Note: Does not include 'family' labour – i.e. men/boys employed in family businesses (shops, bars etc.).

from Lower Bay were employed in these occupations during my period in the field.

Women experience even greater difficulties than men in securing public sector employment. Limited opportunities do exist for women in administration, teaching and health care, but no Lower Bay women were employed in these occupations in 1980–81, although three worked as teachers in the privately run Lower Bay primary school. (Table 3d). Those indigenous women who have secured public sector employment tended to have an overseas education, from North America or Europe, being members of the dominant classes in Bequia.

Lower Bay people are resentful of the lack of opportunity for employment in the public sector and their resentment usually takes the form of criticisms of Vincentians and the government:

Table 3d: Female wage labour employment, Lower Bay community, 1981

	January 1981					May 1981				
	No.	%	FT	PT	Perm/temp	No.	%	FT	PT	Perm/temp
School teacher (private school)	3	2.70	1	2	1 2	3	2.70	1	2	1 2
Domestic – tourist/resident non-national houses	6	5.41	0	6	0 6	3	2.70	0	3	0 3
Hotel – chambermaid, waitress, barmaid	8	7.21	6	2	0 8	4	3.60	3	1	0 4
Restaurant/bar waitress/barmaid	7	6.30	5	2	0 7	4	3.60	4	0	0 4
Shop assistant	2	1.80	2	0	0 2	3	2.70	2	1	0 3
Over 60	17	15.32	–	–	– –	17	15.32	–	–	– –
No wage labour 15–60	68	61.26	–	–	– –	77	69.37	–	–	– –
Totals	111	100.00	14	12	1 25	111	100.00	10	7	1 16

Note: does not include women/girls 'employed' in family businesses (shops, bars etc.).

Man, you think it right dat dem Vincees doing jobs in Bequia dat we people is able for do? We done have plenty need for work and dere endless people willing for do dat kind of thing. De only time dey ever looking for gif job to Bequia man come before a election when dey repair de road for one or two week. Den dey for pay we $10 EC a day to work like slave. Dat government dey know dat even if every man and woman in de Grenadines done vote against dem it ain't for make no difference to dey strength. So dey give all de work to Vincees and dem people will do anything for make a dollar. Dey ain't care dat we Bequarian can't even find job in we own island.

It is a misconception to argue, as does Gibson (1981), that Bequarians are averse to manual labour. Lower class Bequarians certainly aspire to manual skilled and white collar work, but they are acutely aware of their increasingly marginal position in the island's system of production. When a government scheme to repair the roads in Bequia was announced just prior to the by-election of 1980 large numbers of Bequia men applied for work, but most of the jobs went to Vincentians who accompanied the vehicles and machinery from Kingstown.

However it is predominantly in the private sector, dominated by transnational companies and expatriate businesses, that the lower classes depend for wage labour.

3 Private sector employment

Wage labour in the private sector exists largely within two spheres: seamanship (sailing) and tourism/real estate.

The adult male population of Bequia has been employed as seamen to varying degrees of full time employment since the establishment of the whaling industry in 1875. As we have seen, the most significant development in the seaman labour market came in the late 1950s with the first recruitment of Bequia men to the US-owned National Bulk Carriers. Prior to the creation of this labour market the most prominent form of seaman wage labour was aboard inter-island trading schooners. Although wages were low in comparison with the merchant seaman wages offered by the foreign companies that began recruiting small numbers of Bequia men in the mid-1950s (notably the US Harrison line), work aboard trading schooners was an essential part of the lower class employment structure. 'Giant' Thompson, a 50-year-old Lower Bay man, recalls his years as a 'sailor':

> In de 1950s we done earn about $10 EC a month. I work almost ten year on dat kind of wage. My family couldnah survive dem days widout it. It wasnah just de money dat help we, nah. Once de skipper know you was alright, den he let you take things from de cargo when you reach home. Dat mean every month we haf food, clothes, sugar, rum and even some timber for we family.
>
> If you ain't haf work on schooner in dem days, den you hafi fish hard. But you know you gonna catch enough for keep

yourself, and family too. It ain't so dese days. If you ain't got work (wage labour) den you fighting for survive. Fishing ain't so easy today. It like we come round in circle. Wid so many foreign ship in de area de Jameson and Taylor ain't for bother wid schooner no more, and now a Bequia man mus'a look for other work. It like dis when dem rich family first done build de schooner – cos den dey only taking on family and we poor folk done wait plenty year afore we get for working dem schooners ...

The analogy drawn by 'Giant' with regards to the contemporary situation in inter-island trade throws light on the inequalities inherent in the class structure of the island. No Lower Bay men were employed as crew aboard inter-island schooners during the period 1980–81, but descendants of the planter families of Southside and the harbour still operate a small number of inter-island and fish export trading schooners, essentially in the peak tourist season, depending solely upon family labour as they had done before World War II. This reflects the changing nature of work in the maritime industries. With declining opportunities for wage labour aboard foreign vessels and the ever-increasing restrictions placed on emigration to North America and Europe, younger members of the ex-planter families have returned to inter-island trade.

The most significant of the post-war developments in labour markets was, without doubt, the recruitment of Bequia seamen to National Bulk Carriers of the USA. This has been documented extensively in the previous chapter and here I wish to relate the contemporary state of merchant shipping employment to the overall employment structure of the lower classes.

During the peak of its operations, NBC employed approximately 25 per cent of the island's adult male population (Frank, 1976:38). With communities such as Mount Pleasant, La Pompe and Paget Farm, as we have seen, virtually excluded from these figures parts of the harbour area had over 50 per cent of their adult male population in full time merchant seaman employment with NBC. Lower Bay, whilst not accruing the benefits of NBC labour demand to this extent, had as many as 30 per cent of its active adult male population in employment with NBC alone during the mid 1970s. By 1980 the total number of Lower Bay men employed in merchant shipping (i.e. with *all* companies operating in the region) had dropped to 19 (18 per cent of the adult males: see Table 3e) although a small number of younger men secured seasonal work as crew on foreign-owned and controlled charter yachts in 1980.

Table 3e: Adult male employment, in relation to seamanship, for Lower Bay community

Age[a] (years)	15-20 1980	15-20 1981	21-30 1980	21-30 1981	31-40 1980	31-40 1981	41-50 1980	41-50 1981	51-60 1980	51-60 1981	61+ 1980	61+ 1981	Total 1980	Total 1981	Total % 1980	Total % 1981
At sea	4	1	4	6	4	6	3	3	2	2	0	0	17	14	16.5	13.7
Contract signed – awaiting call or less than 4 months ashore	0	0	1	2	4	3	1	0	0	0	0	0	6	5	5.8	4.9
Seeking seaman employment having previously been a seaman, but over 4 months ashore	2	4	7	8	3	2	1	2	0	0	0	0	13	16	12.6	15.7
Seeking seaman employment for first time	5	6	3	0	0	0	0	0	0	0	0	0	8	9	7.75	8.8
Retired from seamanship and relying upon alternative work	0	1	7	2	2	2	4	3[b]	3	3	8	8	24	24	23.3	23.55
Never having been employed as seaman – still working	15	14	3	7	4	4	4	4	4	4	3	3	33	32	32.0	31.4
Not working – through old age or illness	0	0	0	0	0	0	0	0	0	0	2	2	2	2	1.95	1.95
Totals	26	26	25	25	17	17	13	12	9	9	13	13	103	102	100	100

Source: House to house survey, September 1980 and April 1981

Note (a): For purposes of comparison, age changes between September 1980 and April 1981 not recorded
 (b): One man killed in fishing accident December 1980

'Sailing' represents the highest status occupation for lower class men in Lower Bay. The 1979 List of Electors for the Grenadines, Polling Division No 4, which includes Lower Bay, Lawlers Hill and Lower Bay Gutter, lists the electorate for the district, together with occupation. Only twelve of the total male electorate for the community of Lower Bay listed their occupation as something other than 'seaman'. These included seven 'fishermen' and one each of 'mason', 'electrician', 'carpenter', 'shopkeeper' and 'mariner'. Table 3e shows that a total of 41 men in the community had never 'sailed, including nine who were seeking seaman employment, representing over 40 per cent of the male population. Of the remaining 60 per cent who had sailed, many had gained only a very limited experience of seaman employment. These figures reflect the perceived high status of 'sailing' as a male occupation amongst the lower classes, and indeed of wage labour.

During the 1960s and 1970s there were few alternatives to merchant shipping as a source of wage labour for Lower Bay men, aside from emigration and labour migration. Of those young men who took up apprenticeships with NBC after leaving school, few acquired the skills, techniques and tools/equipment for work within the traditional economy, such as fishing or carpentry/shipwright work, and today experience the strains of unemployment. Some have been successful in securing employment, albeit seasonal and/or temporary, in the tourist sector, whilst others engage in hawking locally produced goods and artefacts to tourists. It is through contact with tourists and expatriate yachtsmen that some of the youth have managed to gain employment as crew on charter yachts.

Chapter 7 contains a detailed discussion of the influence of tourism and property development on lower class employment structure in Lower Bay, set within a historical analysis of the growth of foreign capital in the island. One of the central themes of that chapter is an exposition of the effects of tourism on lower class socio-economic relationships and perceptions. The analysis of work is at the level of categorisation of activities according to the degree of interaction (face to face contact) between indigenes and foreigners. In this section, by discussing the availability of waged employment for the lower classes in the tourist and real estate private sector, attention is given to the impermanent and exploitative nature of such employment. Presentation of empirical material will be kept to a minimum as much of the material will appear in Chapter 7.

Tourism and real estate activity created the first opportunities for female wage labour in Bequia. Such work is, however, seasonal and temporary, influenced by the level of commercial activity in these sectors. As Table 3d, p.63 shows, 23 women from Lower Bay were employed in tourist-related employment during the peak of the 1980–81 tourist season, and this had declined to only 14 by May 1981. It is mostly younger lower class women who gain access to paid employment in the private sector, as chambermaids and waitresses in hotels/restaurants, cleaners/servants in tourist and expatriate houses and as shop assistants in tourist-oriented retail outlets, although many shops still rely on family labour in much the same way as the small community-based provision shops. Administrative and professional jobs for women in hotels and real estate companies tend to go to expatriates employed by trans-national companies, or to educated women from the ex-planter/merchant class. Because of the high demand for work in the private sector, women's wages have remained low: a job as a 'domestic' in an expatriate house, which involves cleaning, preparation of meals and, in some cases, 'nannying', paid $5.00 EC a day in 1981 (approximately 80p); waitressing and chambermaid work paid approximately the same ($20–25 EC a week for 40 hours plus). Although women complained about the exploitative and insecure nature of work in the private sector, they stressed their dependence on such work and their powerlessness in bargaining procedures:

> In de tourist season (in this particular case, from 1 November to 1 March) I get job cleaning rooms and making bed in de hotel. Most week I working about 50 hour for $22 EC. Dis really ain't much wage for all de work I do, but what else can I do? I need de money real bad – I got two young children for feed and I ain't get much other money. I also hafi gif my parents some money for we all living in dey house ... Dere plenty women looking for work, so I just gotta accept dese things and feel fortunate dat I got work.

As already noted, the availability of wage labour for women in Bequia is a recent phenomenon. Traditionally the woman's sphere of work activity was in the domestic domain: agriculture within plebeian culture is classified as 'women's work' and represents an extension of household tasks, i.e. a 'domestic' activity. The increasing commercialisation of the Bequia economy has enhanced the necessity for wage labour and petty-commodity production, and threatened the traditional sexual division of labour amongst the lower classes. As Chapter 4 below demonstrates, the increasing numbers of matrifocal households in the community, in which women are household heads, is related to the recent decline in male wage-earning power and the availability of salaried employment for women. Within conjugal households containing male wage earners, the traditional sex role ideology of plebeian culture pertains, and women are prevented from entering the labour market by their male partners/household heads who wish to maintain their positions as 'providers'. The changes in the sexual division of labour can, thus, only be understood in the context of changes in male involvement in the capitalist mode of production.

The tourist-oriented private sector offers fewer employment opportunities for lower class men than for women. Those that do exist, such as barmen, maintenance workers and drivers for hotels and holiday home complexes, are also predominantly seasonal and temporary. In January 1981, eight Lower Bay men worked in this sector, but only one remained in employment by the off-peak tourist season (see Table 3c, p.62). Wages tend to be slightly higher than women's in this sector, a barman earning approximately $7.00 EC (£1.20) per day in 1981, and a maintenance man up to $10.00 EC (£1.75). Tips and gratuities substantially increased the real earning power of men in these jobs but, compared with rates of pay of merchant seamen, the financial returns from work in the tourist sector remained exploitatively low. Nevertheless, demand for wage labour in this sector was high and, consequently, wages had not risen for several years and workers' bargaining power was minimal.

The real estate sector provides short term casual labouring work for men in land clearance for, and construction of, holiday homes, hotels, retail outlets and private roads. A number of lower class men in the community worked periodically as masons, carpenters and painter/decorators.

The means for securing temporary and seasonal employment in the tourist and real estate private sector is usually through kin and friendship networks (see Chapter 5 below). Networks are essential support structures derived from earlier forms of communal production based upon reciprocity. Loyalty to close kin and friends means that an individual in employment will offer assistance such as information, recommendations, etc., to network members seeking work.

The staffing of Lower Bay Primary School[2] highlights the significant role played by kin and/or friends in securing employment, in this case in the private sector. The school was set up in the early 1970s by an American woman who bought the building and land from Gerald James when he moved to Friendship during the migration in the late 1960s. The school predominantly caters for the children of resident non-nationals and the indigenous élite who pay weekly fees. However, for each two full fee-paying pupils a place is allotted for a lower class pupil on reduced fees. The headmistress of the school, the widow of a recently deceased Lower Bay seine owner, has a full time and permanent post (see Table 3d, p.63). Much of the teaching in the school is done by volunteer expatriates: young American, British or Australasian women who have arrived in Bequia on charter yachts and decided to spend an extended period before returning to their home countries or continuing on their travels. However, in 1979 the fees for expatriates' and fee-paying locals' children were increased in order to stimulate additional capital to enable two local women to be employed as part-time teachers. The headmistress appointed two Lower Bay women for the jobs – one was her sister's daughter and the other a neighbour. Both these women had completed a High School education.

Demand for wage labour amongst the lower classes, however, continues massively to outweigh the availability. In the absence of trade unions, except within the merchant shipping sector, of workers' representation and of government-enforced minimum rates of pay, with the exception of the public sector from which most Bequarians are excluded, wages remain low, working conditions poor, and workers' bargaining power minimal. Declining employment in merchant shipping, restrictions on labour migration and emigration and little expansion in the local labour market means that men and women are forced to rely upon returns from work in the pre- and non-capitalist forms of production, to which I now turn.

Petty-commodity entrepreneurial activities amongst the lower classes

Petty-commodity entrepreneurial activities in Lower Bay are characteristic of a class commonly referred to in Marxist theory (see, for example, Poulantzas, 1975) as the traditional petty-bourgeoisie, engaged in small-scale production, small-scale trade and, in the case of Bequia, provision of services to tourists. The limited returns from these activities mean that Lower Bay individuals and groups involved in such operations remain dependent upon alternative sources of income derived from production in the CMP and the residual forms of pre-capitalist production.

1 Small-scale production

Small-scale production in Lower Bay is predominantly artisanal in nature, practised by young, under- or unemployed men and women with little or no access to wage labour. Artisanal production amongst young men has been stimulated by the recent increase in tourists in Bequia and includes macramé, coral jewellery and ornaments, and model 'gum' boats. All these activities require little or no capital outlay, the producer relying predominantly upon local natural resources. Production is characteristically male only and involves no co-operation, each man being singularly responsible for his own product. This individuality tends to further characterise disposal of the products, with young men hawking their artefacts to tourists on the beaches and/or around the harbour. Recently, however, a small number of young men have managed to secure outlets for their products through local shops or bars on a sale-or-return basis.

Small-scale fruit production and sale has recently been affected by tourism. Many lower class households, although unable to produce surplus vegetable products, have surplus producing fruit trees. Traditionally, some fruit would have been taken to the market in Kingstown where it would fetch higher prices than in Bequia. Tourism, however, has created new markets, with young men hawking fruit to visitors on the beaches, while some households sell direct to hotels and restaurants locally. This latter practice has led to intra-community conflict as traditional channels for the disposal and exchange of fruit, through community networks, have virtually closed and many members resent the lack of access to seasonal fruits.

Small-scale production amongst lower class women takes the form of fishing-net knitting and charcoal production. Both of these forms of production were traditionally for household use and limited exchange within kin and friendship networks. With the increased need for money in the local economy many women now produce for sale to households in need. Although the art of small net making is dying out as a result of the availability of cheap imported nets, charcoal production is still a popular activity as it requires no capital outlay, the women collecting wood from the densely forested hills above the village.

2 Small-scale ownership: trade and services

The provision of services and involvement in trading activities by the lower classes in Lower Bay, like small-scale production in the community, have recently been stimulated by tourist demand and the decline in wage labour opportunities.

Small-scale trading by the lower classes chiefly involves retail activities in which the owner of the 'stock' assisted by family labour *not* wage labour, is engaged in the circulation of goods. The only sector of small-scale trading which has not been affected by increased tourist presence in the island are the rum/provisions shops, which continue to cater almost solely for the needs of the local community. There are three rum shops, two provisions shops and three combined rum/provisions shops in the community, and not one represented the only source of income for its owner. Apart from the rum and supplies shop owned by Gerald James, a descendant of the Southside planter family, at Friendship Gap, the remainder of the shops were owned and run by lower class community members. Three of these shops were owned by regularly employed merchant seamen who relied upon household members to run the shops during their 'sailing' contracts. All shop owners in the community stressed that they could not depend solely upon their enterprises for the support of their households. As one merchant seaman who owned a small rum shop explained to me:

> De rum shop ain't really making much-a-dollar for me and my family. But I man feel better for knowing it dere to bring in a little money. When I at sea de money it make go toward food and clothes for de family. Tania, my sister (see Case 3a above) who done run it, she doing a good job. None of de rumshop in Lower Bay making much, and unless dey trying for attrack tourists, like de Reef, dem ain't never gonna get rich from rumshop.

Many shop owners complained about the excessive overheads that small retailers face in Bequia. Despite the presence of laws requiring liquor licenses in the state for many years, it is only since the mid 1970s that the laws have been rigidly enforced. On top of licensing costs, shop owners are faced with transportation overheads from St Vincent and import duties on much of their stock. Consequently, smuggling, or the 'sellin of bobol'[3] as it is known locally, is an important aspect of small-scale retail trade in Bequia. All shops in Lower Bay depend upon smuggled goods supplied by locals using sloops and small schooners to smuggle duty free liquor and cigarettes from the US Virgin Islands.

The most numerous small traders in Lower Bay are those involved in hawking their own products. Also a number of resident non-nationals who have 'retired' to Bequia have, since the mid-1970s set up small tourist-oriented businesses. These are discussed in Chapter 7 which deals exclusively with the impact of tourism and property speculation on lower class social structure and culture. One small-scale enterprise recently entered into by three Lower Bay men, as a response to regional, rather than local, tourism is fish trading. The case below discusses the major factors influencing the establishment of this enterprise and highlights the restrictions faced by small entrepreneurs with insufficient capital and limited access to credit.

Case 3b   A small fish trading enterprise
Danny is a 30-year-old Lower Bay man who lives with his unmarried mother and four younger siblings. In 1979 his mother's brother, who owned and operated a small restaurant in St Vincent, died and bequeathed Danny his small sloop. With his savings from work as a seaman (he was made redundant in 1976) he equipped the sloop with icing facilities for storage of fish, and with his two cousins (his mother's sister's sons, aged 25 and 21) started buying fish locally and transporting it to Martinique in January 1980. This is Danny's account of the early months of the enterprise:

> When we start de business I say to de other two dat it all equal when it come to making money. Even though I done pay for de equipment outa I saving it ain't seem worth trying to make a share system: plenty people fed up of shares wid de seine and I ain't want argument to start. So we tell de Lower Bay fishermen dat for a couple of days every month we gonna be looking for buy fish at de same cost dat dey getting from de big traders in de harbour. De boat ain't really big and we cannuh carry much fish.
>   The first three month we make about $300 EC each after paying for gas (petrol), ice and thing, and we happy wid dis. It ain't much compare wid sailing but it better dan nutting. It good for me cos my mother ain't haf much a money coming in. Things looking good. Den we meet we first problem. One month de seine start for catching tuna so we waiting for take as much of dis fish as we could to Martinique – dis sell for $5 US a kilo dere (almost $7 EC a pound) and we only paying $2.50 EC a pound to de fishermen. So we reckon for make over $1,000 EC between we on dis trip. But we meet real bad weather when we sailing

up and it take we so long for get dere dat all de fish spoil.
If we ain't try for carry so much fish things would haf been
OK. So we learn from dis mistake ...

Unable to afford expensive freezing equipment, the enterprise
was forced to operate on a very small scale compared with the major
exporters based in the harbour. The men repeatedly talked of the
hard work involved in sailing up to Martinique, taking three days to
reach port. The cost of petrol meant that, when possible, they
travelled under sail only. The operation continued throughout 1980
with the men averaging about $100 EC a month each, net profit,
allowing for two months when they were idle because of Hurricane
Allen.

In early 1981 the sloop began 'taking in water' and Danny took
it to the dry dock in St Vincent. At the time of my departure from
Bequia the vessel was still awaiting repair: the keel needed replacing
and the hull considerable restoration before it would be seaworthy.
The three men were trying unsuccessfully to raise the money needed
for the repairs and were talking about scrapping the sloop:

> Man, de kind of money dey talking about for fix de boat
> gonna take we six month for earn even if we done find
> someone for lend we it. We ain't really sure dat it worth all
> de problem, and since we stop buying fish de big traders
> raise de price dey paying. Dis is always gonna happen to
> small businesses in Bequia. De big man gonna make things
> real hard and de bank ain't wanna know you when you got
> problem ...

In addition to small-scale trading activities, lower class entrepreneurs are also involved in the provision of services to tourists. As
with most small enterprises in Lower Bay it is the most marginal of
the lower classes, viz. women and young men, who have taken up
service provision.

Women have begun offering laundry services to tourists and
resident non-nationals. The most common way of attracting laundry
business is through networks based upon reciprocal alliances between kin and friends. Daughters and other female kin who have
secured part-time work as 'domestics' offer laundry services to their
employers and, if successful, pass the work onto their female household heads, if they live in matrifocal households, or to other close
female kin living without a resident male money earner. This is an
integral part of the economy of matrifocal households (see Chapter

4 below). One young woman, who found work as a 'domestic' to an American family who spent four weeks renting a house in Lower Bay in January–February 1981 explained:

> When I done start work, dey aksing me for wash dey clothes every two day or so. My mother done hear about a woman in de harbour who putting a sign up saying 'laundry here' so she say to me dat I should aks dese Americans if dey prepare for wait til dey haf a bag full of laundry and den gif it to her. Dey agree to dis thing and so at de end of each week I taking clothes and sheets and all thing to my mother. Dis way I ain't feel dat I hafi gif she (her mother) so much of de money I earning. She making $10 EC a week cos I done help she get de laundry work. We ain't really haf too much-a-money come in to de home, dere only my mother and me and my two brod'ers. One of dem still in school and de other ain't find much work.

A very recent form of service provision entered into by the most marginal of the lower classes has been the renting of rooms or houses to tourists. Absenteeism of members of a household (fishing being the predominant cause of periods of absence of men, although some women have recently found 'living-in' domestic employment), coupled with the shifting of household members into neighbour's or kin's households, allows for whole houses to be let for short periods to tourists. This, however, is an infrequent practice; far more common is the renting of a room to a tourist. Lower Bay persons involved in such activities stress the expedient nature of having to resort to 'letting part of my house to strangers' as a means of supplementing an insufficient household income.

This form of service provision refers here specifically to the lower classes and does not include the ex-planter/capitalist classes who construct houses and apartments for the sole purpose of renting to expatriates or tourists. However, it does include the upper strata of the lower classes, those who have maintained regular waged employment such as merchant seamen who invest their savings in the construction of buildings suitable for letting to tourists on short stay terms. Only one such case had occurred in Lower Bay by the completion of my fieldwork (see Case 7b, p.218) and demonstrated the potential, albeit limited, for class mobility amongst the lower classes. All cases of lower class provision of tourist accommodation depended solely upon family labour to maintain the property i.e. cleaning, laundry, etc.

In all small-scale entrepreneurial activities amongst the lower classes, the same agent is both owner and possessor of his/her means of production as well as being the direct producer, in the case of small-scale production. Consequently there is no economic exploitation in the Marxist sense, as no wage labour is employed. Labour is provided by the owner and sometimes family members, who are not remunerated in the form of a wage. This production draws profit from the sale of goods and through the overall distribution of surplus value, but it does not directly extort surplus value (Poulantzas, 1975:285). Hence, these forms of production and exchange do not belong in the CMP, but are part of a petty-commodity form of production. As Marx and Engels have stressed, the tendency is for the class of traditional petty-bourgeois entrepreneurs to be undermined by the dominance of the CMP and its reproduction: petty-commodity production being characterised as a form of transition from pre-capitalist to capitalist mode of production. However, the dependence of the CMP in Bequia upon movements of international capital, predominantly under the control of American and European multinational companies and property speculators/financiers, has meant that entrepreneurial activity in the petty-commodity form has tended to increase during periods of high unemployment. This is well illustrated by the number of lower class men and women engaged in such production and exchange since the decline in seaman wage labour opportunities during the mid-1970s.

The unstable nature of the CMP and its inability to provide regular employment for the lower classes in Bequia has led to continued economic activity within other residual forms of pre-capitalist production, viz. fishing, agriculture and communal (labour exchange) production which, as they relate to the Lower Bay Lower class economy, are considered below.

3 Fishing[4]

Fishing is a male economic activity currently characteristic of petty-commodity production. The fisherman, as direct producer, owns the means of his labour, the boat, fishing equipment etc., has limited access to the means of subsistence, and so engages in production for exchange, requiring a market for his product. With the recent decline in wage labour opportunities, fishing has become increasingly important for the lower classes' means of livelihood.

In all but the single-person fishing activities (see below), fishing is organised on a share basis, crews receiving a pre-arranged share of the revenue for catches after marketing. The majority of boats engaged in fishing are owned by one member of the crew. Recruitment to crews is based on kinship and/or personal networks, not on a formal labour market. Unlike wage labour, petty-commodity production involves no separation of capital and labour or, in seine fishing, a partial separation. The fisherman achieves his means of subsistence by production and exchange of the product of his labour, viz. fish, on the market, not by selling his labour for a wage. Petty-commodity production can be distinguished from peasant forms of production, typified by household agriculture and subsistence fishing, by use-values:

> Compulsion to produce for the petty-commodity producer comes from his need for a range of use-values not met by his own product ... through the medium of the market he may attain the use-values not met by his own product.
> (Deas, 1981:60)

In subsistence agriculture and fishing the products (food) are consumed by the household, i.e. the use-values are met by the product and require no market intervention.

Most households own one small, 9–12 foot, double-bow fishing boat (see Table 3f) modelled on the original whaleboat design. These fishing boats allow households to catch sufficient fish for domestic consumption; any surplus is sold to tourist outlets (restaurants, hotels) or at the local market in Port Elizabeth. In the past these small 'Bequia dinghies', as the fishing boats are known locally, were built by Lower Bay men, but in 1981 no one in the community was engaged in work as a shipwright, and fishermen depended upon Southside shipwrights for new boats. However, the recent economic demise has meant that most lower class men find the cost of new boats prohibitive, only regularly employed seamen and seine-owners being able to afford new boats.

(i) Small-scale petty-commodity fishing

Single or one-man fishing activities are characterised by low labour input and involve the setting of fish pots, small floating (tramil) nets and handlining from an anchored boat. All one-man types of fishing are done fairly close inshore, in or around Admiralty Bay and, because of depleted fish stocks, produce little surplus or marketable catches. One-man fishing activities exist, therefore, in both peasant and petty-commodity forms of production, for although geared primarily towards household consumption, catches of marketable seafood, e.g. lobster, red fish, will be sold to local restaurants or on the beach to tourists.

Table 3f: Boat ownership by household, Lower Bay, 1981

No. of boats per household	Date built	Size/type	Approximate cost (EC)	Date bought if after construction date	Origin
3	1935	Seine	$100	1951	La Pompe
	1957	15' double ender	$40		La Pompe
	1958	12' flat stern (fillet)	– (built himself)		
4	1935	Seine	– (built himself)		
	1940	Seine assistant	– (built himself)		
	1970	12' double ender	$450		Paget Farm
	1973	18' square stern speed boat	$1,200 (without engine)		Hamilton
2	1963	12' double ender	$200		Friendship
	1972	17' double ender	$750		La Pompe
2	1950	10' double ender	$250	1970	Lulley
	1979	10' double ender	$700		Reform
1 (brothers)	N/A	Seine	$1,300	1972	Paget Farm
1 (brothers)	N/A	Seine assistant	$1,000	1972	Paget Farm
1	1958	13' double ender	$200		Hamilton
2	1935	16' double ender	– (built by father)		
	1963	17' double ender	$1,200	1979	Lower Bay
1	1958	12' double ender	$400	1978	Lower Bay
1	1954	10' square stern	$40		St Vincent
1	1976	13' double ender (racing)	$900	1979	La Pompe
1	N/A	15' double ender	$750	1976	Paget Farm

1		1930	9' flat stern	– (built by father)	
1		1951	8' double ender	$50	1966 Friendship
1		1967	13' double ender	$500	St Lucia
1		1976	18' double ender (speed boat)	$2,100 (with engine)	1979 Paget Farm
1		1976	19' double ender (speed boat)	$800	Paget Farm
1		1978	17' double ender	$1,200	Built by German man in La Pompe
1		1960	12' double ender	$20 (labour charge – built by brother)	
1		1979	15' double ender	– (built by himself for racing)	
1		1974	10' double ender	$350	Paget Farm
1		1963	12' double ender	$160	Paget Farm
1		1980	12' double ender	$950	Paget Farm
1		1951	14' double ender	– (given by uncle: built himself)	
1		1937	10' double ender	– (given by father: built himself)	Lower Bay
1		1981	13' double ender	$1,100	Paget Farm
1		1960	15' square sterned	$100	St Vincent

Total households: 27
Total boats: 35

(ii) Small-scale crew fishing

Involves co-operation between two or more men in a single boat. It takes a number of forms, including trolling (pulling a lure or live bait behind a moving boat to catch migratory fish); bottom (tramil) netting; spear-fishing (with one man required to row the boat to collect the fish in case of sharks or barracuda); hand lining (which is more commonly done with two to six men in the boat); and fillet net fishing, which is discussed, along with seine fishing, below.

All small-scale crew fishing, except the fillet net, involves co-resident men or close kin/friends and, with the exception of hand lining and fillet fishing, the catch is distributed according to a share system of one share for each fisherman, one extra for the boat owner who is normally present in small-scale fishing, and a half share if there is an outboard motor used. The shares are calculated after expenses have been taken out for fuel, replacement tackle, etc. In the case of hand lining, when two or more lines are in operation in a single boat, each fisherman marks the fish he catches according to his own system, e.g. cutting the tail, notching a particular fin, etc., which he claims when fishing is complete. Each fisherman is required to provided his own fishing tackle and bait and, if an engine is used, each will be required to contribute to the fuel, usually prior to setting off. No share is taken for the boat because, as I was told, the more men fishing the more fish that will be attracted to the area by ground bait.

With the depletion of fish stocks around Bequia some fishermen have chosen to spend long periods fishing in the Southern St Vincent Grenadines and around Carriacou, where they have kin with whom they stay. They are within easy access of French traders on the islands of Canouan and Union to whom they are able to sell their catches. Tourist demands have led to higher prices being paid for conch, lobster and red-fish, so when in the Southern Grenadines most dive or hand line for these sea foods.

The inter-relationship between the different fishing activities described above is illustrated by the case below, which draws out the effects of declining fish stocks, and other measures, on fishing in the community.

Case 3c   Small scale fishing: competition and co-operation

N is a 48-year-old married man whose household is made up of his wife and nine children (see Case 6a below). Although he periodically works as a carpenter within the tourist and/or expatriate housing sector of the economy (furniture making, repairs, etc.) he depends largely upon fishing for his family's means of livelihood. He owns a small double ended fishing boat which he bought in 1966, which he fishes along with one of his sons who has recently left school. With the boat he and his son set a floating tramil and fish pots, and regularly hand line. He is widely regarded as one of the finest fishermen in the community. N is suffering from the effects of depleted fish stocks in Bequia, as this excerpt from a conversation highlights:

> Ten year ago we was able to manage from my fishing and pot making and de wife work on Friendship (sharecropping). Today it real hard for catch enough for live. Wid such a big family I ain't feel it fair for leave de wife look after dey on she own, so I ain't much go down de Cays or Canouan wid de seine. Man, it hard for make a catch dese days ... Sometimes you finding men trying for get more of dey share from lining and trolling. It hard times dat making people bad like dis ...

This increased competition following from scarcity of fish has led to a number of disputes amongst fishermen in the community and attempts at juggling shares. N is no longer able to make a living out of fishing his small boat with family labour and regularly gets involved in larger crew fishing activities such as trolling and seine fishing.

> I ready for go fishing wid anyone dese days. It ain't possible for me to make enough dollar just fishing wid de lad, so I for using my boat wid de seine (see below) and for going trolling and hand lining around de point wid de wife brod-'er cos he haf a outboard. Now I ain't mean for show no respeck, but some of he friend dey ain't real trusting. One guy he try for tell me dat de way I mark me fish is de same way dat he done it – dat was when I find he putting some of my catch in he bag after we beach de boat. Man, we all haf problem and we ain't gonna solve dem if we ain't working together.

Co-operation between fishermen, which is essential to the most productive of fishing activities, is clearly being undermined by the increasing pauperisation of lower class fishermen.

(iii) Seine and fillet fishing
The single most important source of income for community fishermen, albeit insufficient to sustain a household, is the purse seine. There are three purse seines owned by community members,

descendants of planters, one of which is now operated out of Canouan, where the owner spends two to three weeks of each month fishing, sometimes with crews from Lower Bay. Seine fishing requires a more complex social organisation than other community fishing activities. A seine boat, 25 feet in length and modelled around the whale boat, with a large square stern to hold the net, which is 1,000 to 3,000 feet in length and 50 feet in depth, requires a crew of seven, four rowing and three casting the net, plus the owner. Four or five other small fishing boats assist in pulling the net when cast around a shoal of fish, each boat containing two or three men. The total number of men engaged in the process varies from 16–23.

The most lucrative catches from the seine are migratory fish such as tuna and couvali, although because of the restrictions on the use of purse seines to water depths of no more than 50 feet, the most common catches tend to be of jack-sprats and robin. Adams (1970:184) reports that in 1965 Bequia fishermen contributed about 60 per cent of the fresh fish retailed in Kingstown. Since the proliferation of the fish trading industry, owned and controlled by the ex-planter/merchant class, this figure has dropped to an estimated 15–20 per cent (St Vincent Fisheries Office, 1980) being essentially jackfish and robins which have no market value in Martinique and Guadaloupe.

Cash from the sale of the fish is shared according to a system which gives half of the total sale to the owner of the seine boat and net, the remainder being shared equally amongst all others involved in the exercise, with additional shares for boat owners and divers. The average number of shares, after half the money had been taken by the seine, over the period of my field work, was 23. Over a four month period (January to April 1982, see Table 3g) when I recorded detailed figures for seine catches, the average *single* monthly share for a fisherman working the seine was $58.30 EC (£1.00 sterling = $6.00 EC in 1981). Many of the community fishermen, especially the young and poor, consider the share system outdated and exploitative, although for many there is little alternative to working the seine.

Case 3d   A seine share-out dispute
In September 1980, the first time the seines had been out since the hurricane of early August, a number of separate but related instances of dissatisfaction broke out amongst the crew of one of the seines.

Table 3g: Shares from seine fishing, January–April 1981

Date		Total catch (EC)	Number of shares	Single share value (to nearest EC dollar)
Jan 1981	Seine 1	$4,100	21	$98
	Seine 2	$3,500	24	$73
Feb 1981*	Seine 1	—	—	—
	Seine 2	—	—	—
Mar 1981	Seine 1	$6,200	24	$130
	Seine 2	$1,800	23	$39
	Seine 1 and 2 (combined)	$2,300	26	$44
April 1981	Seine 1	$1,500	22	$34
	Seine 2	$4,000	23	$86

Average number of shares   23
Average value of shares $58.30

* Exceptionally high 'ground seas' restricted fishing activities and also meant few fish migrated into shallow water around Bequia to feed.

For two months the fishermen of Lower Bay had been unable to engage in production because of climatic conditions and the subsequent erosion of the beach. When the seine finally set out in mid-September, many households were in need of cash. Although the catch was comparatively small it nevertheless represented an opportunity for many to clear their debts with supplies shops and to buy much-needed provisions, including seeds and seedlings to replace their lost or damaged crops. Two days before the scheduled seine shareout J-L, a 58-year-old single man with no other source of income than a small, badly-worn tramil net and an eight foot fishing boat, approached Len Lafayette, the seine owner, to ask for a small 'sub' from his forthcoming share with the seine. J-L has a reputation in the community for being a 'worthless drunk' and many who heard that he was going to approach the seine owner for a pre-payment of his share felt that he was behaving improperly because, as one man put it:

> ... we all needing money bad right now. Since de hurricane all of we suffering endless problem wid raising money. J-L he ain't got no family for feed and he ain't even want for wait two day. All of we haf plenty more a need dan he but we got more respeck dan he. Len (the seine owner) ain't never gonna give he afore de day, dat for sure. He only want it for spend on rum and come on bad wid everyone, cussing and de like.

Popular opinion turned out to be correct, and after he was refused a 'sub' J-L was subjected to mockery from many, which climaxed in a small skirmish outside a rum shop when J-L attempted to get a drink on credit. J-L expressed his grievances in terms of the power held by the seine owner, and that being refused a 'sub' was indicative of exploitation:

> J-L: All of dey (the other men involved in the seine enterprise) just f—kin' afraid for aks for dey share afore time. If dey was all to stand up for things den de seine gonna change. But dey like frighten fowl wid nutting for do essept make bad word about me
> ...

After the share out two days later arguments in a rum shop seemed to support J-L's claim that he was not the only man who felt the system was unfair. Many expressed their dissatisfaction with the size of their shares. This brief quote illustrates the feelings of a number of crew members:

> So de seine ain't catch much dis month. You think Len haf some kind of heart, knowing we is all short after de problem of de last couple month. But he ain't even gif we a bit extra just for dis month. Most of we trying for feed we family and he ain't care ...

Giant, who operates the other seine since the death of his brother, attempted to defend the system on the basis of the cost of maintenance to the net and boat. Violent verbal arguments ensued.

The following interview with a young man was conducted a few hours after the rum shop arguments and illustrates the feelings of animosity and hostility towards the seine owner:

> Me: How much did you make from the seine this month?
> R: Man, I only get $30 EC. And dat's only after I make

	plenty problem in de share out.
Me:	Why was that?
R:	We make two small catch dis month. On one of de days I ain't diving for I man cut I shoulder and I ain't want for get de wound and strapping wet. De other days I diving and rowing like everyone else. When de share come out it $20 EC. So I reckon my share to be plenty more dan $20 EC cos I done dive. But I only given $20 EC and I stand up and say dis unfair. After plenty arguing I manage for get a half share extra.
Me:	What did the other men say when you asked for more than a single share?
R:	Man, dey ain't really say nutting. Every man frighten for say things to de big man. Dey all know things ain't fair in de seine, like de way it always take half of de money straight out. Seine owner can'eh work de seine alone ... All dem guys in crew should stop working and see he change quick like hell. True, he gotta repair and add to he net and boat but he make plenty more dan he need. He already have de only cassava mill, and rented house. What he want wid all dat money for? He getting richer and we all is suffering.

Lower class fishermen engage in most, if not all, of the available fishing activities. The case below, involving a 'small scale' fisherman with no access to wage labour, highlights the dependence of such men on the seine, despite ownership of the means of small-scale fishing production.

Case 3e   A Lower Bay fisherman's dependence on the seine
Vincent is a 60-year-old man who lives with his wife, two of their children and one of their son's children (the boy's father, Andrew, emigrated to the Virgin islands in 1981, see Case 5a, p.141.) A second son emigrated to the USA in 1970 and regularly sends money to his parents.

Vincent has no experience of wage labour apart from three months in the 1950s when he worked on a small inter-island trading vessel as a favour for a friend who had injured his back in a fall. He owns a small fishing boat, a number of fish pots and a small floating tramil. He works these, plus his hand lines, alone, preferring not to have to depend on anyone.

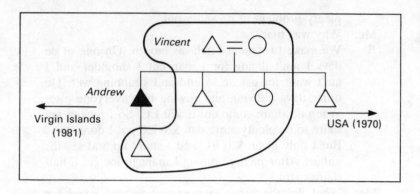

He is regarded by all in the community as the 'best fisherman in Lowbay' and, like N in Case 3c, p.80 is frustrated by the decline in catches from his 'one man' fishing activities. For the past four years he has worked the trolling season with two other men, one of whom bought an outboard motor and a large, 16 foot, double ender when he retired from sailing in 1976. This, together with his regular work with the seine and remittances from his son in the USA, allows him to maintain his household:

> I ain't really like for work wid others. But de way things is today I ain't have no choice. Some years de trolling ain't make much money at all, and my son ain't able for send money if he got debt for pay in America. Den it all down to how much I can make in de seine. Sometimes I just wish dat I could buy me own seine cos I know how much dollar dey can make. But in my life I ain't never gonna have dat kind of money. I suppose I lucky cos I got me a boat dat earn a extra share, but I too old for dive dese days so I cannah make de extra dollar dat way. My youngest son he gonna be a real fine diver soon and den we gonna have a little extra if he can get diving work wid de seine. But time a come for change in de share out from de seine. I ain't criticising cos it always been dat way for shares. But in dose days de seine making plenty and no-one bother cos dey getting enough for live. Dat ain't so today and so much a people getting fed up wid only a few dollar for a month work dat dem seine owners gotta start giving more ...

Smaller shoals of jackfish and robin are caught using the fillet net, a smaller version of the seine net (about 100 yards long and 10 feet deep) operated from a fillet boat, a scaled-down model of the seine boat. Fillet net fishing requires the assistance of two or three smaller vessels to manoeuvre the net around the shoals. Both fillet nets in the community are owned by the two respective seine owners that operate out of Lower Bay. The share system is that of the seine, although the owners rarely fish their fillets, taking half the catch, but no individual share. Because of the relative ease of operation, including the launching and beaching of boats, the fillet nets are used more frequently than the seines although they produce far less marketable surplus than the seines.

Seine and fillet fishing, despite the appropriation of half the product by a single individual (the owner) and their dependence on market forces, nevertheless represent forms of petty-commodity production: the share system excludes any notion of wage labour.

(iv) Supplies, costs and maintenance of fishing gear
All new fishing gear used by Lower Bay fishermen is today purchased from a resident American who has lived in Bequia since 1965. He imports fishing gear and outboard motors from Florida and Europe, and operates a supplies shop from his home in Lawler's Hill. The most productive fishing technology is prohibitively priced, excluding most members of the community from purchase. A seine net and boat today would entail an initial outlay of $7,500 EC (see Table 3h).

Table 3h: Seine equipment retail costs, 1939–1981

Year	Seine net price (1,000 ft)	Seine boat	Total
1939*	$500 EC	$120 EC	$620 EC
1965[†]	$2,000 EC	$1,000 EC	$3,000 EC
1981	$5,000 EC ($500 per 100 ft section)	$2,500 EC	$7,500 EC

* Source: Brown H. H., 1945:26.
[†] Adams, 1970.

Local fishermen who complain about the prohibitive costs and inflation calculate that a 100 foot section of a seine would take six months to knit and cost $200 EC in seine twine, making it unviable to attempt to build up one's own seine net. A new fillet net currently priced at $2,000 EC, a bottom tramil at $200 US ($550 EC) and a floating tramil at $400 EC, are all prohibitively priced for most fishermen, who are unable to secure any credit facilities. Consequently, a great deal of time is expended on repairing old and damaged equipment, notably tramils and boats, leaving most fishermen dependent on the few individuals who own the most productive fishing gear. Most of the equipment/boats used by lower class fishermen were purchased through the co-operative[5] in the 1960s with loans.

(v) The articulation of petty-commodity fishing with capitalism
The relationship between fishing, as a petty-commodity form of production and the planter/merchant controlled capitalist mode, dominant during the development of commercial fishing, and international capitalism, can be understood by a closer examination of the market and the means of production in fishing. Deas (1981) in a study of the Scottish inshore fishing industry, distinguishes two elements in fishing: the producers' raw materials (fish) which constitute the objects of labour, and the producers' tools and implements (boats and fishing gear), the means of labour.

In Bequia the planter/merchant class was, by definition, unable to monopolise the objects of labour, but instead exercised control over markets and the means of labour. During the first half of the twentieth century fishermen found markets outside the control of Bequia's dominant classes, notably in Kingstown, St Vincent, where local demand exceeded supply. As production increased, new and more lucrative markets became available as Martiniquan fish traders arrived in Grenadine waters. The planter/merchant class and other powerful groups, notably the new 'aristocracy' of schooner operators, responded to this external threat by converting trading schooners to include fish freezing and/or icing facilities. This effective monopolisation of the market means that most fish caught in and around Bequia today is purchased by these traders for export to French tourist islands. The introduction of large purse seines (and recently SCUBA, outboard motors, etc.) has undermined the traditional lower class work-ownership patterns within fishing, has increased social differentiation, and led to the growing dependence of many fishermen on the planter class. As already shown the share system in fishing where new technology and/or the seine is used, benefits the owners of the technology.

Marx considered all forms of petty-commodity production as transitional, because under the pressure of production for the market they allow for a direct transition to capitalist class relations. But as long as households can periodically gain access to cash and other resources outside the sphere of petty-commodity fishing, then despite its instability, petty-commodity production will continue to be an important and necessary economic activity for the lower classes.

Agriculture

Within all lower class economic activities there are inherent inequalities as a result of a system of stratification based upon sex, age and class. However, within agriculture these inequalities are most clearly recognisable.

Age, as a distinguishing factor in full-time wage labour is legally enforced by a school leaving age of 15. Employment opportunities in the public sector and seaman labour market favour men, although within the tourist sector women are able to compete favourably with men for jobs. The nature of most petty-commodity entrepreneurial activities precludes women because of the required informal interaction with tourists and expatriates: women engaging in such relationships would be effectively breaching plebeian norms covering the gender-based public/domestic dichotomy. Similarly, age is significant within many small-scale entrepreneurial activities: the quality of the relationships between hawkers and 'customers' demanding a loose correlation of ages between the parties (see Chapter 7 for a fuller exposition of this relationship). Fishing is an exclusively male economic activity; age and physical fitness limiting involvement in specific types of fishing; for example, older men are unable to dive, and young boys lack the strength and skills for most tasks. Traditionally, a boy's socialisation included the teaching, by father, male household head, or senior male kin, of fishing skills and practices so that when the boy reached the age of 15 or 16 he would be considered, and have proved to be, a proficient fisherman. He would then be given the concomitant responsibilities of his status, such as manoeuvring fishing boats, setting nets, etc. and equal shares with other fishermen.

It is upon women, children and older male dependent household members that agricultural production relies. It is considered inappropriate and improper for adult men to engage in agricultural work, for to do so is to demonstrate failure in the expected male role of 'provider'. The types of agricultural production entered into by women and dependants in Lower Bay can be classified into two distinct forms: peasant production and sharecropping. Of the two, sharecropping is the more significant for the lower classes, both symbolically and materially, yielding higher returns. The marginality of agricultural forms of production in Bequia means that such production remains limited to residual forms derived from earlier modes of production and, as will be shown below, involves no capitalist relations of production.

All households in the community own or have access to land, usually in the form of small garden plots of less than half an acre that surround the dwelling place (see Table 3i). Sporadic and erratic rainfall, plus the marginality of land, in terms of size and soil quality, restricts peasant production on household gardens to consumption/subsistence crops such as pigeon peas, maize and cassava, and 'cash crops', such as tomatoes, peppers and groundnuts. The only surplus agricultural product that enters the market from

Table 3i: Land ownership and agricultural production by household (Lower Bay), 1981

Land ownership		agricultural production	
Size	No. of households	Type of product	No. of households
Less than ½ acre	39	Household production of pease, maize and cassava with small livestock production	58
½–1 acre	16	Cassava mill ownership producing surplus for sale	2
1–5 acres	5	Cash crop production (tomatoes, groundnuts, etc.) producing surplus for exchange/sale	11
5–10 acres	1	Fruit trees, producing surplus for exchange/sale	7
10+ acres	2	Meat production (pig farm)	1
Total	63	Ownership of sharecropped land	2

household gardens is fruit, which is taken to St Vincent or to local hotels for sale, or, as we have seen above, is hawked to tourists by young male household members. Planting and harvesting of crops take place at the end of the 'dry' season and during the 'rainy' season respectively (see Appendix III), and are undertaken by women, sometimes with the help of young and old household members. Most households are engaged in rearing small numbers of livestock, viz. sheep and goats, which are tethered on uncultivated hillside land throughout most of the year, except for a short period following the pea harvest when they are allowed to graze in the peafields until planting begins. All households have a number of domestic fowl, for meat and eggs, and raise a single pig in a pen beside the house. Piglets are purchased from Gerald James, who breeds pigs in Lower Bay Gutter. Community-produced meat is sold locally and there is rarely enough meat available for members to consume it more than once a week: Sunday being a day on which, traditionally, people in Bequia eat meat instead of fish. The slaughter of an animal brings women from all three settlements to the household where the slaughter takes place, for the purpose of buying their meat requirements, and represents one of the few opportunities for women to congregate publicly. Livestock rearing, consistent with peasant production, is a household activity: children, and older men and women being responsible for the tethering and grazing of sheep and goats and the tending of chickens and pigs.

The production of subsistence crops, such as peas, maize and cassava), is not limited to household gardens. As a legacy of the post-slavery economy, fragmented ex-plantation land still supports a sharecropping system. Changes in the social relations of production following the decline in commercial agriculture in the late nineteenth century established a sexual division of labour within the lower classes whereby men rarely worked the land. Sharecropping, although it involves production outside the household domain, is considered 'women's work'. During the labour intensive processes of planting and harvesting (and in the case of cassava, processing) women receive support from dependent household members, notably children and old men, who are otherwise peripheral in the local system of production.

As already noted, sharecropping often involves the apportioning of labour and resources between households from the three settlements in Lower Bay community. There is no land in Lower Bay village for sharecropping, due to the hillside nature of the settlement, although some of the larger gardens are worked by the owners' independent relatives and by members of their personal network for a share compatible with the standard sharecropping arrangements, which is two thirds of the crop.

The unfragmented land on Diamond Estate is currently sharecropped on a basis previously described, the land being jointly owned by a pair of siblings: an elderly sister who lives at the foot of Lawler's Hill on the outskirts of the estate, and her brother who emigrated to the USA in the 1950s. On Friendship Estate, which has been divided into smaller sections, sharecropping and household gardening are carried out by subsistence and kin groups from Lower Bay community as well as from Lower Friendship.

With the exception of the four ex-planter families in the community there is little differentiation of ownership, or access to, land and other agricultural means of production (fruit trees, livestock, etc.). However the ownership of cassava mills by two members of the ex-planter class constitutes a form of social differentiation based upon exploitation and dependence. There are only two cassava mills available to the people of the community, one in the village owned by Len Lafayette, and one at the top of Lawler's Hill owned by Gerald James.

The following case highlights the dependence of the lower classes on the planter-controlled cassava processing facilities and the extent of perceived exploitation. It further draws out the significance of cassava harvesting as a sphere in which it is culturally acceptable for women to congregate and interact publicly.

Case 3f   The Lower Bay cassava harvest 1981
Sharecropping in Lower Bay produces very few cash crops, such as tomatoes, groundnuts, peppers, etc. because of the higher risk of loss with such crops which are dependent upon regular rainfall during the summer months. The 1980–81 cash crop was even lower than usual due to the damage caused by Hurricane Allen in August 1980. Subsistence crops were also affected by the hurricane, maize and peas being most adversely affected. As cassava is a root crop only a small portion of it was lost through erosion from the heavy rains. Of all the crops produced by the lower classes, cassava is the most important, constituting the major carbohydrate staple in the diet. In its processed form (*farine*) it can be stored for the year following harvest: many households through sharecropping and home production manage to grow sufficient cassava to last the year.

The first stage in the cassava harvest is the gruelling task of picking: women gather in the fields at dawn to pull the long roots and remove the stems. During the middle of the day when the sun is at its hottest the women return to household chores, returning to the fields in late afternoon, thus avoiding the debilitating period of the day. In 1981 the bulk of the cassava in Lower Bay was picked during the month of March, after which it was dried in the sun for a few days. Once dried the cassava was scraped to remove loose soil and the outer skin. The scraping, like the picking, was done predominantly by individual women or household groups, without adult men. The remainder of the processing, however, was characterised by women coming together into small groups: one of the few spheres of social life outside the church and Friendly Society where this occurs amongst the lower classes.

When scraping is complete, the cassava has to be ground, and for this the women are dependent upon the two ex-planter owned cassava mills in the community. I concentrated my observation of this stage of the process on the mill in Lower Bay village owned by Len Lafayette. Grinding, or 'ginning' as it is known locally, took place during the first weeks of April 1981, with Lafayette, in accordance with the traditional share system for mill owners, taking one third of all the cassava brought to the mill. During the period 29 March to 9 April 1981, the mill was in constant use. As the mill is manually operated, it is at this stage that older children contribute most to supporting their women kinsfolk. Use of the mill is on a daily first-come-first-served basis, women and children arriving shortly after dawn with their cassava in hessian rice and flour sacks. Also at the mill were those older men and women who, because of no land or lacking the stamina required to plant and harvest, had no cassava crop. In return for grinding some of the mill owner's cassava, these people receive a small share. Lafayette, although not owning any sharecropped land, amasses a large surplus from those using the mill, plus a substantial domestic crop which his wife, and some of her female kin, produces. Some of his surplus is sold to local supplies shops and to other individuals in need.

The ground cassava is pulp-like and contains a toxic element. The next stage was to wring the ground pulp in large sheets or hessian sacks to extract some of the poisonous liquid. Again, older children and retired male household members lent support to the women during wringing. When the cassava had been wrung the women formed into groups of four or five on the basis of sharecropping groups, or for non-sharecroppers close female kin and neighbours grouped together, to construct small, easily-erected shelters out of bamboo and corrugated iron. The ground cassava was stored in these during the final stage of processing, the baking. Baking took place in large copper pots outside the shelters, which removed the remaining toxicity and produced a fine dried flour-like product, known locally as *farine*, from the French word for flour. Although the pots were owned by individual households, no share system for using the pot existed; as one pot owner said: 'We is ordinary women working together and we need for be fair'. Baking is traditionally a female only activity, and the nine shelters which I counted in the Lower Bay community during April were all consistent with this arrangement.

Baking took place over a very small flame, to avoid burning the cassava, and most groups took about six days to complete their baking. I concentrated my observation at a shelter constructed on wasteland just outside the house I was renting, at which four women gathered, two sisters, one of their daughters and a neighbour, from a Monday morning until the following Sunday afternoon. Each morning they would arrive with fish and vegetables to cook their daily meals, household responsibilities being allocated to other dependants for the baking period. The lifting of other family and household responsibilities for this week of the year is a time that most senior female household members look forward to: a time to exchange ideas and stories without fear of sanctions governing women's role in the extra-domestic sphere. Because of the women only nature of these social/work groups, I was unable to participate in any way in the activities, relying for data upon chance encounters with the women in shops or on their porches in the evenings.

Although cassava processing remains traditional in its division of labour and technical production, one group of women in Lower Bay Gutter responded in 1981 to the impact of tourism. This particular group, who were all sharecroppers in Friendship Estate, had produced a surplus and set up their shelter and cassava pot on the side of the main road to Friendship Bay. This attracted the interest of tourists using the road to get to the beach bar and bay: the women selling a little of their surplus *farine*, at considerably inflated prices, to the passers-by.

Production of cassava, then, highlights the inequalities that characterise residual forms of production. Despite being required to provide their own means of production, in the form of seeds, tools, manure, etc., women are required to give up one-third of all sharecropped subsistence crops to the owners of the land. A further share is taken for use of the mills, upon which all cassava producers are dependent.

Maize and pigeon pea production requires no such elaborate

processing, but nevertheless is subjected to sharecropping regulations. Any surplus is disposed of through the same channels as cassava; pigeon peas, when dried, last the whole year and are stored for household consumption, whereas maize is consumed in its unprocessed form, as 'corn'. Both these crops were seriously affected by hurricane damage and no surplus was produced in 1980–81 by the lower classes.

Agricultural production in a subsistence mode remains an integral part of the economy of the lower classes of Lower Bay community, as indeed it does for the lower classes throughout the island. Previously characterised as a 'residual subsistence element' of post slavery peasant and sharecropping production, agriculture (producing essential foodstuffs), has taken on increasing significance since the recent demise of the seaman wage labour market. Few lower class households were able to afford imported foodstuffs in 1980–81. This illustrates the relationship of dependence that exists between the lower class economy and local and international capital. When wage labour opportunities arose, lower class households, notably in the harbour, turned away from food production in the residual agricultural and fishing sectors, using their purchasing power to obtain foodstuffs from foreign and local capitalist-owned and controlled supermarkets. Redundancies from wage labour employment forced lower class men and women back into the traditional sectors of agriculture and fishing. Lower class participation in the 'modern' economy, then, is one of marginality and dependence and represents confinement to a sector which traverses traditional and capitalist forms of production and which makes access to land, albeit barely productive, essential.

Communal forms of production: 'casual' work and labour exchange

The construction, maintenance and repair of houses, boats, nets and other fishing equipment, and land clearance are characteristic of communal production, involving labour and resource exchange between community members and based on kinship and/or personal friendship network obligations. Exceptions to these obligations, resulting in the use of non-community members' labour or resources are infrequent.

Cash remittances were formerly paid only for casual work when the unit under construction or repair was an integral part of an entrepreneurial activity, e.g. the construction of a shop or house for renting, or maintenance/extension work to tourist-let houses. In such cases a daily wage rate in line with that paid for unskilled labour in the public sector would be paid by the 'employer'. Community pressures on the employment of local labour would still be effective. Private house construction or repair, maintenance of fishing equipment, and clearance of land for peasant production were considered as non-profit orientated and non-entrepreneurial activities, and work done for the owner of such structures or resources would incur a labour-time debt which could be recouped when necessary. Should the 'debtor' be unable to repay, then a cash payment, or equivalent payment of an item of material value, would be made upon the demand of the 'creditor'. Whilst working under the labour-debt system, the 'employer' would be expected to provide daily food and rum supplies for the labour force.

Today, this distinction between waged and reciprocal work is not made by many men. The advent of temporary (daily) wage labour in, for example, the construction, maintenance and decoration of expatriate and resident non-national homes, means that only a small number of men are prepared to work on a reciprocal basis, and these are predominantly older community members with well-developed networks, through which obligations can be instigated, and repayments attained, with relative ease and without the formality which can lead to disputes.

Amongst older fishermen, labour exchange is still regularly practised, most commonly in the repair of nets and boats. The following extract indicates the nature of the social relations operative within such reciprocity and the perceived value of such exchanges for older men in the community:

> Since I done lose a finger, it ain't easy for mend my nets. But 'Reds' and me we go back long time helping each other out. We always done work together on fixing we boats and things. So now he willing for help repair my nets, and though I ain't always able for do things in return for he, I done give he fish sometime, or send my son for work wid he when he needed. Dis is how things should be in Bequia not like dose guys who always aksing for dollar for dis and a dollar for dat. How I gonna pay someone for help me fix de net, when I need de net to make a dollar?

Reds was killed in a fishing accident during January 1981, and the strength of the friendship bond that had existed between him and the informant was illustrated by the support given to Reds' elderly mother after the death:

'Man, I owe Reds plenty when he die, and he mother ain't really have anyone else for help she out, so I give she fish whenever I able and me and my son help fix she roof.

This reflects the continuation of reciprocal labour/time debts even after the death of a member of an individual's network. In contrast to older men's continuation within communal production based upon reciprocity is the following case of a number of young men who rejected the system outright:

Case 3g   Young men's rejection of traditional, communal work arrangements

When Stephen Walters began construction of a guest house in the village in January 1981 (for full details of the circumstances surrounding this project see Case 7b, p.218) he attempted to recruit a labour force on the basis of traditional labour-exchange. This system involves, not only accruing a debt to be repaid in labour or kind, but the provision of meals and rum to the labour force. During the weeks leading up to the commencement of work on the project he had recruited five young men from the community, all unemployed with little or no access to traditional means of production. Discussions about payment for the work had, as one of the men involved informed me:

> ... not bin good. Stephen he done refuse for say how he plan for pay we. We done tell he dat we ain't prepare for rum and food only, dat we want for see dollar before we gonna break we back in de sun. But he say he gonna think out a way dat good for everyone. So we agree dat we meet on de day he want for start, and before we do any work we gonna be sure we getting fair payment.

When the men turned up to start work on the arranged morning, Stephen's wife was preparing goat pillau, a rice dish with goat meat, and Stephen offered them all a drink of rum before they started. An argument ensued almost immediately, during which the men stated emphatically that they were not prepared to start work until a wage had been negotiated. Stephen explained that, because of problems in securing a loan from the Caribbean Development Bank (again, see Case 7b, p.218) the men would have to work for a while on the traditional arrangements of communal production, whereby he would either repay them in cash, if he could afford it, at a later date, or he would 'find other ways for make thing all right'. He emphasised that his sons would also be able to contribute their labour and skills to any venture that the men may enter into which would require a labour force. After an hour or so of heated discussion the men decided they would work only if they were guaranteed $10 EC a day, the rate for unskilled work in the public sector, to be paid at the end of each day. Stephen reiterated that it was not possible for him to pay this sort of money, and the men left.

For three weeks following the dispute Stephen invoked a few outstanding labour debts which, together with a small contribution from his sons and some network members, meant he was able to get some of the land clearance done in preparation for the construction of the foundations. However, progress was slow and, eventually, Stephen agreed to pay the original five men a wage, which he negotiated to $5 EC a day plus food and rum. The men's decision to compromise on their demands stemmed from their marginality and powerlessness:

> We ain't happy about it. $5 EC really ain't much a wage for dis kind of work, but what we can do? We ain't have no other way for making a dollar so we for take dis chance, otherwise he gonna find plenty of men who gonna take de work. And anyway Stephen real close to my family, so I feel dat I have for show respeck for he. But it ain't right dat we is forced into dis position of working for dis kind of wage.

The decline in communal forms of production, then, has taken place within the context of changing production relations and ideas relating to specific work relationships. This complex inter-relationship between traditional ideas and values and 'modern' ones is discussed in further detail in Chapter 6, but in economic terms the threat to 'reciprocal' work relationships is a further example of the effects of a modern economy on traditional forms of production. To acquire the range of commodities necessary to exist within their rapidly changing society and to maintain monetary commitments, households increasingly require a flow of cash, through sale of labour power or entrepreneurial/petty-commodity production. It is in this respect that the hierarchy of production activities with which I started this chapter becomes more clearly recognisable. Communal production and agricultural activities with little or no marketable surplus are engaged in only in times of absolute need as a means of subsistence when opportunities for work in the CMP or petty-commodity form are unavailable.

Inequality and marginality: the continued dependence on residual forms of economic activity

The analysis of political economy presented above has shown that the CMP is combined with forms of economic activity embedded in the traditional division of labour. The CMP reproduces the social relations of production upon which these residual forms are structured, leading to the persistence of inequality in the shape of hierarchical class relations. Perceptions of inequality are expressed locally through feelings of resentment. Such expressions are responses to increasing impoverishment and dependence, and reflect perceptions of inequalities. Within the CMP, lower class men and women are critical of the lack of opportunities for stable employment, and in the tourist sector hostility and anger are expressed with regard to powerlessness and diminished bargaining capability over wages and working conditions. In entrepreneurial activities competition for markets and access to resources leads to open conflict often directed at groups in similar class situations, such as Vincentian hawkers. Frustration and resentment are continually expressed in relation to the traditional economy: lower class men and women pointing to the exploitative nature of the share systems in petty-commodity production and sharecropping and the outdatedness of communal labour exchange in an increasingly commercial society.

The potential for change in such contradictions will unfold in the chapters to follow, which provide specific examples of areas of plebeian social life in which structural transformation have become, or are in the process of becoming, evident. Despite the increasing resistance towards participation in traditional economic forms by many groups in the lower classes, dependence upon community-based organisations continues. The analysis of modes of production presented in Chapter 1 showed community in Bequia to be a legacy from slavery, which took on increasing importance following the exodus from the estates. Community remains a significant category for the lower classes as a means of coping with minimal subsistence in a social formation in which wage labour opportunities are dependent upon movements of international capital. During periods when wage labour is unattainable the lower classes are forced back, often reluctantly, into community-based production within residual forms: production essentially for use/consumption, rather than exchange. The instrumental activation of kinship and network bonds (see Chapter 5) which effects production relationships within the traditional economic sector, draws individuals and groups from the three settlements of Lower Bay village, Lawler's Hill and northern Friendship, into co-operative work activities.

Migration to northern Friendship (Lower Bay Gutter) was a response to forces within and outside the village of Lower Bay; the pressure of increased population coupled with the concentration of village land in the hands of a small number of powerful individuals decreased the amount of land available to the lower classes. Land is a significant means of production within the traditional sector and, consequently, the division and marketing of a large area of land in Friendship in the 1960s led the lower classes to:

> ... push off surplus population into newly formed daughter villages ... Internal population surpluses can be pushed off into daughter villages only as long as *new land* is available (Wolf, 1957:12–13, my emphasis).

In this respect, migration out of the village was a response to the perceived continuation of dependence on production within the residual agricultural sector, constituting an extension of the relations of production and exchange within a form of production derived from earlier modes. Migration was also effectively a form of lower class protest towards continued inequality in land-ownership.

The continued importance of community-based organisation reflects the insecure market participation, economic marginality and powerlessness of the lower classes in respect to regional and international forces. The provision of services within the community, on the basis of kinship and friendship networks, the Friendly Society, etc., acts as an insurance against this powerlessness and marginality. In this context the household also remains a significant category, acting as a fallback system within residual forms of production. The lower class household is an effective mechanism for reducing risks, with responsibility for economic survival not falling on the individual.

The following chapter examines household form in the context of specific economic relationships and forces. It is not concerned with kinship *per se*, but with the institution of the family and the residential category of household as coping mechanisms for the lower classes on the periphery of the CMP. It will demonstrate how female-centred households allow women to maximise their chances of material survival through a flexible response to fluctuating resources in periods of economic demise. It further analyses the effects of the changing nature of the sexual division of labour on conjugal households, as women find wage labour and extra-domestic sources of income.

Notes

1. The Commonwealth Immigration Act of 1962, passed by the British Conservative government, was aimed at restricting the entry of coloured commonwealth immigrants, effectively excluding Eire. The Act introduced the Work Voucher system whereby coloured commonwealth citizens were granted one of three types of voucher: those intending to take up skilled employment, unskilled employment, and those with no guarantee of work. Vouchers were granted for a period of six months initially, after which time the immigrant was required to re-apply to the Home Office.

    The White Paper of August 1965 (Cmnd 2739) abolished the latter two categories of work voucher and reduced the total number of vouchers for coloured immigrants taking up skilled employment to 8,500 per year. The same White Paper also introduced strict tests of eligibility for the wives and children of immigrants.

    The legislations of 1962 and 1965 represented effective barriers to Afro-Caribbeans entering Britain but the figures (see Peach, 1968) indicate that emigration was already declining during the first two years of the 1960s.

2. The local education system is not discussed in any detail in the thesis as it is not relevant to the main argument as the lower classes invariably move straight from school to work.

3. The term 'bobol' appears to have been derived from the abbreviation 'bbl' used to indicate weights of flour, sugar and rice transported on cargo ships (details in *St Vincent Blue Books*).

4. A fuller account of fishing practices and techniques in Lower Bay appears in Price (1984:131–157).

5. A fishing co-operative was set up in Bequia in 1959, one of four in the St Vincent Grenadines between 1957 and 1960 (one in Barrouali, St Vincent in 1957, one in Canouan and one in Union, 1960). The co-operative in Bequia was set up to assist the whaling industry, but the Government later that year appointed a fisheries officer to assist members in the processing of loan applications for marine engines and other equipment. On establishing the co-operative in Bequia, the Government provided a loan of $5,000 EC for the establishment and stocking of a fishing supplies shop in Port Elizabeth. By 1962, three years after its formation, the Annual Report of the Registrar of Co-operative Societies (1962:3) stated:

    ... the fishing co-operative in Bequia is showing signs of inefficiency.

    By 1964 the co-operative was disbanded and the shop closed. The official report states that the shop in Bequia:

    ... was never a success due principally to the fact that its turnover was not sufficient to pay overhead expenses. The stock of goods was sold out and the amount realised paid on the loan. (1964:3)

CHAPTER 4
Household and family in Lower Bay

This chapter analyses the lower class household in the context of recent economic developments, focusing specifically on the institutionalised practice of matrifocality. Household form is viewed as a consequence of economic variables from prevailing market forces and production relations. Emphasis is placed on the household as a flexible and significant unit in the context of fluctuating opportunities for work.

Unlike the model of the typical peasant household, characterised by Chayanov (1925) as a unit '... based upon the identification of the family and productive plant ...', the domestic unit amongst lower class Afro-Caribbean Bequarians is rarely coterminous with the elementary family. It is, therefore, important to distinguish betwen the concepts of household and family.

I use the sociological term household or domestic unit to refer, as does the lower class term 'house' or 'home', to the physical structure, where people eat, sleep and live, and the immediately surrounding land and provision grounds, plus the people normally resident within it. As a residential unit the household represents the basic unit of property holding and socialisation.

The sociological concept of the family has a history of methodological debate. Central to this debate is the socio-biological dichotomy. I shall be using the concept of family analytically to refer to the relationships that constitute the elementary kinship unit of husband, wife and children, biologically or socially defined, who are not necessarily co-resident. All other socio-biological relationships that constitute the kinship structure of Lower Bay will be qualified according to the nature of that relationship in structural terms, e.g. father's brother, adopted son, foster (social) mother, mother's brother's son, etc. This is not intended to express the idea that the elementary biological family constitutes the point of departure from which Lower Bay plebeian culture elaborates its kinship system. For, as Levi-Strauss (1972:50) points out:

> ... what confers upon kinship its socio-cultural character is not what it retains from nature, but, rather, the essential way in which it diverges from nature.

Instead, the concept uses the biological relationship as its central referrent because family and domestic unit do not consistently coincide. The aim is to make analytical distinction as accurately as possible.

Within plebeian culture, the term 'family' has a number of contextually specific meanings. At its widest, and least kinship specific, it can refer to all members of Lower Bay community, as illustrated by the expression '... we is all family in Lowbay ...' This is a reference to co-residency and to a common sense of belonging and solidarity (see Chapter 6). As a direct kinship term, the word is not used to refer to kinsfolk as a group, but to one's kinship tie to another individual. In this sense it can refer, as does my sociological concept, to the kinship relationships stemming from the biological or elementary family. 'He is family to me' refers to a recognised socio-biological relationship. Even the term 'my family' refers to a relationship with one person, as in 'He is my family'. It can further refer to persons of non-biological relationship, such as foster/adoptive parents and to their biological kin depending upon the quality of the relationships (see Chapter 5 for fuller details). The implications are that ties between particular individuals are more important than ties to a group of kinsfolk. This is clearly illustrated in the value placed on the 'home' or 'house' (to refer to members of a household), reflecting the fact that co-residency, regardless of relationships of kinship, is distinguished from all other personal relationships.

Households, of course, are not enduring. They have a cycle of development, they can be dissolved and formed, and are not corporate units. Nevertheless, the concept of the household is a fixed concept in the plebeian meaning system and is linked to concepts about the person: notably (as will be shown), to a person's relationship to the system of descent and inheritance, and to her/his position within groups and institutions contained in the community.

Before proceeding with a discussion of household structure and formation it is necessary to clarify the sociological concepts of household headship, including specifically matrifocality, and affinal and consanguineal households. Household form and size in Lower Bay varies to the extent (see Tables 4a and 4b) that these concepts become important sociological classification tools.

(i) Household head

The continually changing form of relationships within households during their developmental cycle is such that classification of household types according to headship allows, as M. G. Smith (1962:20) notes:

> ... the study of factors which influence the development and change of domestic units.

By household head, I am referring to the 1970 British Caribbean Census (BCC) definition (Vol 9:xiii) which states that the household head is the person acknowledged as such by the other members of the household, the role of such a person being to '... carry out the main responsibilities in affairs of the household' (*ibid.*). The role, status and characterisation of household head in Lower Bay is, in reality, far more complex that the BCC definition indicates, as we shall see. The inherent problems of identification of household head, through a house-to-house survey, stem from the complexity of relationships of power and authority, contained in ownership patterns and other material factors, and these are further discussed in subsequent sections.

Matrifocality, as used here, refers to female role dominance in household decision-making and authority structures. The term 'matrifocal household' refers to the residential unit in which relationships between members are defined in terms of the 'mother-child' dyad (see Gonzalez, 1970:236). The role of the mother figure is structurally central: she exercises control over the domestic unit's resources and is involved in the decision-making process. It is not, as will be shown, genealogical but 'cultural' motherhood that is significant in lower class matrifocal households. The mother in matrifocal households is economically significant and ideologically and structurally central.

In emphasising that the matrifocal household is a predominant form, for the purpose of analysis this refers to the existence of a number of households in which the household head is female, as well as fulfilling the conditions laid out in the definition above.

Because of the instability of conjugal unions amongst lower class Bequarians, where the tendency is for men to leave the household, through search for employment or in entering new conjugal relationships, or to die earlier than women, authority can pass to the mother figure as a direct result of changes in household structure. When this occurs a patrifocal household becomes matrifocal. Matrifocality therefore, should be recognised as a particular point in the domestic cycle rather than an absolute or unchanging characteristic of the system as a whole.

Table 4a: Frequency distribution of household sizes (Lower Bay) 1981

No. of persons in household	No. of households			Percentage of households		
	Total community	Lower Bay village and Lawler's Hill	Lower Bay Gutter	Total community	Lower Bay village and Lawler's Hill	Lower Bay Gutter
1	8	8	0	12.12	16.33	0.00
2	6	6	0	9.09	12.24	0.00
3	8	6	2	12.12	12.24	11.76
4	9	7	2	13.64	14.29	11.76
5	10	7	3	15.15	14.29	17.65
6	5	4	1	7.59	8.16	5.88
7	4	2	2	6.06	4.08	11.76
8	6	3	3	9.09	6.12	17.65
9	5	5	0	7.59	10.20	0.00
10	1	1	0	1.52	2.04	0.00
11	1	0	1	1.52	0.00	5.88
12	1	0	1	1.52	0.00	5.88
14	1	0	1	1.52	0.00	5.88
16	1	0	1	1.52	0.00	5.88
Totals	66	49	17	100	100	100
Mean household size	5.05	4.41	6.88			

(ii) Affinal and consanguineal households

The majority of households in Lower Bay can be classified as either affinal or consanguineal (see Table 4c).

Affinal households are defined here as those in which the household head has a spouse or concubine co-resident in a stable union. The ideal family-household form in Bequia, as defined by the dominant ideology of the planter-descended class, is that of an

Table 4b: Household composition by frequency of structure and sex of household head (H/H) Lower Bay 1981

Household composition	Total				Lower Bay village and Lawler's Hill				Lower Bay Gutter			
			Household head				Household head				Household head	
	No.	%	Male	Female	No.	%	Male	Female	No.	%	Male	Female
Single adult	8	12.12	6	2	8	16.4	6	2	0	0.00	0	0
Affinal households:												
Nuclear family: H/H + 'partner'	2	3.02	2	0	2	4.1	2	0	0	0.00	0	0
Nuclear family: H/H + 'partner', issue of H/H and/or 'partner'	7	10.6	6	1	5	10.2	4	1	2	11.76	2	0
Nuclear family: H/H + 'partner' + issue of H/H and/or 'partner' + outside child(ren)	3	4.53	3	0	1	2.05	1	0	2	11.76	2	0
Nuclear family; H/H + 'partner' + outside child(ren) only	1	1.51	1	0	0	0.00	0	0	1	5.88	1	0
H/H + 'partner' + grandchild of H/H and/or 'partner'	2	3.02	2	0	1	2.05	1	0	1	5.88	1	0
H/H + 'partner' + single issue + grandchildren { Children of daughters / children of sons / children of sons and daughters }	10	15.16	5	5	6	12.3	2	4	4	23.53	3	1
H/H + 'partner' + issue + issue's spouse	1	1.51	1	0	0	0.00	0	0	1	5.88	1	0
H/H + 'partner' + issue + mother of H/H	2	3.02	2	0	1	2.05	1	0	1	5.88	1	0
H/H + 'partner' + issue + issue(s)' spouse + issues' children	1	1.51	1	0	1	2.05	1	0	0	5.88	0	0

Household and family in Lower Bay 107

Female household head + issue	8	12.12	0	8	7	14.35	0	1	1	0	0	1
Female H/H + issue + outside child(ren)	1	1.51	0	1	1	2.05	0	1	0	0	0	0
Female H/H + outside child(ren) only	1	1.51	0	1	1	2.05	0	0	0	11.76	0	0
Female H/H + issue + issue(s)' children { Daughter's issue												
Son's issue	10	15.16	0	10	6	16.30	0	8	2	0	0	2
Female H/H + issue + daughters's husband + issue's children	1	1.51	0	1	1	2.05	0	1	0	0	0	0
Female H/H and issue + daughter's issue + daughter's grandchildren	1	1.51	0	1	1	2.05	0	0	0	0	0	0
Male H/H + issue	1	1.51	1	0	1	2.05	1	0	0	0	0	0
Male H/H + daughter + daughter's issue	1	1.51	1	0	1	2.05	1	0	0	0	0	0
Male H/H + issue of deceased sibling	1	1.51	1	0	0	0	0	0	1	5.88	1	0
Sibling group (two sisters)	1	1.51	0	1	1	2.05	1	1	0	0	0	0
Sibling group (mixed sex) plus issue of one sibling and daughter (of same sibling's) issue	1	1.51	1	0	1	2.05	1	0	0	0	0	0
Sibling group (mixed sex) plus issue of one sibling	1	1.51	0	1	0	0	0	0	1	5.88	0	1
Sibling group (two brothers) + 1 brother's daughter and husband	1	1.51	1	0	1	2.05	1	0	0	0	0	0
Totals	66	100	34	32	49	100	22	27	17	100	12	5

Table 4c: Distribution of household types, classified according to internal structure and sex of household head, Lower Bay, 1981

Type	Total community						Lower Bay village and Lawler's Hill						Lower Bay Gutter					
	All No.	All %	H/H No. M	H/H No. F	H/H % of total M	H/H % of total F	All No.	All %	H/H No. M	H/H No. F	H/H % M	H/H % F	All No.	All %	H/H No. M	H/H No. F	H/H % M	H/H % F
Single	8	12.12	6	2	9.09	3.03	8	12.12	6	2	9.09	3.03	0	0.00	0	0	0.00	0.00
Affinal (Conjugal)																		
a) Nuclear	13	19.69	12	1	18.18	1.51	8	12.12	7	1	10.61	1.51	5	7.58	5	0	7.58	0.00
b) Extended	16	24.25	11	5	16.67	7.58	9	13.64	5	4	7.58	6.06	7	10.61	6	1	9.09	1.51
Consanguineal	29	43.94	5	24	7.58	36.36	24	36.36	4	20	6.06	30.30	5	7.58	1	4	1.51	7.58
Totals	66	100.00	34	32	51.52	48.48	49	74.24	22	27	33.34	40.90	17	25.76	12	5	18.18	7.58

H/H = Household head; M = Male; F = Female

affinal household containing the elementary (nuclear) family. Less than 20 per cent of households in Lower Bay can be classified as nuclear family households, i.e. containing a couple in a stable mating relationship, with or without children, demonstrating the deviation from ideal form. In fact, in less that 44 per cent of all households, including extended families of three and four generations, are household heads in a permanent mating relationship with a co-residential concubine or spouse. The head of such households is usually male: of the 29 affinal households, 23 (or 79 per cent) were found to be male-headed.

Consanguineal households, in which the effective and enduring relationships are those existing between consanguineal kin, are predominantly based on mother-child and/or mother's consanguineal kin relationships. Table 4c shows that 29, or 44 per cent, of households in Lower Bay are consanguineal, of which 24 are female headed. This supports the claim by Gonzalez (*op.cit.*:238) that although '... matrifocality has nothing to do *per se* with the consanguineal household ... most consanguineal households also tend to be matrifocal'.

Table 4d shows there are 29 households (43.94 per cent of the community) in which a female household head and her child(ren) are present – representing the *matrifocal* households in the community, of which 24 are consanguineal (see Table 4c).

Matrifocality, as a specific stage in the household cycle, is, as suggested earlier, a consequence of economic variables. To examine this further, within the specific context of the material position of

Table 4d: Distribution of households according to sex of household head, Lower Bay, 1981

	Total community		Lower Bay village and Lawler's Hill		Lower Bay Gutter	
	No.	%	No.	%	No.	%
Male	34	51.52	22	44.90	12	70.58
Female	32*	48.48	27	55.10	5	29.42
Total	66	100.00	49	100.00	17	100.00

(* includes 2 single female households and one household containing 2 sisters with no children)

Table 4e: Distribution of households according to age and sex of household head, Lower Bay, 1981

	By number							By percentage						
Age	Total community H/H		Lower Bay and Lawler's Hill H/H		Lower Bay Gutter H/H			Total community H/H		Lower Bay village and Lawler's Hill H/H		Lower Bay Gutter H/H		
	M	F	M	F	M	F		M	F	M	F	M	F	
21–30	3	1	3	0	0	1		8.82	3.13	13.64	0.00	0.00	20.00	
31–40	6	6	3	5	3	1		17.65	18.75	13.64	18.52	25.00	20.00	
41–50	7	9	4	7	3	2		20.59	28.12	18.18	25.92	25.00	40.00	
51–60	7	6	5	5	2	1		20.59	18.75	22.73	18.52	33.33	20.00	
61+	11	10	7	10	4	0		32.35	31.25	31.82	37.04	16.67	0.00	
Total	34	32	22	27	12	5		100	100	100	100	100	100	

lower class men in the community, it is necessary to look closely at the process of household formation.

Household formation

In Lower Bay, as in most lower class Afro-Caribbean communities, procreation generally precedes household formation. Despite efforts on the part of the mother, and sanctions by the household head (in households where the mother's partner has formal authority in the home) to prevent young unmarried females from engaging in premarital sex, most girls and boys in the community have had sexual experience by the age of 16 years. The first pregnancy of a young, unmarried woman in the household brings disgrace (see Chapter 6) to her parents, especially the household head who, being responsible for the sexual conduct of childless young women in the household, views the pregnancy as a reflection of his/her ineffectiveness as leader. Subsequent pregnancies are treated less harshly, even if the girl remains unmarried and at home. After initial threats of expulsion from the household and demonstrations of anger at the girl's 'foolishness' the parent(s) usually agree(s) to accommodate the girl and her child in the likely event of the father not being willing and/or materially able to establish a separate household based upon cohabitation or legal marriage.

The father of the child will be expected to contribute to its upbringing both socially and materially, although rarely is a young man in Lower Bay able to support his offspring and their mother(s) fully. If the child, and subsequent children, together with the mother are resident in her parent(s) household but maintained by the father(s) of the children, they operate as a separate unit, relying upon the other members of the household for shelter only. This is illustrated by the introduction of a second cooking pot: in lower class Bequia households food is eaten from a single communal pot[1] at least once a day. The newly formed unit is responsible for managing its own affairs and meeting its own expenses, with the exception of repairs and upkeep to the house itself. As provider, the absent father, although he lacks the formal authority of household head, is, nevertheless, responsible for ensuring that his children receive a school education and attend church; and, as such, he will visit the household regularly. Formal authority over who visits the homestead and the daily activities and household tasks, however, remains with the head of household within which this separate unit lives.

It is more common for the man to be unable to support fully the mother and child, especially amongst teenage couples. In these cases the girl may either turn to her parents for support, the household remaining intact and fully operative as a single unit and the child raised as a sibling to its biological mother or, in less frequent cases (see Case 5a, p.141) the father's mother or other maternal kin will informally adopt the child and bring it up as her own. In such an event there is little, if any, contact between the mother's family and the child.

Should the unmarried daughter continue to bear children whilst living at the household of her parent(s), and these children receive some but not full material support from their biological fathers, she may decide to enter into affairs with other men, based upon (as Greenfield 1966:119, noted in Barbados) '... presents in exchange for companionship and sex ...', whereby she will be forced to acknowledge her position in the household of her parents as that of dependent daughter; and subject to her parents' approval, will see her children raised as her siblings.

Although the dominant ideology in Bequia emphasises marriage as the preferred union between men and women in association with the care and socialisation of children, the most common form of relationship between lower class islanders of procreative age is 'visiting', where the man, usually from outside the community, visits the house of his mate who may or may not be the mother of his children. When the woman does not live in her own house, sexual intimacy will only be possible at times when the woman's parent(s) and/or other senior members of the household are absent, notably during Friendly Society meetings, other ceremonies, or at work.

The age at which couples in Bequia enter permanent, common law or legal marriage is dependent to a large degree upon the material wealth of the man. Very few men under 40 years of age in the community own land or other means of production, relying upon older fishermen for work aboard their fishing boats. Those who were successful in finding, and keeping, work aboard National Bulk and other shipping companies in the 1960s and 1970s have been able to purchase small plots of land and build, or are still in the process of building, houses. Table 4f shows that, of men under 40 years of age, only five own houses and are living in legal or common law marital unions. All of these had regular wage labour employment with shipping companies at the time of the survey.

This demonstrates quite clearly the effect of the division of labour, experienced locally, on the social position of men in the community and highlights the material and cultural preconditions

Table 4f: Distribution of affinal households according to relationship between partners and age of head of household, Lower Bay, 1981

Age of H/H	Total community							Lower Bay village and Lawler's Hill							Lower Bay Gutter						
	Married		CL (2+)		CL (2–)		Married		CL (2+)		CL (2–)		Married		CL (2+)		CL (2–)	
	M	F	M	F	M	F	M	F	M	F	M	F	M	F	M	F	M	F
21–30	1	0	0	0	0	0	0	0	0	0	0	1	0	0	0	0	0	0
31–40	2	0	2	1	1	0	1	0	0	0	0	1	1	0	0	1	0	0
41–50	5	1	1	0	1	1	2	1	2	0	1	1	3	0	0	0	0	0
51–60	5	2	0	0	0	0	3	1	0	0	0	0	2	1	0	0	0	0
61+	4	2	0	0	0	0	2	2	0	0	0	0	2	0	0	0	0	0
Total	17	5	2	1	3	1	8	4	2	0	2	1	9	1	0	2	0	0

Notes: CL = common law
CL (2+) = common law union of two or more years
CL (2–) = common law union of two or less years

for lower class marriage. The extent to which the increased earning power of men in the 'economic boom' of the 1960s and early 1970s affected marriage rates in Bequia is borne out by the Caribbean Population Census figures which showed an increase in the number of married women in the St Vincent Grenadines, from 16.4 per cent in 1931 to 41.9 per cent by 1970. Table 4g shows the rate of increase in married women in Bequia over the ten years between 1960 and 1970, although it should be stressed that these figures are higher than the Lower Bay ones, due to the less significant effects of National Bulk and other shipping companies on the employment structure of Lower Bay community (see Table 4g), compared with Port Elizabeth and Hamilton. Nevertheless, marriage rates did increase in the late 1960s, but today the decline is such that only six men under 40 (8.8 per cent of eligible age) and seven women under 40 (10.6 per cent of eligible age) in Lower Bay are married (see Table 4h). The marked difference in the percentage of legally married men and women in Lower Bay Gutter, compared to that in the village (30.56 per cent of men compared to 22.38 per cent, and 37.93 per cent of women compared to 19.25 per cent respectively, again see Table 4g) emphasises the importance of the acquisition of resources as a determining factor in marriage. Availability of suitable housing is one of the most significant of these factors; those individuals and domestic groups that moved to Friendship in the mid to late 1960s were those from the village who were able to purchase their own land and build new houses.

Inheritance

The acquisition of significant resources through inheritance is an important determinant of household form in Lower Bay. Matrifocality, as a lower class response to marginality, pre-supposes the transfer of property to women. This is in direct opposition to the statutory laws of inheritance in St Vincent and the Grenadines, which Patchett (1959) classifies as of the 'Modern English Pattern', based essentially upon English Common Law with modifications contained in the Judicative Acts of 1873–75. For the purpose of this chapter I am concerned with the law and customs pertaining to the inheritance of land, houses and fishing equipment, as little other property is commonly held by people in the community. With regard to the law in St Vincent, these laws may be listed, briefly, as:

Table 4g: Percentage of married women* in Bequia (adapted from Gibson, 1981:88)

Date	Age (in years)	
	15–44	45–64
1960	17.5%	35.3%
1970	33.9%	50.6%

* Only figures for rates of marriage amongst women available from Gibson (op.cit.)

Table 4h: Number and percentage of persons legally married in Lower Bay community, 1981

	Total community				Lawler's Hill and Lower Bay village				Lower Bay Gutter			
	Male		Female		Male		Female		Male		Female	
Age	No.	%*	No.	%	No.	%	No.	%	No.	%	No.	%
15–40	6	8.82	7	10.60	4	8.34	3	6.38	2	8.34	4	21.05
41+	20	57.14	20	44.45	11	47.83	13	37.13	9	75.00	7	70.00
Total	26	25.23	27	24.32	15	22.38	16	19.25	11	30.56	11	37.93

NB Number of married women over 40 years is lowered due to widowhood. I made no age distinction at 45 years in my survey, which affects comparability.
Table includes widows and widowers, of which there are 7 in the community.
* Represents percentage of age group

(a) marriage legitimises the children of a couple born in wedlock, and the law recognises the rights of legitimate children *only* to inherit;
(b) in cases of intestacy only legitimate children inherit, the law stating that, whilst provision may be made for the maintenance of a widow/widower and dependent children,

all property passes to the eldest son, and specifically excludes daughters over 21 years;
(c) in the absence of legal heirs, intestate property shall pass to the siblings of the deceased and their lawful descendants. Illegitimate children of the deceased received no share of his property.

In practice, the law is generally ignored and in cases of intestacy, settlement is made outside the formal judicial system: children dividing the property, including land, of their parents equally amongst themselves. In such cases the rules of primogeniture and the denial of rights to illegitimates are disregarded. The disjunction between law and practice is illustrated in the cases that follow, being a necessary and economically rational response to marginality and scarcity of resources. Patchett (*op.cit.*:677) notes that:

> ... legal provisions ... are patently ignored by a large section of the population ... The law makes no concessions to the negro family structure: it grants no recognition in any form to other relationships than legal marriage: it draws a rigid dichotomy of legitimacy-illegitimacy in situations where it is disregarded: it insists upon principles of inheritance out of touch with social facts and customarily ignored: it makes no provision for rights customarily observed.

The partible nature of intestate land and property is a major cause of conflicts over the division of property between siblings, both full and half, most notably when one sibling wishes to sell his or her portion of land, or establish the exact boundaries between his and other siblings' shares. Few individuals can afford the cost of the lawyer and surveyor needed to establish a Registered Title on land, and as a result disputes over boundaries, ownership of fruit trees, etc. persist for years. Anyone wishing to sell land in Bequia requires a Registered Title by law before the transaction can take place. Because the value of land in the past was so low, titles were very rarely taken out. However, with the increase in the value of land since the early 1960s small plots are now worthy of investment in a Title, and many men who found employment on National Bulk have taken out Titles and had their land surveyed during the past 15 years to establish rights and minimise the risk of subsequent disputes over ownership. This is illustrated by the sharp increase in the number of Titles listed in the St Vincent Registry over the period 1965–1981.

There is, then, a clear disjunction between the law and economic reality in Bequia. Few individuals understand the intricacies of the legal system and unless the legal heir, usually the eldest legitimate son of the deceased, is present in the island and familiar with the primogeniture clause, intestacy statutes are never followed up.

One of the most overt disjunctions between the law and lower class practices is in regard to 'family land'. Family land, as defined in English Common Law as it relates to land in the Colonies, refers to land inherited from an ancestor who was bequeathed it as a gift from a slave owner after Emancipation. The fundamental principles governing inheritance of family land are:

(a) it is inalienable;
(b) it passes to all children;
(c) any member of the family, through 'name or blood' has rights of use, not lost through non-exercise of those rights for any period (see Clarke, 1966:44).

Disregard for the law has meant that over generations family land in Lower Bay has been divided and even sold, and claims to individual ownership have been recognised and practised within the community. In many of the case studies I made of inheritance and its associated disputes it became clear that what people in Lower Bay referred to as 'undivided family land' was, in most cases, land that had been owned by a single individual who had not bequeathed it in a will. It appears, however, that areas of uncultivated hillside land qualify as family land, as evidenced by older members of the community whose ancestors had acquired it as gifts from the ex-plantation owner, Walters; but, as far as I was able to ascertain, there were no disputed claims to this land as it was unsuitable for cultivation or housing. The conflicts over inheritance in cases referred to locally as 'undivided family land' stemmed not from a failure to recognise the customary rights of both legal and illegitimate children, but from the failure for full division of the land to take place at the time of death. Part settlement of undivided land and confusion over boundaries are amongst the recognisable symptoms of the time lag between the death of an owner and attempts at establishing individual rights over un- or loosely divided land and property. The following case highlights many of these points – specifically focusing on intestacy and customary inheritance rules.

Case 4a Disputed 'family land'

Roland Walters, whose descent is traceable to the ex-plantation owner of Lower Bay estate, owned a large area of land, mostly steep hillside, to the west of Lower Bay village. When he died in early 1980, he left no will. At the time of my fieldwork the land was uncultivated, with the exception of a small plot where his widow lives with her young grandson, in a house Roland built himself (Household A below). His wife works a garden of approximately one and a half plots.

This is the account of the dispute that followed Roland's death, given by his grandson, Monty. Monty is the legitimate son of Roland's son, Samuel, who was born to a woman that Roland never married (see kinship diagram below).

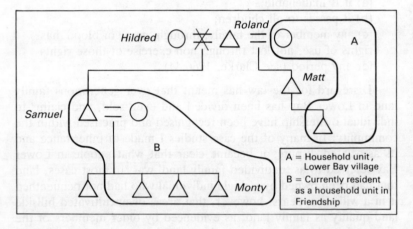

Kinship diagram

The story was confirmed by several members of the community.

> When we was young, we (his three other brothers plus his mother and father) lived in Hildred's house in the village. Roland was my father's father, but he nah marry Hildred (his father's mother). When my father done born, Roland gif Hildred de home we all done live in, but he still nah marry she. Old-man Walters (Roland) done marry dat other woman and build de house where she done live today. We all done move out of de village in 1966 (land bought in Lower Bay Gutter in 1964) for now we getting too much for live in Hildred's house (by now Monty's parents had four children). Land was cheap in Friendship and my father done save a couple hundred dollar from sailing. (See above kinship diagram, viz. Household B).

> My father done aks Old-man Walters for a plot of he land up dere but dat man evil and tell my father no.
> Dat land been doing nothing for de people of Lower Bay and I so fed up for live wid my parent dat I plan for do something about it. I a man and it ain't no good for me to be relying upon I-man mother all de time (two of his brothers also live with their parents, the other has emigrated to the USA). My father done nutting for get any of dat land and I know it family land. If I done haf de money I get me a lawyer and build a house up dere in de trees.

Whether the land was family land is impossible to determine as records in the St Vincent Registry date only from 1867 and post-Emancipation gifts of land would have been made 30 years prior to that. It is, however, reasonable to assume that, even if the land was originally part of a family land estate, it has subsequently been divided and subject to individual rights because of the size and exclusive rights exercised by Roland Walters. By the law of intestacy, Roland Walters' eldest (and only) legitimate son, Matt, who has a house in the harbour, and who had been away at sea since the death of his father, has exclusive rights of primogeniture to the land. The customary means for dividing land would give an equal share to Samuel Walters (Monty's father) who could then divide it equally amongst his sons. Should Monty invoke the law in order to secure his rights to land, he will discover, unless the land is registered as family land, of which I could find no trace, that neither he, nor his brothers or father have any legal rights to the land. At the time of my departure from Bequia in May 1981, a bitter argument had developed between Monty and Roland's widow. Monty had gone to her house one day and asked her permission to begin clearing some of the less-severely sloping hillside land in preparation for building a house. She had refused, apparently mocking Monty and maintaining that he had no right whatsoever to the land. As the argument developed, much abuse was exchanged between the two, to an ever-increasing audience. Monty later told me that he 'knew' he had legal rights to the land, but had approached the woman in the hope of avoiding the expenditure and formalities of a legal case.

Walters' widow maintained that she recognised no 'family relationship' with Monty or his household, i.e. his father, and, therefore, he had 'no right to de land, nor even de right to come cussing on my doorstep'. Another major factor which people in the community considered was instrumental in her decision, was the escalating value and demand for land in the village, especially by foreigners.

This is an unusual case in as much as the custom is for intestate land to be divided equally amongst all children of the deceased at, or as near as possible to, the time of death. This case was complicated by confusion over the land being 'family land', the absence of Roland's legitimate son, and the grievances held by the parties as a result of previous disputes. Nevertheless, it does highlight many of the factors involved in inheritance, and a further aspect: that of 'favouritism' towards kin and even non-kin in decisions over choice of benefactor.

Unless the death is unexpected, intestacy is rare in the community today. In drawing up a will, it is the personal relationships with other community members, and outsiders, that influence an individual's choice in disposal of property and not legal or blood relationships. As Rodman (1971:144) noted in a Trinidadian village:

... it is the nature of a man's relationship to his kinsmen and non-kin that influences his attitudes and behaviour ...

and consequently the choice of benefactors in his will. Extended to the case of Roland Walters the strained relationships that existed between him (and his wife) and Hildred (and Monty's nuclear family) could be seen to stem from his marriage to another woman and his refusal to offer land to his son.

Personal relationships, dependant upon quid pro quo elements, mean that parents frequently show favouritism to a child or more distant kin or non-kin, justifying it in terms of the respect, loyalty and material support shown and offered during their lifetime, especially in later years. The death of a small-holder in the village in the late 1970s illustrates this point. He had lived alone and had been crippled for the last years of his life. His children – two by his wife who had died some years before, and one 'outside child' by another woman – were all living outside the community and rarely offered any material or emotional support. His sister, who lived nearby, apparently took food to him regularly and tended his small garden. When he died his will bequeathed his house and garden to one of his daughter's children, who, I was told, came to see him after church every week, and a four-acre piece of hillside land to his sister.

The freedom of choice of beneficiaries, within the limits imposed by law, (ensuring 'reasonable provision for dependants' such as children under 21, disabled sons and daughters, and legal spouses), influenced by the expected, reciprocal nature of personal relationships, leads to great rivalry amongst full and half siblings. The practices of marital shifting and child shifting, which often mean that full siblings grow up in separate households and half-siblings are raised in the same household, sometimes with distant or non-kinsfolk, also places strain on sibling relationships. Of all the kin relationships in the community, none was as tenuous or subject to as much conflict as the sibling bond. Favouritism undoubtedly leads to hostility between siblings as a result of competition for valued resources:

> The deteriorated quality of sibling relationships is easily explained. The opportunities for affection and material necessities in the lower class home are severely limited. In the struggle to obtain a share of these scarcities, the ensuing rivalry is bitter and enormously exaggerated ... (A. Kardiner and L. Ovesey, 1962:68, as cited in Rodman, *op.cit.*:94).

Clearly, then, the economic and political baseline for a patrilineal social life, i.e. co-operation and exchange between male kinsfolk in work and leisure activities, is absent because of the marginal position of lower class males.

Obligations between siblings, unlike those between parents and children, are vague and undefined. There are few opportunities for siblings to work together in household production, with the exception of sharecropping. As Rodman (*op.cit.*:98) notes:

> ... there is no common lineage or other strong kinship tie to bind them together tightly. They work as individuals not as a group. As adults, and frequently as children, they live in separate households ... These things, together with the rivalry that may result from scarce parental resources and from overt parental favouritism, do not permit the development of a strong sibling bond or a stable sibling relationship.

However, there are situations and contexts in which siblings offer emotional and material support. In the event of absence of parents, through death, emigration or temporary migration, an older sibling, usually the eldest sister, will take responsibility for the care and socialisation of the younger ones in the household as illustrated below:

> Upon the death of her mother in 1977, the eldest daughter of a co-resident sibling group of seven in Lower Bay

Gutter took on the role of household head. She was 24 years old at the time with a 3-year-old son. Since the death, one sister has married and lives in the harbour, and the youngest brother has gone to live with his mother's sister in St Vincent. The household receives material support from a number of sources: the father of the household head's son, two brothers with limited income from fishing and hawking to tourists, and from the sister of the deceased mother who also visits the household regularly. The sibling group as a unit work the small household garden, and one 16-year-old sister sharecrops a small piece of land in Friendship. Although the eldest sister cannot provide materially for the entire household, she has clearly adopted the authority and responsibilities concomitant with the position of household head.

Female sibling groups exhibit more cohesion than male or mixed groups. A woman's sister will offer support through fostering or adopting the child(ren) if her sister is materially unable to maintain them. There was no evidence of a sister adopting or supporting a brother's child; and a brother raising his sister's child was unusual amongst lower class sibling groups. This latter phenomenon can be explained within the context of the material position of most lower class men who have difficulties maintaining their own children and supporting their mothers. Although the avuncular bond does not prescribe financial or material responsibilities, there was evidence that some less poor male household heads were prepared to provide shelter and support for sisters' children, or, in one case, a brother's child, see below. One man in Lower Bay Gutter, who still sails regularly with Caribbean Steamships (in 1981) bought a piece of land in 1967, and whilst sailing sent remittances back to Bequia, his brother and other network members (see Chapter 5) providing the labour to build him a house. When the house was complete in 1970 he married a Jamaican woman he had met whilst shipping bauxite from Jamaica. They now have four children but they also look after his sister's 15-year-old daughter. His sister lives and works in St Vincent with her three other children.

This form of avuncular support, in the shape of fostering/adoption is just one example of a widely practised response to declining material resources: that of child shifting and parental role replacement.

Child shifting and parental role replacement

In Bequia, as in many lower class Afro-Caribbean societies, there is no strong plebeian ideological or normative prescription on biological parents to bring up their children. As already noted, the biological father is often absent from the household into which his children are born; and the biological mother is often unable materially to support her children so will turn to kin or friends for assistance in the form of fostering or adoption. It is usually the woman's mother or sister who takes on the role of social motherhood, but dependent upon the material circumstances, and the strength of personal relationships, other female kin or friends will replace the biological mother's role. If the shifting of children is intended to be temporary there may be some continued financial assistance to the household in which the child is being raised. In such cases the biological mother will seek wage labour, or alternative forms of income, and may even leave the community for this purpose. It is not unusual for some of the children of a couple living in a stable conjugal relationship to be placed in other households if the material means are insufficient to meet the needs of all members of the household, which is illustrated by the brief case below.

Case 4b **Children displaced from a household suffering material deprivation**
(i) One married couple in the village have 12 legitimate children. The eldest son lives in Italy, where he stayed after completing a contract with a shipping company. One daughter married a man from Lower Bay Gutter at Christmas 1979 and emigrated with him to Tortola, in the Virgin Islands. Eight of the remaining ten children live in their parents' household. One six-year-old son lives in his father's brother's household. At the time of my fieldwork, the brother's household was one of the more affluent in the community as a result of sustained income from 'sailing' with Barbados Shipping Company (14 years), and a marginal income from his rum shop which is run by his wife. It was not possible to ascertain whether the child was only temporarily fostered, although he referred to his social parents as mother and father and had lived with them since he was two years old. The other child, the youngest, lives with a young widowed teacher in the village along with her two children. Again this child was placed with its social mother at an early age and was assumed by people I spoke to, to have been adopted.

In cases of adoption, no material support is expected of the biological parents, and only in special cases is any legal adoption procedure followed. An interesting example which I witnessed whilst in the field does, however, illustrate the types of instances in which legal adoption is sought.

(ii) Keith is an 8-year-old boy whose mother died in 1978. For the three years since the death he has lived with his mother's sister and her husband and children. His mother's other sister lives in the USA and in wanting Keith to live with her in the US, she was forced to undertake legal adoption procedures through a court in St Vincent. She returned to attend the hearing in May 1980, which granted her legal adoption of the child and at the time of my departure from Bequia, Keith was still living with his foster mother in the village, awaiting clearance to emigrate to the USA and live with his legally-adopted mother. During the time he lived with his mother's sister in Lower Bay, the other sister in the USA sent remittances to the household for his support, thus distinguishing quite clearly between the role of one sister as temporary foster mother, and the other as adopted (social) mother.

It is more common for the displacement of children from their natal household to be a structural manifestation of matrifocality. As I have suggested, matrifocality is often the result of the failure of men to provide steady support for their spouses/mates and children, and women will often shift their children onto their mothers or, if they live in someone else's household, to the senior female member. If a biological mother continues to reside in the same household as her children, yet they are being raised by another member of that household, such as the mother's mother, then her children will be raised as her siblings. Should the woman later enter into a common law or legal marital relationship involving taking up new residence, her children will normally remain with their cultural mother/parents:

(iii) A young woman in the village who entered a common law union with a man, also from the village, took up residence with him, along with her one-year-old daughter by another man. Her other child, an 8-year-old son, also by a former relationship, remained in his maternal grandmother's household where he had been raised and where his biological mother had previously lived. It is significant that the elder child, as a result of having been raised by his mother's mother, and, consequently, as his biological mother's sibling, was placed in a quite different relationship category to that of the younger child. The difference was given existential recognition by the maternal grandmother, the biological mother and her partner who, although not the biological father, was willing to accept the younger child into his household.

The exchange of children in Lower Bay can be recognised as an adaptation to economic marginality, alleviating the pressure on mothers, and to a lesser degree, fathers, unable to support and raise their children independently. Meillassoux (1981:58–60) argues that child shifting practices in domestic communities, by which he means communities divided into households, each of which disposes of all or part of its own produce, is a direct response to the constraints on production. As there is no centralised redistribution of produce, and most households have relatively equal productive capacities, the redistribution of children, rather than produce, allows a harmonisation between production and reproduction:

> Since the number of children born in each household is bound to vary more often and more rapidly than does production the redistribution of dependants allows human energy[3] to be shared more equally between productive cells and balances the proportion between productive and non-productive individuals. This strategy of redistributing people ... by manipulating kinship relations, encourage(s) permanent reconstitution of the relations of production (Meillassoux, *op.cit.*:59).

Lower Bay is clearly not a community characterised by a domestic mode of production of the sort defined by Meillassoux. However, the lower classes remain dependent upon residual forms of pre-capitalist production in which the household is a crucial category. The recent return to subsistence production for household consumption, as a result of the decline in wage labour opportunities, is indicative of this continued dependence. Whether the 'economic boom' and the subsequent effect on relations of production in the 1960s led to a reduction in the degree of child shifting is not clear, but certainly there is sufficient evidence that the plebeian ideology of the family, extended to the notion of classificatory kinship, pre-figures institutionalised circulation of children. Together with the problems of maintaining production and material support for many over-crowded and under-productive households, the system of child shifting and social parenthood acts as an adaptive and stabilising institution in a community experiencing economic decline.

Because of the personal nature of kin and network rela-

Table 4i: Dispersal of children in households not containing their biological mother, Lower Bay 1981

	Total community	Lower Bay village and Lawler's Hill	Lower Bay Gutter
No. of children	25	17	8
No. of households	19	13	6

tionships, the majority of child shifting practices occur intra-community. Of the 25 children in the community living in households where their biological mother does not reside, only three came from outside the community, and were all in households containing maternal kin. Although I have no accurate data on children being placed in households outside the community, this was undoubtedly an infrequent practice. Again, figures for the number of children being raised as siblings of their biological mother were unattainable, due to the extremely qualitative, personal and transitory nature of such shifting. There was, however, a tendency towards such practices within the community, especially in the context of the recent decline in the earning power of young under-employed men in the community.

Changes in household composition: responses to material marginality

A brief look at the lower class household cycle, focusing on changes in household membership over time, illustrates the flexibility of residential arrangements vital for the survival of the most materially marginal of the lower classes.

The development of a household group is, as we have seen, generally preceded by the birth of children. As a result, the most common form of household grouping containing lower class women of procreative age is the joint or 'split' household, where a young woman with children, supported to varying degrees by men outside the household, resides in a residential unit of which she has previously been a junior member. Although a separate residential unit is not created, in all other senses – materially, symbolically and in terms of decision-making, authority and socialisation of children – a distinct household grouping exists. This is shown up clearly by the introduction of a second cooking pot. It is not until later life that conjugal households are formed, reflected in the high percentage of household heads over 40 years of age (see Table 4e p.110).

In the early stages of the development of households based upon conjugal relationships in a newly-established residential structure, the woman is tied to the home and garden, engaged in the birth, care and socialisation of children, and in domestic tasks. In the community, the majority of conjugal households are male-headed (see Table 4c, p.108), most notably amongst recently-formed households, reflecting the dependency of women in conjugal relationships upon men for material support of the domestic group. Women are restricted to the domestic sphere, men taking little part in the daily activities of the household until they reach old age, when they become physically dependent upon household members for care and support. Men's only household tasks are the material support of household members, maintenance and repair to the physical structure and, as part of their duties as household head, ensuring that young dependants receive a proper upbringing, such as a school education and regular church attendance.

In female-headed households, especially those in which the household is consanguineal, the woman is still tied to the domestic sphere unless less senior members are old enough or physically capable of assisting with the running of the household to allow her to engage in part-time work in or outside the community (see Chapter 3). Alternatively, she may be forced to supplement the household income by accepting gifts or payments from visiting men. In households in which there are too few, or no, members to care for children or to assist with domestic tasks, individuals may be accreted to the household solely as extra labour. These are usually the collateral kin of the household head, such as young siblings or children of siblings (or friends) who have died, left the community, or who are unable to support their offspring (see Case 4b, p.123). Many accreted members take up residence on an expediatory and temporary basis.

Case 4c   An elderly woman dependent on her grandson for assistance in running her household

This brief case illustrates the expediatory and temporary nature of accreting household members when there is a shortage of labour to carry out domestic tasks.

Veronica is a 68-year-old woman whose husband died in 1979 and who was left alone in her house in the village. Her daughter, who had once lived in the house with her two children, had married in 1973 and had since had two more children. Following Veronica's husband's death, the daughter sent her eldest son (G) to Veronica's house to help on a daily basis, running errands and assisting with the garden and other domestic tasks. G would usually eat his evening meal at Veronica's house after school; he was 13 at the time. Veronica became ill in 1980, the year that G finished school, and G took up residence in Veronica's house. G's sister now visits the house to do some of the domestic work, while G goes fishing with his mother's husband and/or other maternal male kin, and has recently found a part time bar job in the harbour.

G told me that he did not intend to stay for much longer in his grandmother's house and as soon as his sister was old enough to leave school (she was 14 at the time) she would move in and he would be 'free for choose where I done live'.

The inability of young people to be materially independent of parents/senior household members means that the emergence of separate residential units for junior household members is often delayed, sometimes until the death of the household head. Within lower class households it is extremely rare to find that all junior members and dependants have left. Maternal pressure and lack of economic opportunity or lack of access to land and other means of production mean that, by the stage at which the household head (and/or partner) has reached old age, there are invariably junior members present in the household. One of these members, often the eldest female, will, upon the death of the household head, inherit the physical structure and contents of the house and take on the position of head in the new household unit. The death of a household head and partner marks the dissolution of the household unit: the resulting change in household structure is not a part of the continuous process of the household cycle, but is rather an overlap of two households in time. The new household head is quite likely to have surrendered her parental duties to the previous head and partner during the development of the household, i.e. when no joint or 'split' household has been formed, and/or left the household at some stage of the cycle to seek employment or establish a conjugal relationship. On returning to the household, due to a failure to secure a stable income or a breakdown in marital union, a daughter's parental duties may be reinvoked as a result of the age of her social or biological parents. The death of these parents marks the dissolution of one household and the establishment of another.

Child shifting, parental role replacement, and temporary accretion of collateral kin all represent lower class household responses to poverty, marginality and dependence. The effective survival of many of the most impoverished and those at greatest risk due to susceptibility to fluctuating resources (the very small and very large households) depends upon the effective redistribution of individuals between households and the manipulation of kinship relations in times of need.

Towards a materialist perspective on family and household

The characteristics of family and household form in Lower Bay are flexible and adaptive, in accordance with the unstable and fluctuating material conditions experienced by most lower class members of the community. The choice of conjugal relationships open to men and women, determined by economic factors and plebeian cultural norms relating to sex roles, along with the partible and bilateral nature of descent and inheritance, give to the family its unique character, observable in the form of:

(a) household heads of both sexes;
(b) the marginality of men in many households, as a direct consequence of their marginality in the productive sphere, leading to
(c) increased numbers of matrifocal households characterised by the centrality of the mother-child dyad and an independent productive role by some women, requiring
(d) a high degree of child shifting (21 per cent of the children in the community living in households not containing their biological mother, plus many more raised as siblings to their biological mother with whom they are co-resident), coupled with
(e) a flexibility and variability of maternal (and paternal) roles; the strength of the parent-child bond, more overtly, the mother-child bond, being dependent upon quid pro quo elements, illustrated by cases of children 'supporting' social (adopted/fostered) parents rather than biological ones, and by cases of favouritism in the bequeathing of property;
(f) a relatively low rate of legal (church or civil) marriages, especially amongst people under 40 years of age, despite the dominant ideology.

The latter point requires some elaboration, within the context of a discussion of the inter-relationship and interaction between ideological (cultural) and material factors. Conjugal relationships, *per se*, do not form alliances between groups in Bequia. Forms of conjugal relationship can be ranked according to cultural values relating to 'properness', as expressed through the dominant ideology. Whilst choice of union is dependent upon material factors, most notably the material wealth of the man, most individuals express aspirations towards church marriage, followed by, in order of properness, civil marriage, permanent common law unions, and temporary common law/visiting relationships. Connubial relationships can be distinguished from all other types of relationships in the community by the nature of the combined exchange of economic, sexual and companionship services. The high rate of break up of non-legal, conjugal unions results from the unfulfilment of one or more of the above services – most commonly the inability of the male partner to fulfil his economic role, leading to the withdrawal of other services by the female partner. Cultural ideas about the person are contained and expressed within the economic relationships between mates (the sexual division of labour at household level): of man as the material provider, woman as the recipient of material support and the provider of services. A man's economic and social sphere lies in activities outside the home, a woman's should properly be limited to the domestic sphere of house and garden. A man unable to fulfil his role in the public sphere, or a woman forced to seek wage labour, whilst not subject to sanctions, are considered to be acting improperly within the terms of plebeian ideas relating to work and sex roles, although there is increasing acceptance of such actions (see Chapters 6 and 7 below).

Cultural ideas about the person, then, are articulated within the institutionalised patterns of household residence, mating and exchange of children/parental roles. In considering the meanings attached to household and family organisation by lower class members of the community, material factors continually emerged. I have repeatedly referred to the flexibility of the family form in coping with the material pressures associated with the situational conditions of dependency and marginality, and I would here further suggest that, within the limits imposed by plebeian cultural ideas about proper behaviour, *a direct relationship exists between the material base of production and household and family form*. A brief examination of the relationship between production relations, including the sexual division of labour, and household and family form, located within the theories of the Afro-Caribbean and Afro-American family and drawing on the contemporary ethnographies of the Caribbean, will illustrate and add support to this assertion.

Three theoretical approaches can be broadly delineated: historical (determinist), structural-functionalist, and marxist-feminist. In the first approach historical evidence is invoked to explain the contemporary empirical form of the lower class Afro-Caribbean/American family. There are two schools of thought within this approach: one which considers slavery to be the determinant of the Negro family form, the other seeing the Afro-Caribbean family form as a vestige of matrilineal and polygynous African, tribal, social organisation.

The slavery school is typified and influenced by the work of Frazier (1939, 1957) who maintains that, as slaves in the Southern USA, Negroes were restricted from forming legal marital unions if they were considered to interfere with slave owners' property rights over women: slave paternity being effectively denied by the planter class. The permanency of the mother-child bond, arising from the specific social relations of slavery, was an all-determining factor in the origin of the matrifocal family structure:

> The bonds of affection between mother and offspring were generally developed in the slave cabin where the Negro mother nurtured her brood and was mistress ... On the other hand, the father was often a visitor to the cabin ... (and) he was compelled not only to recognise the mother's more fundamental interest in the children but her authority in the household. (Frazier, 1957:309)[4]

The overtly deterministic theories of the slavery school are illustrated by Matthews (1953:64, 65):

> The New World plantation ... is in a very real sense the originator of the non-legal union. It certainly was its matrix.

and:

> The disorganised family ... (is) the outcome of detribalisation and disintegration of the African family.

The tenet that African tribal forms and cultural values relating to family and kinship were destroyed by slavery is in direct conflict with the hypotheses put forward by M. J. Herskovits (1937, 1941) and by M.J. and F.S. Herskovits (1934, 1947) who relate the low rate of 'legal' marriage and the dominance of women in lower class Afro-Caribbean households to African vestiges. They consider marriage to have been organised flexibly in order to adjust from polygyny to monogamy; and the central role of women in the domestic sphere, a facet of West African social organisation, remained effective throughout slavery.[5]

The work of Kobben (1973), Bastide (1971) and Robinson (1969) on Caribbean Maroons stands as a challenge to the overgeneralisation and crude determinism of the historical theses referred to above.

Kobben's (1973) ethnography of the Djuka, a bush Negro tribe in the interior of Suriname, who take their name from the plantation from which they escaped in the early eighteenth century, shows that the West African heritage of the slaves, most of whom were first generation out of Africa, may have contributed to their family organisation, but did *not* determine it. The Djuka practice polygyny within their matrilineal kinship structure, the lineage representing a corporate group. Although some of the original Maroons came from the strongly matrilineal Akan tribe, others came from patrilineal African societies. In addition, Kobben points to major differences between the matrilineality of the Djuka and the Akan, amongst which are:

(a) the Djuka, unlike the Akan, do not maintain a clan exogamy;
(b) the Djuka practise partible inheritance, the Akan maintain that a dead person's estate belongs to a single individual;
(c) marital residence amongst the Djuka varies and includes endolocal, uxorilocal, ambilocal, autolocal, virilocal and neolocal patterns, which contrast with the exogamous residence practices of the Akan and other matrilineal and patrilineal African tribes.

The Boni, of French Guiana, were the last of the black refugees (Bastide, 1971:37) and, unlike the Djuka, many of whom had escaped slave plantations as first generation Africans, the Boni had been subjected to generations of slavery. In fleeing to the jungle they were forced to organise into bands in order to survive:

> There is no hint of even an initial moment of anarchy, no wavering between rival systems of kinship and alliance ...
> (Bastide, *op.cit.*:38).

The Boni, like the Djuka, organised into matrilineal clans incorporating new forms of marriage and property inheritance.

Amongst the mountain Maroons of Jamaica, many also organised themselves into modified matrilineal systems similar to the Bush Negros of the Guianas, while others practised an enforced form of monogamous social organisation, based on a hunting and gathering mode of production, supplemented by seasonal pastoral activities: the men hunted and reared livestock, the women engaged in deforestation and wild crop gathering (Robinson, 1969:68–70). Despite a polygynous ideology, most Maroon men had one wife/mate only, due to the marginal nature of production.

Despite the differing degrees of conditions of slavery to which the Djuka, Boni and Jamaican Maroons were subject, and the diversity of their tribal African origins, all turned to a form of social organisation based upon modified matrilineality in which polygyny was not ideologically prohibited: a form of social organisation *shaped by their similar material circumstances.*

Structural-functionalist theories of the Afro-Caribbean family and household form consider mating patterns, child care arrangements, and household organisation as functional adjustments between the family and other institutions in the total social system of which it is a part. The work of Edith Clarke (1966), Greenfield (1961), Gonzalez (1970), Rodman (1971) and R. T. Smith (1956) is characteristic of this approach which is clearly influenced by the work of Radcliffe-Brown (1952:181ff.). Structural-functionalists consider economic variables to be central to the interaction between the family and the wider social system. These include: lack of economic opportunity for men, male marginal occupational position and the absence of kin groups of a corporate nature engaged in production.

Kunstadter (1963) criticises historical and structural-functional/economic approaches as too specific and ethnocentric to account for the worldwide distribution of matrifocality. In reference to the Mescalero Apache, the Nayars of South India, and to the Caribbean, he discusses the significance of the high ratio of females to males at community level, resulting from male participation in a wider economic system:

> ... the proportion of matrifocal families in the community appears to be a function (in the mathematical and social sense) of the degree of physical separation of adult males and adult females involved in the division of labour (Kunstadter, *ibid.*:62).

Kunstadter, in effecting a universal explanation of matrifocality, is simply reducing the number of economic variables specified by structural-functionalist theories of the Afro-Caribbean matrifocal family to one: the degree of separation of sexes within the division of labour,[7] clearly a characteristic of the West Indian lower class economy[8] which, to varying degrees, is the product of dependence on extra-community production and international capitalism. Structural functionalist accounts of the matrifocal family, then, consider the practice to be one of adjustment and consequently fail to provide a dynamic explanation which can account for social change.

Whilst accepting many of the theoretical premises of the structural-functionalists on the relationship between economic structures and family form, recent Marxist and feminist anthropologists of the Caribbean area have stressed that matrifocal household patterns and 'unstable' mating arrangements are to be seen as *conscious* decisions on the part of women in conditions of economic deprivation and changing systems of production and male unemployment. Anna Rubbo (1975) characterises black Carib peasant households in rural Colombia as:

(i) commonly headed by women;
(ii) based upon the sexual division of labour of 'women's work = domestic work', 'men's work = outside work';
(iii) high degree of 'visiting' or extra-residential mating patterns, coupled with a recent decline in the rate of 'legal' or church marriages.

These characteristics are also those of the lower class Afro-Caribbean Negro societies, including the community of Lower Bay. Partible inheritance gives women land and property and, says Rubbo (*ibid.*:341–343) many peasant women have relative economic independence. As the relations of production change from those of small scale peasant production of coffee, cocoa and household crops to the capitalist production of 'green revolution' crops such as corn and soyabeans, landlessness has increased, especially amongst males, who have sold their plots of land or had them confiscated for inability to repay loans on capital-intensive machinery and seeds. Under such circumstances women have come to regard marriage as a 'severe restriction' on their liberty and independence as agricultural work on their own small plots can be, and often is, done by women, and their offspring, alone. Men are seen as an unnecessary and risky addition to households that can survive and function without them.

Susan Brown (1975) follows a similar line of argument in her work on poor black families in a Dominican Republic community, and maintains that the family form of female household head is a strategic device on the part of women, aimed at maximising the means of subsistence available to them (*ibid.*:324):

Here the multiple mating pattern for women is neither deviant nor an undesirable variation of the middle class, single partner pattern. Rather, it is a dynamic female adaptation to life under severe poverty. In fact, it appears to provide these women with a *better* existence than the single mate pattern could under the same circumstances.

Child shifting through temporary fostering, or permanent adoption, by kin or friends gives women the independence to seek work outside the village. Men who fail to fulfil their roles as 'providers' are dropped for those who can potentially fulfil such roles and, says Brown (*ibid.*), if poverty continues to increase in the Dominican Republic, more women are likely to adopt a multiple mate pattern in order to increase their effectiveness under such conditions.

In concluding this chapter a brief comparison of family and household form in rural communities in Trinidad and Barbados with that of Lower Bay highlights the relevance of the above materialist theories. The historical theses fail to consider whether sub-cultural patterns of residence and mating constitute differential survival strategies and modes of adapation and resistance to specific material and cultural factors. Whilst the contemporary family and household forms of lower class sections of Afro-Caribbean societies have clearly been influenced by African cultural vestiges and by slavery, further factors, specifically material, appear to have had a more far-reaching influence.

Amongst the poorer rural communities of Barbados and Trinidad, where the independence of men as wage earners is greater than that of men of similar age in Bequia (Barbados because of its sugar cane estates, Trinidad because of sugar, oil and asphalt industries), there is a considerably higher rate of legal marriage. Rodman (1971:44) states that, in the village of his study, one of the poorest in Trinidad, approximately 33 per cent of men and women between the ages of 15 and 64 were legally married. Likewise, Greenfield (1966:188) reports that 47 per cent of people over 15 years of age in the village of his study had been legally married. These figures far exceed the comparable rates for Bequia where less than 25 per cent of all people over 15 are presently married (see Table 4g, p.115). Harding (1981:67) reports that in Cleavers Hill, a lower class Barbadian village, only 22 per cent of households were consanguineal, compared with 44 per cent in Lower Bay (see Table 4c, p.108). Despite the comparative poverty by national standards, of the communities cited in Barbados and Trinidad the presence of socialised labour, availability of wage-based incomes for some men and the differences in systems of production (Lower Bay has a high level of production for household consumption, socialised labour is scarce and wage earning capacity of most men has declined) can be seen to *increase the rates of legal marriage and the formation of nuclear and affinal households directly.*[9]

As with Maroons, the family and household form of post-Emancipation Negro societies in the New World is influenced by material conditions, specifically the degree of marginality and economic dependence and the effects these have on the economic position of men and women. The variations in family form and household composition that exist amongst the dispossessed sectors of these societies is a point that has been overlooked by many sociologists and anthropologists, and has led to over-systematic and over-generalised explanations for what is a highly complex institutional arrangement. Practices such as multiple mating patterns, child shifting, and flexible household composition are strategies for survival that have developed in response to specific material conditions, such as unemployment, landlessness, and low level production in residual forms, which have generated inequality and poverty, and have led to the marginalisation of the lower classes. Such material conditions have been shaped historically and culturally and continue to be structured by relationships of dominance and dependence producing resources of a shifting and unstable nature.

Notes

1 Chayanov (1925:21) notes that the family to the Russian peasant at the beginning of the twentieth century was generally '... the people who eat from the same pot'.
2 The Anglican priest in Port Elizabeth set up a fund in the early 1970s (exact date unknown) to collect money, essentially from resident non-nationals and affluent visitors, to help children receive further education, either at the Bequia High School or abroad. In 1981 one young man from Hamilton received sufficient grant to be able to go to Canada to undertake a teaching course.
3 Meillassoux defines human energy as '... all the energy produced by the metabolic effects of foodstuffs on the human organism ...' (1981:50). As such, it is a more comprehensive concept than 'labour power' which is only that portion of human energy with exchange value.
4 Frazier (1957) further acknowledges that abhorrence of plantation work, coupled with the social acceptability of temporary mating unions, was instrumental in maintaining a high number of female-headed family forms: '... the stability of the rural Negro family was undermined by the migration of men and women (from the plantations)' (Frazier, 1957:637) (my brackets). See Gutman (1977) for a revision of Frazier's thesis on the negro family.

5 Herskovits (1941) suggests that '... the elasticity of the marriage concept among Negroes derives in a measure, largely unrecognised, from the need to adjust a polygynous family form to patterns based on a convention of monogamy' (p.170). And furthermore '... such specialised features of Negro family life ... as the role of women in focusing the sentiments that gives the family unit its psychological coherence, or their place in maintaining the economic stability essential to survival, correspond closely to similar facets of West African social structure' (p.180).

Arensberg (1957) who also bases his understanding of Caribbean and Afro-American lower class family structure on historical evidence tends to support the Herskovits' thesis of 'cultural vestige', in opposing the 'conditions of slavery' hypothesis and states emphatically in a short article on the subject that, as a specialist in the culture of the Old World, he is:

> ... less likely to be sure that Caribbean marriage customs, ... or matrifocality and grandmother families, are simple responses to colonialism, plantations, and slavery ... they may be traits, reworkings or traits, that must be pushed back to the base line which the classification 'Caribbean culture' gives. (p.97)

6 The Maroons had sexual access to slave women, reports Robinson, (1969:68–70) for the planters believed they would father stronger children!

7 Kunstadter does stress, however, that he considers causal relationships between unbalanced sex ratios and the presence of matrifocality not as direct or simple:

> '... the unbalanced sex ratio might easily be handled in several other ways, including polygyny, female infancticide, or reduced age of marriage for males ...' (1963:63)

8 Data collected during my fieldwork shows the level of male absenteeism from the community:

Male-female population ratios in Lower Bay community, 1980–1981

Total adult male population = 103
Total adult female population = 111   Ratio female/male = 1.08:1

Male population at time of August/September 1980 survey = 76 (17 sailing, 10 fishing away)
Female population at time of August/September 1980 survey = 109 (1 in Canada, 1 working on St Vincent)
Ratio of female to male at this time = 1.43:1

Male population at time of April/May 1981 survey = 82 (14 sailing, 7 fishing)
Female population at time of April/May 1981 survey = 111 (no women away from island)
Ratio of female to male at this time = 1.36:1*

(*Note: fewer men were fishing in April 1981 because of unusually high seas; normally it is during the first four months of the year that many men fish in the Southern St Vincent Grenadines [the Cays] or around the Northern Grenadan Grenadines of Petit Martinique and Carriacou, diving for lobster, conch and turtle before the season closes in later April.)

9 Dirks (1972) reports a similar process in the Virgin Islands in the 1960s and early 1970s following increased wage labour opportunities in tourism: '... this period of relative wealth found more and more couples formalising their relationships through marriage ...' (p.582).

CHAPTER 5
Kinship and friendship networks: extra-domestic relationships in Lower Bay

The reproduction of relations of production within residual forms of economic activity and the resultant marginality of the lower classes forces them to rely on self-help organisations, one of which, the household, has already been considered. Kinship and friendship networks represent further organisations of self-help upon which Bequia lower classes fall back in times of need, and constitute a social resource for the continued survival of the lower classes.

Networks in Lower Bay are formed on the basis of personal alliances: of individually established relationships between friends and kin involving reciprocity and quid pro quo arrangements of a material and symbolic character. There is a considerable sociological literature on networks,[1] but the following definition will suffice:

> (A network) ... is a set of interconnected points. The points are people and the connections social relationships ... All members (of a network) do not recognise relationships with all other members but are linked with varying degrees of closeness depending on the number of relationships involved. (Harris, 1969:85, my brackets)

In this respect, networks differ from groups, the latter being characterised by all members recognising relationships with all other members (e.g. peer groups, see below); groups have readily identifiable boundaries, networks are as large as the number of effective relationships involved.

Kinship patterns

Although as I have argued above, the forces of expansion of international capitalism, during its mercantile stage of development, effectively dissolved the African kinship systems of the slave population in the Caribbean, the marginality and impoverishment of the lower classes require them periodically to utilise relations with kinsfolk for specific ends, including the temporary and permanent placement and care of dependent children; the provision and exchange of labour and resources in times of need; the distribution of property, land, houses and productive equipment, through inheritance and gifts; support during crises, including the provision of essential services such as accommodation, food, etc.; and the provision of jobs in family businesses such as supplies/rum shops and fish trading.

It must be stressed, however, that kinship relationships and obligations are non-institutionalised, ties to individual kinspersons being considerably more important than ties to groups of kin. Kinship groups are not engaged in corporate activities in Bequia: relationships with kin not being part of a wider sanctioning system. This contrasts with corporate kinship systems which provide social frameworks for politico-ritual and economic activities and, as such, function as ideologies: symbolic codes which express and sanction social relations.

The non-corporate, individualistic (person-to-person) character of kin relationships in Lower Bay is based on quid pro quo, which is clearly illustrated in inheritance patterns. Kinship links, aside from the parent-child link in cases of intestacy, do not provide a person with rights to property. It is, instead, the personal quality of the relationship between kinsfolk that influences bequeathment and transference of property:

> ... the individual may ... exercise a great deal of choice in disposing of his money or his property. The primary obligations of an individual are to his wife (married or 'living') and to his children ... and it is the *nature of a man's relationship to his kinsmen and non-kin* that influences his attitudes and behaviour. (Rodman, 1971:143–144, my emphasis; this statement applies equally to women in Lower Bay, notably in cases of intestacy.)

The parent-child relationship remains, however, the single most important kinship relationship in terms of responsibilities and obligations. Because of flexibility in child rearing arrangements, it is social recognition of parenthood, notably motherhood, based upon the qualitative (emotional and instrumental) nature of the relationship, not biological parenthood, that is of crucial importance. Quid pro quo forms the basis of the parent-child relationship. The degree of assistance and support offered by a person to his/her social parents depends upon sentiment and ability: sentiment being influenced by the degree of material, emotional and social support given by the parent; ability being largely dependent upon the material position of the individual. There are few obligations binding kinsfolk together unless they are co-residential, or have been symbolically and instrumentally strengthened by relationships and obligations characteristic of household membership. For example, the temporary placing of a child in its grandparent's household will usually cement a bond between the child and grandparent(s) of a quality quite different to that normally, and normatively, expected between two such kinspersons.

An individual will only recognise kinship relationships outside the household when such relationships are of a quality quite distinct from relations with other community members. The lack of prescribed obligations between kinsfolk outside the domestic sphere is reflected in the system of kin terminology used in plebeian culture (see Chater 6). For example, 'uncle' or 'tanty' (aunt) do not denote kinship relations, but are terms of address signifying deference and respect to senior community members. Recognised kin relationships are denoted by precise descriptive expressions such as 'my mother sister', 'my father mother', 'my mother brother son', etc.

As noted above, grandparent-grandchild relationships tend to be weak unless strengthened by quid pro quo elements. This is particularly true of paternal grandparents. Case 4c, p.127, concerned the raising of a child by the maternal grandmother in exchange for material support (labour and domestic help) and companionship, and demonstrated quite clearly the importance of kinship ties in times of social and economic need and the personal and reciprocal quality of the relationship. The matrifocal nature of many households means that maternal grandmothers are often co-resident with their grandchildren, or are frequently the source of support for their daughters' children in times of material deprivation. Paternal grandparents, however, play such a role very infrequently and, unless the relationship with their grandchildren is cemented early on, by material support and/or symbolic support, such as regular visits to the child when young, then reciprocity of any sort by the grandchild is unlikely in future years and the relationship will be confined to one of 'distant' deference in public.

During my fieldwork, however, an exceptional case arose, in which a child was placed in his paternal grandparents' household because of the inability of the father, mother or mother's kin to support and raise the child adequately. This case highlights the importance of extra-domestic kin in caring for dependent children.

Case 5a   A child raised by his paternal grandparents
Andrew is a 30-year-old man who, until September 1980, lived with his parents in Lower Bay village. In June 1980 he was made redun-

dant from his part time job as line maintenance man with the St Vincent Electricity Co (CDC) in Bequia, after which he spent more of his time fishing, which he had done previously only as a supplement to his wages from CDC.

In 1979 he had a child by a young woman who lived in her maternal grandmother's house in La Pompe. Also resident in her household were two children from previous relationships, and the woman's three younger siblings together with two of her sister's children (see below). The woman's mother had died earlier in 1979 and I was unable to ascertain the whereabouts of her father, but if any material support was provided by him it was minimal. Upon the birth of the child the grandmother apparently only accepted the child into the household with considerable reluctance, because of over-crowding. Andrew told me that at the time of the birth the woman's grandmother had spoken to him about ensuring that he materially supported the child and mother.

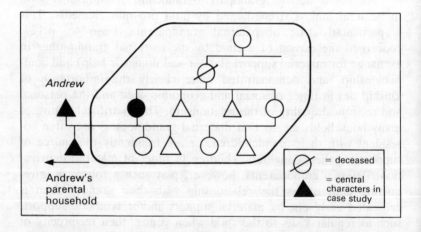

The household in which the mother of Andrew's child resided

The new baby lived in the maternal gradmother's household for 12 months. Andrew told me of his feelings during this period:

> I man done be hope for full time work with CDC, so dat I might make good for dis woman and she children. Wid full wage de bank gonna lend me money for buy land and den I gone build house for dey all. Dere too much a problem wid dem living over dere in La Pompe.

All these aspirations dissipated when, in June 1980, he lost his job. Unable to support his child materially, and under pressure from the mother's grandmother, he turned to his parents who agreed to have the child live with them. After the child moved into Andrew's parents' house in July 1980, the biological mother had little contact with her child. Andrew became very depressed during this period, which he expressed essentially in terms of his dependence on his parents. In September 1980, as a result of a contact made through one of his friends working in St Johns (Virgin Islands) he left Bequia to work, illegally, as an electrician with a construction firm. When I left Bequia in May 1981 he had not returned. People with whom I spoke in the community assumed that the child would remain with Andrew's parents who would eventually 'adopt' him.

A further kinship relationship which is only recognised/utilised in exceptional circumstances is that of the sibling bond to which I now turn. As we have seen in Chapter 4, 'favouritism', based on quid pro quo elements in a life-long relationship between kin, is often the source of conflict between siblings competing for scare resources. Relationships between siblings are so fraught with rivalry and competition that they are usually only invoked in times of crisis. This is particularly evident between non-co-resident brothers and reflects the precarious material position of many lower class men. The following case illustrates this rivalry and the extent to which specific crises can produce co-operation between siblings whose relationship is otherwise hostile or, at best, indifferent.

Case 5b   Co-operation between brothers: the activation of a sibling bond following structural damage to a house

This case involves two non-co-resident brothers, heads of their respective households. Although they drank in the same rum shop, one less frequently than the other, there was never any noticeable interaction or co-operation between them, which is not unusual in Lower Bay.

As a result of Hurricane Allen in August 1980, one brother's homestead suffered extensive damage: the roof was blown off, part of the back of the house collapsed and his maize crop was damaged. During the hurricane the family stayed at their neighbour's house. When the storm had subsided the other brother, together with his two young sons were the first to offer support in repair and spent three days working on the house. Two weeks later, when the second brother's maize was harvested by his wife, one of the sons took some of the crop to the brother who had lost his. When the worst of the crisis had been surmounted and the household was again restored, the social distance between the two brothers was resumed: in the rum shop they continued to behave with indifference to one another, drinking in mutually exclusive groups.

This illustrates two aspects of the contradictory nature of kinship in lower class impoverished societies. On the one hand competition for scarce resources and the absence of a group context which could provide a basis for corporate solidarity leads to estrangement of kin: siblings represent the kin categories standing in the most heightened competitive relationship within lower class Bequia. Conversely, impoverishment and marginality, when extreme, can produce co-operation: the sibling bond being sufficiently strong to ensure effective action in times of need.

This contradiction was excellently illustrated by a woman whose comments to me on this particular case, proved eloquent and enlightening:

> In Lowbay, you see, we is all family ... It espect dat if someone done fall on bad times, dey gonna get help from somewhere. If de Friendly Society ain't able for help wid de problem (and in the case of the hurricane limited support was given by the Society, viz. food supplies to households most seriously affected) den de people alway done get together ... It may look like dese two brothers done hate each other, but y'know dey share de same blood and live in de same house when dey was small boys and you can't change dat, nuh. Dey gonna carry deyselves like dey ain't wanna know about de other agin now dis trouble done pass, but dey alway dere if dey really need each other and dat ain't gonna change never ... (my brackets)

Relationships between non-co-residential kin are often never activated. Close informants in the community told me how one sibling group of two brothers and a sister had not spoken to each other for ten years, following the death of their father who left most of his property to his daughter and the rest to one of the sons. The hostility between the siblings reflects the pressure of material circumstances which are far stronger than any kinship norms. Kin relationships, then, are optative, in contrast, to those between household members which tend to be prescribed and constraining.

Kinship alone does not provide a framework of enduring groups; kin outside the household are rarely of paramount importance except for parents and, in exceptional circumstances and times of need, siblings and grandparents. Far more significant for material, social and symbolic support are friends. Lower class men in particular develop extensive friendship networks: the wider a man's network of personal friends the more security he has against economic and social failure. The most significant stage in the development of friendship networks is the formation of peer groups during and immediately after the years spent in school. The following section begins by contrasting boys' peer groups with those formed by girls, before proceeding to a discussion of the friendship networks to whch peer groups are a precursor.

Friendship networks

Network relationships amongst the lower classes are, because of plebeian normative controls, essentially male. The nature of the dichotomy of sex-specific spheres places restrictions on women forming lasting and meaningful extra-domestic relationships. Dyadic ties between women are, on the whole, restricted to domestic bonds, the most significant, as we have seen, being between mother and daughter. The only extra-domestic relationships that women can form without threat of local sanction are within the formal institutions of the Church and Friendly Society. In contrast, the public sphere is almost exclusively male.

Unsurprisingly, then, the sex-specific peer groups formed early in life by boys and girls fulfil markedly different functions for the two sexes.

Girls' peer groups

A girl's peer group is formed shortly after she starts school. Attendance at school is considered by a girl's senior household members as a concession to household duties, the values of formal education being in direct opposition to female household duties. Relationships within a girl's peer group are developed through continued interaction with classroom peers and through Church and, later, Friendly Society activities. Harding (1980:204) notes that the practical, normative resources necessary for a girl, in Cleaver's Hill village, Barbados, to negotiate a relationship with a boy are not provided by relationships with household members. This is equally true of Lower Bay. A girl's peer group socially sanctions attitudes to the opposite sex, quite distinct from those contained in the household ideology, which emphasise avoidance of men and abstinence from sexual relationships because of the disgrace that a pregnancy resulting from such a relationship will bring on the household.

Peer groups perform an integrative function for girls in Lower Bay, where attitudes and values operative in the household differ from those orientations and values associated with the adolescent girl's involvement in the public sphere in which she is also required to participate.

Once a girl has established her first sexual relationship with a young man her peer group ceases to be of any significance. On completion of her schooling (no girls in Lower Bay attended school past the age of 15 years whilst I was there), a young woman is expected to confine her social life to the domestic, private domain of the household. However, the recent changes in the sexual division of labour, notably increased male unemployment and the rising demand for female labour in the tourist sector, have created social contexts in which lower class women are able to interact publicly. As we have seen, matrifocal arrangements enable a woman with children to undertake waged employment; the increasing involvement of women in the public sphere, albeit outside the community, represents the exercise of choice by women in the face of opportunities and constraints resulting from the marginalisation of lower class men. Whether such strategies by women will effect enduring changes in plebeian cultural values relating to the private/public dichotomy is a theme explored in subsequent chapters.

Boys' peer groups

In contrast to girls, boys are required and expected to develop 'worldly' attitudes and meanings in order to participate in and reduce their chance of failure in the extra-domestic sphere. Whereas the female social role has been traditionally limited to the household, males are excluded from this domain after leaving school. Their peer groups provide the normative resources necessary for the development and continued effectiveness of relationships in the public domain.

As for girls, school is the arena in which boys begin to develop relationships with their peers. But, unlike the constraints placed on young women, boys gain increasing freedom from domestic duties as they grow older. Boys and girls of school age are required to assist in domestic activities, such as tethering of sheep, feeding of pigs and fowls, running errands, etc. But as girls face increasing responsibilities for the daily running of the household, boys nearing school-leaving age, are given more freedom to spend time in out-of-school activities with their peer groups such as sport and 'liming'[2]. Such activities are carried out in the absence of girls of equivalent age, the ethos of peer groups being based on manliness and competitiveness.

'Being a man' in Lower Bay includes aspirations to the male stereotype prescribed in plebeian culture. As in many Afro-Caribbean societies (see Wilson, 1973) the Lower Bay male is ideally aggressive, unbending in his demand for personal attention and vigorous in his defence against personal insult; he is agile, strong and competitive in sports and games. Male peer groups regularly gather on the beach to demonstrate their prowess at athletics, martial arts (popularised by the local cinema), football and cricket. The Lower Bay man should be able to partake freely of alcohol without it 'getting de better of he', be popular with women and adept at courtship, dress well, dance stylishly and have 'class' (see Chapter 6, note 8). These values, attitudes, orientations and attributes are learned and acquired within the peer group: a young man's reputation being dependent upon his aspiring to and achieving the qualities inherent in the male stereotype. Prescriptions for male behaviour are deeply internalised through the socialisation process: public image being closely linked with a self-image of strength, virility, etc., and elaborated ideologically in terms of the value codes of respect.

The observation of a cricket match between a Lower Bay team and one from Port Elizabeth extracted verbatim from my field notes, illustrates the above points and puts them in context:

> The match was played in a very competitive manner. Members from each team used aggressive language when addressing opposition members, and errors or failures were mocked. One Lower Bay batsman out for a duck was jeered by the opposition and by their supporters. Knowledge of an individual's life history and family is often invoked in these cases to further insult and denigrate the person concerned. The player out without scoring was subjected to references to his recent dismissal as bar assistant in a local rum shop: 'My man play cricket like he serve drink ... he can't make it happen ...' and 'You can't keep job and you can't keep you wicket no ...' Both teams and their rival supporters sat around opposite sides of the almond tree on Lower Bay green, this being an

expected part of demonstrating membership of the respective groups, as well as showing willingness to play, even if not selected. Insults from opposing players/supporters were always challenged, demonstrating loyalty to the team, reflecting loyalties to the peer group.

Girls from Lower Bay and a few from the harbour sat around the boundaries and youths fielding near them engaged in chatting and telling jokes. Familiarity and bravado with girls from the opposition team's locus was expected and acknowledged by fellow members, although remarks made to the girls were always such that they could not be overheard by others.

In effect, youths who are marginal, or excluded from the productive process – participation in which is a source of reputation and respect in Lower Bay – depend upon the public display of the qualities of manliness which such cricket matches allow in order to achieve recognised social worth both publicly and within their specific peer groups. As we shall see in Chapter 6 below, unemployed young men face considerable pressure from older members of the community to engage in traditional work activities, such as fishing, for plebeian values relate worthfulness, and hence status, to work and correct use of time. In effect, young men are continually negotiating their status position within the conflicting expectations of peer group and community.

Male friendship networks are built on the basis provided by these peer groups and represent an extension and continuation of these groups: an extension which reflects the absence of kin groups engaged in corporate activity. As peer groups develop there is, as Eisenstadt (1956:149) noted: '... a definite "going out" of the family'. This transition is temporary and instrumental for girls and a means for establishing first relationships with men. But for both males and females, the peer group provides an extension to and an elaboration of the individual's social sphere and relationships in which he/she interacts with people from wider groups than the household and close kin. For males the quality of relationships within the new sphere involves patterns of behaviour and obligations different from those imposed within household life, and sometimes openly opposed to them. Relationships contained in the household tend to be heirarchical: junior and dependent members, such as children, the old and infirm, have little influence over the decisions that are made within the unit. Their roles and duties, which include menial and time consuming tasks like running errands, tethering sheep and goats, cleaning out the pigpen, are prescribed and demonstrate their positions of subordination in relation to senior household members. In contrast, peer groups emphasise common experience and equality. As one youth told me:

> When you wid you friends you know dat you is de same as dey. You ain't for especk to be put down for being late, or for not coming wid dey some evening. But in de house you looking for plenty licks if you ain't for always doing de things you suppose for do. Me, I just as good as any of my friends, in dey eyes, but in de house it 'do for dis and do for dat' like you ain't no better dan a dog.

In the household, then, relationships are structured according to patterns of authority: values, norms and rules imposed on boys and girls. Peer group membership, however, gives scope for the exercise of influence in decision-making and for independent action: an individual's worth and social standing in the group is his/her own making.

Male peer groups are, however, far more than groups with a common transitory goal (the attainment of status outside the domestic sphere): they are cohesive primary groups based around materially and symbolically supportive relationships. The importance of peer groups for survival in a socio-economic situation of dependency and inequality is recognised by many lower class young men as providing the basis for a valuable social resource, viz. the development and consolidation of friendship relationships. The following excerpt from a conversation I had with a 16-year-old school-leaver about a former class mate of his, who was generally regarded as a loner, reflects the perceived importance of peer groups:

> Me: Why do you say he is foolish for not doing things with all of you together?
>
> G: Man, he gonna haf to make real good in life, if he ain't want nutting for do wid we.
>
> Me: You mean he's going to have to get a good job, or to be well off?
>
> G Yeah, dat it. You know none of we really want turn to other for help but dat de way life is here in Lower Bay. A man should be able to make it on he own. But work is hard for get and food not easy. So you need friend, plenty friend when times hard. A friend who know about work or about cheap land, or about sailing jobs ...

Peer groups continue to be effective throughout a man's life. However, the cohesiveness and solidarity typical of a peer group during its school and immediate post-school period tends to diminish with age, as a direct result of work and marriage (see below). As men grow older they develop friendship ties with a number of adult males in and around the community.

Peer groups are closed, primary social groups which gradually lose their cohesion as men grow older. Male activity becomes increasingly confined to the public domain following school, being organised around leisure, notably in the rum shop, and work activities. Because of the marginal position of most lower class males, it becomes increasingly important for a man to develop close but informal ties with as many others as possible. The universalistic meanings and orientations learned and acquired through activity within the peer group enable a man to develop ties outside the group: most men developing network ties with most other adult males in the community (and some outside).

The mobility required as a result of and dictated by the availability of work, leads to long periods of absence from the community for males, during which time they are unable to sustain face-to-face interaction with their fellow men, although activities such as fishing trips will involve interaction with some of their peer group and network members. Marriage further restricts and places limits on interaction with peer group and network members: the material requirements of maintaining a household means that rum shop participation is often limited for married men. Work and marriage are the two major factors in the reduction of peer group solidarity. But despite absence from peer groups and the proliferation of bonds within networks, relationships with peers are maintained, and along with network ties, are often used for instrumental purposes:

1 Personal ties within peer groups and networks can be used to channel cash earned outside the community back into Lower Bay. Men working aboard merchant vessels, or in the tourist sectors of neighbouring islands, send remittances to friends and kin for banking and/or investment in land or fishing technology. In the former case the remittance of all or part of wages earned as seamen is a means of avoiding taxation on return to St Vincent, as it is the amount of cash with which a seaman returns that is taxed by the state. Investment in land by members of peer groups or kin/personal networks was particularly important during the early 1970s when house plots in Friendship (Lower Bay Gutter) came on the market.

Sending money to friends and/or peers is often fraught with difficulties and misunderstandings and can lead to disputes. Many men, however, have used friends quite successfully to channel cash back into the community, but as the brief illustration below shows, problems do arise, especially amongst impoverished people.

> A young man (K) working in the US Virgin Islands was looking for a fishing boat with outboard motor to purchase ready for use when he returned to Bequia. One of his peer group (A) wrote to tell him that A's father's brother had decided to sell his boat and engine for $2,000 EC (approximately $800 US) but needed the cash before he could guarantee a transaction. There was some delay in K receiving the letter and the cash reaching Bequia, by which time the boat and engine had been sold. When K returned to Bequia he found that A had spent some of the money on paying off debts. A violent argument broke out when K discovered what had happened, despite his friend's promise to repay the money as soon as possible. When I left the dispute had not been resolved.

2   The working of fishing equipment by the friends of men temporarily out of Bequia constitutes a second instrumental function of peer groups and networks, and demonstrates the reciprocal nature of such relationships. Loyalty to a particular small boat/net owner will be rewarded by the owner granting access to the fishing equipment during periods of absence. The men responsible will then be expected to take shares of their catch in line with the share system specific to the type of fishing. The owner's share will be banked or saved for his return. All men who own fishing equipment will make arrangements for their equipment to be worked by network and/or peer group members in their absence. The construction of houses also takes place through network channels. In the past the labour of men who carry on the construction of a house for an absent member of the community would be incurred as a debt to be reciprocated but today, especially amongst the younger men, most of their labour is paid for in cash; a share of the money sent back to the community for the purchase of materials being taken as wages. Such a system was used by a Lower Bay seaman during my stay and the case below shows the value of close ties with peers and friends, which allow flexibility in payment arrangements for work done on house construction.

Case 5c A regularly employed seaman's activation and reciprocation of peer group bonds

At the age of 15 Francis left school and found employment aboard a US charter yacht, the 'Yankee Clipper'. After three years experience in the galley, he was offered a catering apprenticeship with NBC in 1973. On completion of his apprenticeship he was given a full time post as chef with the company (in 1975) since which time he has 'sailed' regularly on 12–18 month contracts, spending periods of 3 to 6 months in between contracts in Bequia.

In 1976 Francis purchased a plot of land on Lawler's Hill while on leave. Clearance and construction work has been undertaken since by peer group members to whom he sends remittances for materials and 'wages' during his absence. In between contracts he participates in the work with his friends, who continue to receive cash for work they do. Whenever the cash from the remittances sent back to Bequia expires the group continue to do whatever work is possible without materials and for no wage. As the house neared completion in 1981 Francis planned to stand it as collateral for a bank loan to purchase a boat and fishing equipment, which he intended to use to fish with his peer group, and to retire from seamanship if it became a viable fishing enterprise. Francis, in planning to establish an alternative material base in fishing, was demonstrating his awareness of, and registering his protest over, the current lack of security in merchant shipping employment:

> I ain't want for be in de position of so much of Lowbay men waiting around wid no work. Sailing good for make money but it ain't last forever. Man, dere endless problem if you ain't haf other way for making money. Fishing de only thing I know essep sailing ...

Francis is able to consolidate his relationships with peer groups by providing them with free drinks, as compensation for unpaid work, when he returns on leave. This is only possible, in light of recent opposition to unwaged labour arrangements, because of the strength of the bonds within his peer group. One service he provides in exchange for the unpaid work is regularly to send details of posts available with NBC. Although this service is essentially symbolic, in that few men are successful in their applications, in 1979 one of the group using the forged discharge papers system (see 3 below) secured a post on Francis' recommendations.

The working of fishing equipment by community-resident members of a man's network and/or peer group in his absence from the community can take on a patron-client type of relationship. One man, who owns a 15 foot boat and outboard motor, and still retains a permanent contract with National Bulk, ensures that his equipment is put to its full productive use whenever he is at sea, taking shares for the boat and for the engine. The three men who are usually engaged in fishing his boat in his absence are dependent upon access to this equipment for a means of livelihood, as none of them owns equipment of comparable productivity. Between contracts the owner fishes with the three men, adopting the role of skipper and taking responsibility for maintenance of the equipment and sharing the catch.

3 Reciprocity between peer group and network members is not, however, limited to payment for work or access to productive technology, but can help to meet other continuous needs such as the provision of information and aid in locating and acquiring access to sources of employment. This is particularly effective amongst networks who have members engaged in seasonal or permanent tourist work in other Caribbean islands, where many work illegally (see Chapter 7, and Case 5a, p.141). Networks in this context allow a flexible and dispersed approach to the exploitation of scattered and temporary employment opportunities.

As employment with merchant shipping companies becomes increasingly competitive, a recent practice has grown up whereby a young man with little work experience as a merchant seaman 'borrows' a friend's discharge papers, which record name, rank/class of sailor, company and length of service. By 'chalking' over the name, typing in his own name, then getting the papers photocopied, by a contact in the bank, an inexperienced sailor is able to apply, successfully in a small number of cases, to companies not listed on the discharge papers.

Effective exchanges within networks are, as illustrated above, predominantly instrumental, based on exchange of labour, resources and information crucial for the maintenance of subsistence and for survival. The importance of networks in a society increasingly pushed towards marginality and dependence is continually reiterated by the lower classes:

> You done know just how many friend you have when thing get hard. I man can sleep easy when I know dat dere someone for lend I net or boat, or give help wid clearing land or fixing de roof. You ain't want for be poor in dis place if you ain't have plenty friend. It ain't just lending

thing dat important ... If you know someone who can help wid finding work (wage labour) den you have better chance of making it.

Friendship bonds, especially those between former peer group members only remain viable by repeated instrumental *and* symbolic exchange. The most regularly used form of symbolic exchange is that of reciprocal rum drinking and game playing in rum shop groups. Young men's drinking circles tend to be wider than those of their older counterparts. Many young men drink in rum shop groups outside the community, constituted by former school friends and/or fellow seamen.

As the machismo emphasis on peer group activities, such as sport, girlfriends, etc., diminishes with age, small drinking groups involved in rum shop games such as dominoes and cards become increasingly significant forms of symbolic exchange for older men. Peer group and network bonds can be said to be cemented symbolically by alcohol: drinking is a social activity and to drink alone is considered 'mean' and 'worthless' within plebeian cultural values (see next chapter). A drinking group contains three to five men, the size dictated essentially by the cost of alcohol. A drinking session begins with one man purchasing a quarter bottle of rum, and continues until all members of the group have purchased and consumed equivalent amounts. Differentiation of incomes clearly tends to weaken the bonds of peer groups, as does marriage, for the emphasis on social and reciprocative drinking acts as an effective sanction against the practice of drinking alone.

For those men who do not drink, or participate only rarely in rum shop activities, usually married or very poor men, symbolic exchanges with members of peer groups and networks take place under the trees which line that section of the beach in Lower Bay where the fishing boats are kept when not in use. In the heat of the afternoon or in the evening period prior to sunset, men lie in boats talking: exchanging ideas and information. The success of fishing in the community is usually reflected by the numbers of men grouped around the boats, the rum shop groups moving to the boats when catches are too low to support the cost of alcohol.

The extent to which networks reflect the unstable material position of the lower classes, especially their restricted access to jobs, houses, means of production and other material necessities, is highlighted by a brief look at ex-planter class involvement, or lack of, in networks and peer groups. The dominant ideology of this class prescribes the centrality of the materially and socially independent nuclear family. Few members of the ex-planter class have a developed friendship network, their secure material position being such that they have no need or incentive to cultivate such bonds. They tend to isolate themselves from the plebeian public sphere in all but specific work activities, e.g. seine operations. The sexual division of labour of the ex-planter class remains rigidly female-domestic/male-public, although the patrifocal nature of the household means that men do not need to enter into extra-domestic social activities. Instead they spend their non-working time in or around their own households and aloof from lower class male pastimes. Len Lafayette, the most powerful and wealthy person in the community, represents the extreme of this class separation, entering into none of the community's social activities, aside from seine fishing and the supervision of cassava processing. Len Lafayette's total rejection of networks and community social groups served to consolidate and demonstrate his class position by emphasising social distance from the rest of the community. The extent to which he remained aloof from plebeian social life and the resentment that this caused amongst the lower classes is borne out in the case below, which describes an incident in which I was directly involved.

Case 5d A dispute between a descendant of a planter family and the author

Following the inheritance of the house where I was residing during my fieldwork (see Case 7a, p.215) I rented the tourist house owned by Len Lafayette. Having been living there for about one month alone, I was unexpectedly visited by a black friend from Reading, England, by the name of Leo. Leo was born in Barbados, but left with his parents when he was three years of age. Following his divorce in 1979 he and his ex-wife decided to sell their house in Reading. He used some of his share of that sale to finance a trip to Barbados, returning for the first time since he left 24 years earlier. After two months in Barbados, he decided to spend what little money he had left on a short trip to Bequia, knowing I was there, before returning to Reading.

Lafayette's tourist-let house has three bedrooms and as I was paying full rent, I offered Leo a room in the house free of charge for the length of his stay in Bequia. The first night after his arrival I took him to some of the rum shops in the community where he met many of the local fishermen and youths who found him affable and pleasant company. The next day he came fishing with one of the groups that I occasionally accompanied. When we returned late in the afternoon, Lafayette was standing on the doorstep of the house I was renting. As we walked up the path to the house he shouted angrily that 'dat black man nah set he feet in my house ...' In the conversation (sic) that followed, Lafayette told me that he had rented the house to me and me alone and that he didn't want anyone else staying there. I apologised, not wishing to enter into any conflict with him because of my position in the community, but he became angrier and told me that I also had to leave when my rent for that month was up. I chose not to pursue the matter there and then, hoping that by giving him time he would reconsider. I had to ask Leo to find somewhere else to stay.

In the rum shop that night many local people gave me their interpretations of why Lafayette had behaved the way he did. These included his 'racism' ('he done hate black people' Lafayette being light skinned), his 'ignorance' ('he ain't want for know people unless dey paying he some money') and his aloofness. In the course of the next few days everybody I spoke to in the community expressed anger at Lafayette's behaviour, these included the other two seine owners, close kin of his, older women in the community, and most vociferous were the younger men. Criticisms of Lafayette became an integral part of my conversations with people in the community during the days that followed the incident. Most common were comments about his lack of involvement with community affairs:

> Just cos he got plenty dollar and plenty land he ain't wanna know any of he people
>
> De man he evil, he nah talk wid anyone essep when he want for dey to work for he.
>
> He ain't in touch wid what happening in Lowbay.

By playing the incident down I managed to dissipate much of the anger and tension that had been generated in the community, and when I approached Lafayette a few days before my rent was up and explained that Leo was a friend whom I was trying to help and that I hadn't realised the restrictions on renting the house, he agreed to allow me to stay. The remarkable thing about the conversation I had with Lafayette at this stage was that he told me that he had not wanted Leo to stay because he thought he was a Vincentian. While virtually everyone in the community had been aware that Leo was in fact British Lafayette's isolation and aloofness had meant he was totally oblivious to Leo's nationality.

Economic security in a materially marginal community like Lower Bay clearly lessens an individual's, and his immediate family's, dependence on extra-domestic support structures. Lafayette's power and relative autonomy in Lower Bay effectively isolated him from the rest of the community and conflicted with plebeian ideals of co-operation and integration.

In contrast to Len Lafayette's non-participation in community social life and total independence from networks, Charles Walters who operates his seine in Canouan, has developed a number of network ties in Lower Bay and Canouan itself. His position in the community is far weaker politically and economically than Lafayette's. He owns little land, has no tourist oriented business and relies totally upon the seine for his livelihood. During the periods he spends back in Lower Bay he regularly participates in rum shop activities, being renowned for his story telling. His status is clearly recognised by the deference and respect shown by members of his drinking group, and correlates with his class position. However, he remains dependent upon a number of men in Lower Bay, both kin and friends, to serve as crew on his seine in Canouan when needed and to distribute and market fish that he periodically sends to Bequia from Canouan.

Amongst all networks the strongest bonds tend to be those developed through peer groups. The quality and strength of bonds between men in the community varies, but men with free access to another's household, whether they are friends or kin, represent symbolically potential members of that household, demonstrating a strong personal element in the relationship. Co-residency in Lower Bay denotes a special kind of relationship distinguished from all others, and if extended, albeit symbolically, to non-household members this reflects the quality of the personal relationship between the household and visitor.

Christmas, funerals and births are the only times when the restrictions on access to another's house are somewhat relaxed. During the Christmas of 1980 J-L, (see Case 3d, p.82) invited himself to a small party held by a young merchant seaman on leave. Although it was the festive season, J-L's behaviour was considered improper; as the young seaman told me:

> Just cos it Christmas it ain't mean I gonna haf every man in de village a come in my home. J-L he worthless, looking for free drink and food ... he know dat any other time he ain't able for come in here, but he think I ain't pay it no heed. But I done tell he it only people dat are special friend or family dat come in here ...

Networks and economic change

The significance of kinship and friendship networks is bound to the ability of kinsfolk and friends to manipulate dyadic relationships in times of need. Engagement in network strategies is a matter of choice in the face of changing opportunities and constraints. The wider a man's network spans, the more chance he has of furthering his interests and reducing the possibility of overall failure. Dispersal of network ties outside the community, such as kin and friends working abroad/in merchant shipping, members of a Friendly Society, kin/friends in Southern Grenadines, etc., allows for spatial mobility, essential in times of economic demise in a community characterised by fluctuating resources and irregular employment opportunities and cash flows.

Network ties can be activated in response to material and social needs. Just as mating patterns stabilised and became formalised during the period of economic prosperity that accompanied high levels of male employment in shipping and inter-island trade, so it would appear that networks became less significant, although clearly not insignificant, for the lower classes in Lower Bay during the 1960s and early 1970s.

Dirks (1972:581-2) reports a similar relationship between network activation and economic prosperity in a small community in the Virgin Islands. With the growth of tourism in the islands in the 1960s came increased employment opportunities:

> ... during this period personal networks acquired a less extensive, more stable character ... men in the labour market took numerous opportunities to secure work close to home negating the need for distant fleeting linkages in more remote employment areas ... During periods of economic depression (or recession) market opportunities are generally scarce and scattered. Networks mirror this condition by expanding in breadth and increasing in fluidity.

While I would not state the correlation between economic prosperity/decline and the use/non-use of networks as rigidly as Dirks does, there is nevertheless sufficient empirical evidence to show that in Lower Bay the effects of marginality and dependence can be alleviated, and partially constrained, in a way which does not deviate from plebeian cultural ideas, by effective and widespread friendship and kinship networks.

Notes

1 See, for example Barnes, J. A. (1954), Mitchell, J. C. (1969) and Boissevain, J. (1974).
2 'Liming' means to stand around in public after dark in small groups and is an exclusively male activity.

CHAPTER 6 | Lower Bay lower class culture

Previous chapters have documented and analysed the socio-economic and political relations into which the subordinate classes in Lower Bay enter in order to gain access to and as a result of work. In coping with and making sense of their marginality in society, the lower classes draw on the meaning systems available to them, using sets of beliefs, values and norms for the careful ordering of ideas to make living experience acceptably meaningful. The concepts of personal worth and properness, as embodied in the notions of respect and shame, are significant in lower class ideology and will constitute one of the central themes of this chapter.

The practices and beliefs which define worthfulness and properness are derived from the ex-planter class ideology, but do not represent lower class submission or compliance with the dominant ideology: the lower classes having been denied the necessary means for legitimising their value systems in ways compatible with their life experiences on the periphery of the system of production and exchange. In this respect, the lower classes are symbolically, as well as materially, marginal in the social formation: the beliefs, ideas and practices of lower class culture are derived, partially, from earlier forms of symbolic production associated with earlier modes and forms of material production in which they have been economically and ideologically subordinate. As the lower classes have limited access to the means of production of discourse, they are unable to give legitimation to a lower class culture in terms independent of the dominant planter ideology and value systems. Incorporation of lower class ideologies and practices into the planter ideology is, however, incomplete: lower class people in Lower Bay are forced constantly to re-evaluate and re-examine their locations in the social structure and status hierarchy as a result of unstable and fluctuating material circumstances.

This is not to suggest a crude determinism between material and symbolic/social production, but that social and symbolic (i.e. normative and ideological) elements are rooted in the material order, and take on an existential quality, and so react upon the material order. This chapter is concerned with an analysis of the symbolic sphere and the extent to which class position structures access to the means of production of discourse and determines and restricts the formation and articulation of a lower class culture. As Marx has stressed (see specifically 'The German Ideology', 1845-6) intellectual production is directly interwoven with material production: meaning systems can only be comprehended in the context of the realities of the political economy.

As discourse and meaning are to be crucial concepts in the discussion that follows, a concise definition and theoretical perspective is offered prior to an analysis of empirical findings.

Discourse, meaning and culture: some theoretical considerations

By discourse I am referring to a particular form of communicative and interpretive activity: a way of constituting the world and communicating with others who constitute the world in a similar way. As such, a discourse is not a way of speaking, which is language, but a way of 'talking' which is dependent upon language for its expression in concrete situations. Language, as the means to the production of discourse, takes the form, existentially, of a palimpsest: a collection of rules, ideas and practices relating to speech, which have been and continue to be laid down over time and exist as residues from earlier modes of linguistic production.

Experiences constitute the raw materials transformed within discourse by the process of intellectual production. In any discourse the way a person constitutes the world and communicates this meaning to others requires selection from the language collection of speech patterns and linguistic structures available to him/her. Experience, however, directly influences the selection of constructs from the collection: the formation of concepts derived from primary experience being determined by access to the means of production of discourse. Such concepts constitute an individual's 'personal' collection, or language, and shape perception of the world by limiting access to alternative language constructs.

An individual's location in the social structure is a crucial factor in determining access to the means of production of discourse: class position structures access to types of experience and hence limits the range of concepts for interpreting those experiences. Class can thus be said to determine the boundaries of consciousness and ideology.

The maintenance of positions of power and influence (dominance) requires the suppression of those discourses through which the social order could be challenged, and the paramountcy of those classes in dominant positions threatened. Dominance entails two related, though distinct types of suppression of discourse:

(i) the suppression of thoughts, i.e. those that lie within the intellectual capacity of the subordinate classes, which, if articulated into a particular discourse or discourses would undermine the power and authority of the dominant classes. This type of suppression is concerned with maintenance of surface reality (or appearance) and takes place through the prevention of access to forms of intellectual production that would enable or could lead to explanations of underlying reality: e.g. in Bequia explanations that would depict the relationship between ex-planter/merchant classes and the lower classes in terms of exploitation. In Bequia positions of power and influence are legitimised by the dominant class and its agents through ideologies which depict such hierarchised social relations as some sort of organic order (as God's will, natural, etc.); ideologies whose major function is one of social control affecting lower class conformity with and acceptance of the system of stratification based on ownership and control of means of production and markets.

(ii) The suppression and/or repression of experiences that people have, but which must be unlearnt or reinterpreted so as to defuse their potential for social unrest or collective action. For example, the experience of slavery or of the workers' riots in St Vincent in the 1930s etc., must be perceived by the lower classes in ways which make them appear distant to the specific life experiences and relationships of the actors. Again it is ideological transmission of norms, values and ideas from the dominant class that facilitates and ensures this unlearning process.

The suppression of discourse does not constitute the suppression of meaning. The suppression of discourse is the deprivation of the means necessary for articulating and legitimising an experience in a particular way, i.e. which could threaten the social order and the hierarchy. The experience, however, remains meaningful, if only in a negative way. For example, as we shall see below, the suppression of a discourse which would relate the social relations of slavery (master/slave) to contemporary social relations in Bequia (ex-planter as 'exploiter' of ex-slaves) is essential for the continued existence of the ex-planter class; but the experience of slavery, as passed on through generations of lower class Bequiarians, remains a meaningful part of lower class culture, albeit perceived in terms of cultural affinity with the colonial powers.

The suppression of discourse allows the manipulation of culture to the political, economic and social advantage of the dominant, ex-planter, class. Through suppression of discourse the dominant ideology is incorporated, albeit incompletely, into the lower class value system, which becomes what Parkin (1971:94) calls a 'negotiated form of the dominant ideology'. Although the ex-planter class controls both material and mental production, through ownership of the means of production of wealth and of discourse, and thus imposes its system of beliefs on the lower class (the ruling class/ruling ideas thesis of Marx in 'The German Ideology') the lower classes, because of different historical experience and economic circumstances, have created their own modes of thought and views of the world determined by class interests (Marx and Engels, 1968:117–118). Consequently the separate interests and material conditions of the ex-planter and lower classes produce *two cultures*.[1] The plebeian culture appears to have a similar ideological form to that of the ex-planter class, but the functions of each remain radically different: the latter based on imposition and social control, and endorsing the existing inequalities, the former on the ordering of ideas and concepts to make experience of life acceptable and meaningful.

The analysis of lower class culture that follows uses and develops the two cultures thesis contained in the dominant ideology/suppression of discourse argument to examine the way in which Lower Bay people make sense of their position of inequality and marginality in, and experiences of, the world. It begins by considering the process of primary socialisation through which young people are taught the values of respect and shame considered necessary for participation in plebeian life. This is followed by a detailed discussion of the ways in which properness is evaluated according to observable actions and beliefs; while analysis of the relationship between work and ideas in plebeian culture provides an insight into age and gender distinctions, as well as class. The conflict between plebeian culture and the values and meanings contained in the dominant ideology is drawn out by detailed investigation of lower class interpretation of the dominant meaning system which is often at sharp odds with the normative system of lower class life. The means through which the powerful ex-planter class limits the articulation of a lower class culture is further highlighted by insight into the system of classification employed by Lower Bay plebeians to make sense of their place in and relationship with the outside world. Lower Bay folk use a trichotomous system of classification which categorises others according to their position in the world outside Bequia, to their position in Bequia society, and to their place in the Lower Bay community. The chapter concludes by drawing together the material presented to show the existence of an authentic lower class culture in Lower Bay.

Honour and shame in plebeian culture: the social and moral evaluation of properness

The central evaluative concept relating to a person's actions and beliefs is that of 'worth' or 'worthfulness'. It is an ordering concept which sums up the total social standing of an individual in the community. The familiar anthropological notions of honour and shame, which describe the social worth of a person, are expressed by lower class Bequarians in terms of respect, shame and their antithesis, worthlessness. Respect in Bequia correlates closely with the Mediterranean value of honour. Like honour, respect is the value of a person in his/her own eyes and in the eyes of the immediate society. Respect is maintained by adherence to the codes governing proper behaviour, and requires the correct use of titles and terms of address for others; appropriate bodily movements and physical appearance/dress; fulfilment of obligations and responsibilities; independence, self-sufficiency and the avoidance of debts; control of sexuality; honesty; work; and correct use of time and social distance.

Respect differs fundamentally from the Mediterranean notion of honour in that it is not achieved at the expense of others: it is not competitive and once attained (at puberty) the individual is concerned with not losing it. However, personal conduct produces consequences for others with whom the individual shares collective respect, specifically household members and close kin. If an individual loses respect through improper actions, beliefs or words then family and household members may be subject to the sanctions and attitudes associated with such loss of respect.

Shame is a concept quite different from that of the Mediterranean value, but in common with the Spanish '*verguenza*' (see Pitt-Rivers, 1977:20–21) and the Greek notion of shame (see Friedl, 1962), it covers a far wider range of meaning than the English equivalent. Amongst Mediterranean cultures, honour and shame are intrinsically linked: shame, according to Aceves (1971:63) is '... lack of honour brought about by loss of honour ...', and can also be synonymous with honour (Pitt-Rivers, 1954:113; Friedl, *ibid.*) in that a person of worth is required to have both. Shame, in Mediterranean cultures can also be a value thought to be proper to women only, as showing timidity or shyness:

> Honour and shame, when they are not equivalent, are linked exclusively to one sex or the other and are opposed to one another (Pitt-Rivers, 1977:21).

Shame in Lower Bay is a less ambivalent concept, linked closely with personal respect, and not limited to the qualities of women. The term is often used to mean embarrassment in children: when a small child acts shyly he/she is said to 'be shamed'. The term is not applied to adolescents or adults in this way. Shame in plebeian culture is a valued characteristic in all senses. It refers to a person's sensitivity to and awareness of proper behaviour and is a personal quality which provides the individual with a recognition of his/her position of respect *vis à vis* others in the community and to the necessity of acknowledging deference to those persons with respect. Shame leads the individual to observe and respect the 'proper order' of society and is then referred to as 'having shame' which is quite distinct from 'being shamed'. To be shamed is to be put in one's place for improper behaviour/beliefs. A person can be shamed by household members or close kin, as well as more distant community members. Whilst loss of personal respect can and often does reflect on an individual's close kin and household, to have no shame is a social recognition of personal failure only. No single term or word describes loss of or lack of respect, although the expression 'worthless' refers specifically to someone without shame, i.e. without regard for or awareness of the rules of proper social behaviour. Worthlessness appears to be culturally analagous with the 'shamelessness' (*'sin verguenza'*) noted by Spanish anthropologists to refer to the loss of respect and shame for an individual who is then considered '... beyond the pale of decent life and decent people. The shameless person will not be trusted, he or she may be insulted almost at will ...' (Aceves, 1971:64).

Respect and shame are prescribed concepts through which a person's worth is evaluated and translated and his/her properness described within plebeian culture. In this sense shame legitimates and respect rewards.[2]

Primary socialisation

The embodiment of shame and respect in the consciousness of the young is, as conceived by the actors themselves, the most crucial aspect of primary socialisation which is the process of induction and training from birth to puberty. During the early period of childhood, characterised by dependence on the mother-figure for feeding and care, the lower class child is considered innocent of the moral code of conduct. Internalisation of the qualities of respect and shame takes place during this stage: initially through language by means of which '... motivational and interpretive schemes are internalised as institutionally defined' (Berger and Luckman, 1967:153). The child is subjected to values expressed linguistically in terms of 'being a good boy/girl', 'being kind, honest', 'behaving proper', etc. These programmes differentiate the child's identity from those of others: the beginnings of differentiation according to age and gender.

By the age of about five years, division of household tasks according to gender commences, the teaching of notions of properness associated with respect and shame being sex-specific. Girls are taught the duties of the mother, such as cooking, washing clothes, cleaning the house and collecting supplies from local shops. Boys, on the other hand, are assigned more 'physical' chores outside the house where possible, such as tethering sheep and goats, pumping water and, as they grow older, they assist adult male household members with fishing, land clearance, etc.

Control of young children is often extremely physical. Neglect of household chores, failure to use correct terms of address to elders, especially close kin and neighbours, or failure to return home at required times will often be punished by beating by the mother. Parents hold strong beliefs in the need to inculcate the values of right and wrong, as one young mother expressed it:

> When you done give dem small children plenty licks (slaps with a twig) dey ain't gonna forget dey done wrong. When I a child my mother done take de stick a me for de smallest of thing wrong. I ain't forget and my children ain't for neither.

A child's obligations to parents and household increase as she/he approaches puberty, during which time the basic elements of legitimation of respect and shame are internalised. The child is taught to feel indebted to parents, especially the mother-figure. Deference to older persons, notably those in close relationships (friendship or kinship) with the parents/household head, is also strongly enforced with expressions such as: 'dey older dan you, so you must show dem respeck ...' and 'you ain't address she so, she taunt to you ...'

Legitimation of institutional arrangements specific to sex roles is constantly reinforced: the relationship between work and respect (for males) and church, household and respect (for females) is reiterated: 'As a man you hafi work for keep respeck ...'; 'it a worthless man who done sit around drinking rum when he family hungry'; 'if you ain't attend church you ain' for have no shame'; 'a woman must have pride in she home'.

At puberty the young person is considered fully responsible for her/his moral, social and sexual behaviour. A youth has acquired the personal qualities of shame and is subject to the requirements of respectability. At this stage youths join peer groups and turn away from the household as their primary frame of reference to identify more strongly with peer group values of achievement, which imply sexual activity.

Although parents/household heads exercise control over the movements of their adolescent daughters and repeatedly warn that they should not 'let boy put question to you', many young women establish covert sexual relationships and become pregnant. The initial condemnation of teenage pregnancies by senior household members, followed later by acceptance, illustrates the point made earlier about plebeian culture being a 'negotiated version' of the dominant ideology. Household heads, and partners if present, are evaluated according to their success in inculcating the values of respect and shame into the consciousness of young household members. The social behaviour of pubescent and post-pubescent young people reflects the effectiveness of their socialisation and, as such, the respectability of the household head. Through the initial outbursts of anger and condemnation over the pregnancy the household head is demonstrating his/her aspiration towards respect as contained in the dominant ideology. With plebeian mating practices sharply at odds with the dominant values of legal conjugality and monogamy, the condemnation is short-lived, for the realities of lower class life make it unnecessary to 'overplay' the properness of sexual activity. Indeed, household heads who outcast their pregnant teenage daughters, which is very rare, will be criticised for refusing to accept the realities of plebeian lower class life. Household heads are effectively 'stretching' the values contained in notions of repectability whilst accepting that deviation from such ideals is a way of life. The early reaction to teenage pregnancies is a response to the fact that, although respect and shame are qualities that must be taught in the domestic sphere, they are evaluated in the public domain.

The following excerpt from an extended case study illustrates evaluation of respect in the public domain:

Case 6a   The implications of a youth's loss of respect for the rest of his household

During the peak of the 1980–81 tourist season an American couple rented the ground floor of a recently completed house in Lawler's Hill, belonging to a Lower Bay woman (W) who had recently built the house with savings from a number of years working in the US. Late one night an intruder made off with $100 US belonging to the couple. W was awoken during the burglary and saw the intruder leaving the house. She identified him as Y, a 17-year-old youth from Lower Bay village who lived with his parents and siblings. Whether or not Y was guilty (which he denied) is not significant in this case, which focuses specifically upon the attitude and responses of community members to Y and his household.

When news of the theft reached the community the following morning it became the talking point in rum shops, fishing boats and throughout the village. Excerpts from conversations (recorded verbatim) reflect the relationship between personal conduct and collective respect, in this case that of household members:

> You know dat Y, he done come a decent family. He father and mother alway bin honest people. Now dey ain't gonna be able for hold dey head up when dey meet people ...
>
> I ain't for think Y could be so worthless, coming a respeckful family ...
>
> Y he done do wrong he parent, who hafi live wid he worthless behaviour. It ain't just he who gonna suffer from people talking but he mother and father. Plenty people ain't for trust dat family again. Y gonna bring endless worry on de whole of he family by dis thing.

The extent to which community members extended their disdain for Y's alleged actions to his parents was borne out some days later in a rum shop when Y's father ordered a half bottle of rum on credit. Rum shop credit is available to, and used by, most Lower Bay men, except for those who regularly fail to pay their debts. Y's father had a reputation of being a good credit risk, but on this day W's brother was in the rum shop and on hearing Y's father ask for credit shouted across the shop:

You mussa hafi plenty money wid dat son of you so busy in other people wallet ...

A heated argument ensued, in which a number of men in the shop backed up W's brother's accusations, albeit in a less aggressive manner, the incident ending with Y's father leaving the rum shop embarrassed and disgraced.

The possibility that respect, or, in this instance, loss of respect, can extend from individual to household and/or family suggests that it is not a single value but a complex of values united at the level of social relations. In an impoverished and increasingly marginalised lower class community, actions and beliefs which constitute a threat to the material survival or symbolic status of an individual or group (in this case W's reputation as a landlady) can lead to the offender and his/her family/household being ostracised locally. This reflects the perceived role of the household, specifically its senior members, in the socialisation process. It is, therefore, essential for senior household members to exercise control over the actions and beliefs of junior or dependent members, for it is only through social interaction that respect is demonstrated and maintained, and ultimately evaluated in the community.

Gender differentiation in demonstrating properness

The modes of behaviour and thought seen as appropriate for an individual within plebeian culture are determined by moral and social factors differentiated according to age and sex categories. Pre-pubescent children are not considered to have acquired the qualities of respect and shame: primary socialisation being concerned with the inculcation of such values. While respect and shame are qualities that both men and women are expected to possess and demonstrate, being a 'proper man' and being a 'proper woman' entail quite distinct requirements. Many of these gender differentiations pertaining to the demonstration of respect and shame stem from the separate spheres which lower class men and women occupy: the public and domestic respectively. A woman should avoid being seen 'on de street, making commess' (loosely translated as gossiping in public). In contrast, men spend much of their leisure time sitting in or around the fishing boats under the almond tree at the west end of Lower Bay village engaged in 'old talk'. 'Old talk' is effectively unsanctioned 'commess'.

There are social pressures on women to display a sober appearance which includes not dressing or walking in a provocative manner. At its extreme this involves women bathing in the sea fully clothed. In contrast, the public domain being male, a man should demonstrate publicly his manliness and attractiveness to women. Despite the widespread practice of sexual activity outside marriage, a woman is expected to control her sexuality. A woman with a reputation of being promiscuous is referred to as a 'busy bottom', a term which equally describes anything of poor quality such as over-ripe bananas, low quality rum, etc. Men, on the other hand, are expected to be popular with women and adept at courtship. Although a man's respect is not threatened by promiscuous sexual activity in the way a woman's is, 'success' with women is more about enhancing reputation amongst fellow men than demonstrating worth or properness. Ideally a man should enter a permanent conjugal relationship to be respectable and show he has shame, but transgression from this norm does not entail the loss of respect (worthlessness) that befalls a woman.

Similarly, marriage is the only institutionalised means for a woman to attain full adult status and respect but, as we have seen, is seldom available until later life. As such, the notions of respect and shame contained in the dominant ideology, and transmitted to young women through the household, conflict with the empirical reality of being a woman in lower class Lower Bay. As childbirth starts the process towards household formation, a woman relies upon visible signs of domestic competence, such as keeping her home clean and tidy, the ability to maintain a stable conjugal union, control over and socialising her children, etc., to gain public esteem and respect and demonstrate shame.

The domestic activities of women in and around the household, although classified as 'women's work' in plebeian culture, are not given social or existential recognition as 'real work'. Only men occupy the world of real work in Lower Bay, circumscribing the role of 'proper man' as material provider through productive activities in the public domain. Respect for men entails individualistic norms: the ability to be independent, self-sufficient, and thrifty, and to avoid debts. A man who constantly undertakes domestic work, whether it is because he lives alone or cannot meet the needs of his household without agricultural work, loses respect.

There are a number of personal qualities associated with properness that are common to both male and female status. Dishonesty, aggression, mis-use of time (see below), impoliteness, especially failing to adhere to the norms of respectable address (again see below), and ignorance of worldly affairs can all lead to loss of respect. Women must not fight (physically) or 'use passwords' or 'cuss' (swear) under any circumstances. This taboo also applies to men, although the demonstration of machismo means it is often necessary and acceptable for a man to show himself able and willing to resort to physical means of defending himself and his family. Although Gibson (1981:133) asserts: 'Drinking, fighting and "cussing" were thought of as manly attributes if subject to control', Lower Bay people were very critical of anyone who engaged in physical violence with another from the community: 'Dat kinda thing for Southside and Mount Pleasant. We ain't want it in Lowbay'. The consumption of alcohol and tobacco is further limited to men: a woman who drinks and/or smokes will be ostracised and considered worthless. If subject to control, then such activities are acceptable for men, but no man wants to be known as a 'drunkard'. Expenditure on rum and cigarettes should be related to the financial position of the individual. In times of hardship a man who spends time in a rum shop or continues to buy cigarettes will be publicly accused of failing to fulfil his obligations to household and family.

As we have seen, loss of respect and shameless behaviour can have implications for an individual's household and other close kin. In the case of women this is extended to their children. A worthless woman is believed to pass on such qualities to her offspring. A common expression in the community is 'Goat can't bring sheep', which refers to the belief that a woman without shame or respect is unlikely to bear children of any more worth than herself. (Lamb/mutton is more highly regarded than goat meat). The expression is only employed when a person whose mother has shown herself to be improper, comes into conflict with ideas about proper behaviour in the community: it is thus a means of identifying causes of worthlessness rather than permanently characterising an individual. A person who shows him/herself to be respectful and in possession of shame by his/her actions and beliefs will not be subject to popular criticism about the personal worth of his/her mother but should he/she lose respect or behave worthlessly then inferences relating to maternal origin will be drawn publicly. A person who has attained adulthood will no longer be subject to ideas relating family origin to worth, provided no evidence of worthlessness had become apparent during the years between puberty and full adulthood. The following short example illustrates some of these points.

A young woman from Lower Bay Gutter was known by the nickname 'Busy Bottom' for her sexual involvement with a number of young men over a short period of time. During a conversation about the woman which took place in a rum shop one night, a Lower Bay man explained to me that such behaviour was not unexpected in view of her mother. As he said:

> You know goat can't bring sheep. Dis woman mother she worthless and all. She lose she husband cos she ain't even able for wait for he to come back from sailing for get she pregnant. How such a woman ever gonna hafi children dat any better dan she?

In considering respect and shame this brief section has demonstrated that, despite the value placed on individualism, self-reliance and social distance, it is essential for a person to participate in community life, albeit in markedly different ways for men and women, for this is the only arena in which shame can be recognised and respect rewarded. In this context, properness and worthfulness are embodied in ideas relating to work, and non-work, and correct use of time, which provide a social base for the maintenance of credibility and legitimation. Work, as a social construction, is meaningful and this meaning is legitimised in the symbolic sphere.

Work and respect

Work for the lower classes is not limited to identification with a means of earning a living (remuneration for time spent working) but extends to include a complex of meanings circumscribing cultural ideas about personal worth. Wallman (1979:20) defines work as '... the production, management and conversion of the resources necessary to livelihood ...', the key term being 'resources'. Resources include 'other-than-economic resources', (Wallman, *ibid.*:7) i.e. not only land, labour and capital, but knowledge, information, identity and status. Failure to work, or the engagement in remunerative activities considered improper or worthless, can lead to loss of, or damage to, a person's worth, status and self-identity. For example, a Lower Bay seaman who made the journey to Barbados in the expectation of finding work with a Barbadian-based merchant shipping company, was forced to sell blood to a private blood bank when he found himself without work or money. Although the incident happened in 1976, during my fieldwork people in the community still referred to the worthlessness of such behaviour:

> It ain't matter how much my man done need money, dere no need for he go sell he blood.

Respect can only be maintained and shame demonstrated in Lower Bay by earning a living within the normative boundaries laid down in plebeian culture. The motivation to work is, thus, based upon a combination of material and symbolic rewards: the value of a particular work activity being measured morally as well as in terms of material reward. Many of the contemporary plebeian values and ideas governing work exist as deposits from forms of cultural production which originated in earlier modes of pre-capitalist material production. Under changing material conditions, stemming from transformations in the system of production and exchange, individuals and groups begin to attach differing degrees of symbolic and material importance to types of work.

Conflicting perceptions of traditional forms of economic activity illustrate this relationship between economic transition and symbolic production. Despite the value attached to community-based work activities by older members of the community and the subsequent attempts at inculcating such values in the consciousness of younger persons, salaried employment and tourist sector entrepreneurial activities have taken on increasing symbolic and material importance for this latter group (see Chapter 7 below). This importance stems from the complex interplay between economic and cultural factors, leading to the rejection by many of non-salaried work in community-based production activities, including petty-commodity and domestic production as well as reciprocal labour exchange.

An integral part of the 'custom' of work in the plebeian community (see Chapter 3 above and Wadel, 1979) has been that work, *per se*, should not be perceived as a solely economic activity but as a plurality of activities circumscribed and held together by community life. Fishing, for example, involves not simply the physical process of producing a marketable commodity and essential food stuff. Activities such as maintenance and repair of boats and equipment, exchanging bait, purchasing and replacing fishing equipment, observing moon-tide phases and other climatic variations, securing markets for catches, dividing the catch and attending share-out meetings, and organising crews, all involve the notion of work, but also of community life. The all-embracing work/community nature of fishing, like other residual forms of economic activity, includes aspects of leisure (e.g. participation in rum shop activities when organising crews or following the share-out), social intercourse (e.g. stopping to chat to friends or kin en route to markets, supply shops, etc.), kinship and network obligations (e.g. presentation of part of surplus to maternal household, responsibilities to others as in assistance with organising crews) and exchange of ideas and information.

Folk ideas relating to the work/community continuum have changed as a result of the penetration of capitalism. Materially and symbolically, the community ethic of production in residual forms has become subordinated to market forces. The increased commercialisation of social relations has produced an increasing concern with 'private' life, a desire to be free of the all-embracing involvement in work. Because of the unstable and fluctuating nature of wage labour, however, the lower classes find themselves continually needing to consolidate their relationships with key kin and friends (as seen in Chapter 5) in order to demonstrate their worthiness of material and symbolic support in times of need. The lower classes, despite material pressures arising from increased dependence on wage labour and the dominance of values relating to self-sufficiency, negotiate a meaning system which allows them to utilise communal and mutual aid structures, as a survival strategy, and, at the same time, maintain their respect and status within the plebeian culture.

Status in the lower class world further entails correct use of time. The normative use of time derives from earlier modes of material and symbolic production formerly articulated in the community/work continuum. The availability of wage labour and entrepreneurial opportunities has effected changes in perception of time use, which recognise the appropriateness and value of alternative, non-community based means for earning a living. However, sanctions are often instigated against persons involved in activities which do not qualify as community-oriented or as proper work. Young men involved in the informal tourist sector are considered improper and worthless, despite the enterprising, and entrepreneurial, nature of their activities. Chapter 7 below provides a number of examples of young men who have come into conflict with older community members because of their involvement in hawking and tourist patronage. The following brief example highlights the nature of such conflicts.

Three young Lower Bay men, between the ages of 16 and 18, who were engaged as crew on a French charter yacht during my fieldwork in 1980 were paid only when the yacht was on charter. When the yacht was not hired out the owner would stay in St Vincent with friends, leaving the men to maintain the yacht and prevent thefts. The three decided to stay aboard the yacht together during these periods and at times invited tourist girls to stay aboard with them. One of these young men came from a large family whose father (referred to in Case 3c, p.80 as N) relied upon fishing and occasional carpentry work[3] to support the household. When I spoke to him about his work I received the following reply:

> My time almost all spent working for my family, dere ain't a day pass when I ain't out checking my pots or catching bait or fixing something. Me, I a shipwright by skill, but just cos dere ain't work as shipwright I ain't stop working. But dat boy of me, he ain't working when he could. It only take one of dem young guy to watch over dat boat but dey all want to stay out, like dey ain't want a be known for Lower Bay. He could be fishing wid me and helping out here at home. I ain't think it wrong for dem work on yachts, nah, but dat kind of life done make dem lazy and worthless ...

The implication of the above statement is that the young man was considered to be failing in his duty to his household, his loyalty to his community of residence and, above all, using time incorrectly in improper activities. Young men, on the other hand, attach little value or symbolic importance to total community involvement, being critical of the lack of privacy and leisure activities and the repetitive and unrewarding nature of traditional economic activities. In the absence of merchant shipping jobs and local wage labour opportunities they look to the informal tourist sector for material returns and status.

The perceived importance and symbolic value attached to salaried work has, as we have seen, stemmed from the penetration of market forces and has furthermore been reinforced by contact with representatives of metropolitan capital and tourists, both in work and leisure activities in Bequia. Preference for wage labour, rooted in the material conditions of marginality and dependence experienced by the lower classes, is intrinsically linked with changing ideas relating to the allocation of time:

(i) unlike traditional work activities within residual forms of production where earnings are irregular – noticeably in fishing – and financial and labour debts are incurred, a salaried job allows the planning of time and expenditure in advance and is not subject to the economic and ecological uncertainty which results from dependence on fluctuating markets, climatic variations and the ability to invoke reciprocal labour arrangements:

> Man, when I working in de hotel in de harbour last year, even though I getting paid really bad wage I at least know dat each week I gonna get dollar for pay for food and thing. An when I finish work I

> know I ain't hafi think about going fishing or nutting. Sometimes when I done have some time offa work I done go fishing for help make extra dollar, and also for help de guys I done alway fish wid in de past ...

This quote illustrates the inability of lower class individuals to reject totally the traditional work arrangements, even those in waged employment. It is not only the incomplete incorporation of the Lower Bay economy, and the island economy, into the international capitalist economy resulting in lack of jobs, but the exploitative wages paid in the island that enforce and maintain dependence on residual forms expressed symbolically through allegiance to friends and kin engaged in traditional work activities.

(ii) A salaried job outside the community, with earnings sufficient to maintain the worker and his/her dependants (e.g. merchant shipping) allows for a clear distinction between time in work and time in leisure; and if household, family, network and community obligations and responsibilities are met and maintained, involvement in extra-community wage labour will not be subject to disapproval or reproachment. Nevertheless, returning seamen are conscious of the symbolic importance of participating in local life, in order to demonstrate respect publicly. Although active seamen clearly do not require the material returns from community-based economic activities when on leave, many will engage in fishing with members of their friendship networks or assist in construction or entrepreneurial activities, usually within a week or so of their return.

Recent changes in the wage labour market and increased foreign commercial activity in Bequia have enhanced feelings of powerlessness and lack of opportunities. Inequalities, rooted in increased marginality and dependence have increased lower class awareness of exploitation and injustice. Responses to developments in the tourist sector are detailed in the following chapter, where we shall see that they are rarely translated into effective lower class collective action.

The reasons for this lack of collective resistance are complex. At one level, the material pressures that stem from dependence and marginality mean that much of lower class life is involved with strategies of survival, which are usually sufficient to get the lower classes to co-operate. At the symbolic level many are concerned with maintaining their public image of worthfulness, demonstrating respect and shame in the community. In this sense, repect and shame constitute ideologies which hinder active and sustained collective opposition to the dominant classes.

Respect and shame as ideology

Respect and shame constitute a system of evaluation arising out of the moral framework of the dominant ideology. Because the dominant classes control the means of production of discourse, the definitions of social reality and properness contained in the dominant ideology are '... far more likely to be blessed with the stamp of public legitimacy than are the social and moral constructs of those in subordinate class positions.' (Parkin, 1971:42). Respect as ideology functions so as to commit many of the lower classes to accept the social hierarchy:

> Like all ideologies, honour and shame complement institutional arrangements for the distribution of power and the creation of order in society'. (Schneider, 1971:2).

However, as we have seen, the social and moral criteria of the dominant ideology are not fully accepted as legitimate by all members of the lower classes: the common language of respect and shame is at variance with many of the realities of lower class life.

As Parkin (*op.cit.*:93) has stressed, the norms underlying many aspects of lower class life are not objectified into 'a positively sanctioned and over-arching moral system'. The lower classes are unable to articulate their subordinate values and belief systems because the generating milieu of such values and beliefs is the lower class community which lacks the institutionalised means to 'legitimise a normative system sharply at odds with the dominant value system' (Parkin, *op.cit.*:94). Values such as respectability, sexual puritanism, independence, self-sufficiency, participation in voluntary organisations, like the church and the Friendly Society, are mediated by the institutions of the lower class world and their meanings are, to some extent, translated and adapted to the conditions of the lower classes. The life conditions of the lower classes effectively contradict the reality of the dominant meaning system and from this contradiction emerges the lower class value system which is unable effectively to challenge the dominant ideology but instead expresses itself as a negotiated version of this dominant ideology. Lower class culture in Bequia, then, should be seen as a subordinate value and meaning system which, because of the distribution of power and resultant inequality, is not a completely differentiated normative construct but expressed as an adapted, stretched and negotiated form of the ex-planter culture.

The suppression of lower class discourse and action cannot, however, (as Gray, 1976:184 also noted of Victorian working class institutions and aspirations) be explained simply in terms of a hegemonic conspiracy theory, but rather in terms of the 'incoherent and fragmented nature of ideology' (Gray, *ibid.*) which restricts the articulation of lower class practices and beliefs into a generalised system. According to their positions in the social hierarchy and their immediate circumstances and experience, lower class individuals may accept, reject or reinterpret values contained in the dominant ideology. Thus, practices such as co-operation and reciprocity may co-exist with individualism and self-sufficiency. The ability to rely upon one's own resources to make personal provision for oneself and one's dependants, prescribed in ideas about self-sufficiency and individual effort in the dominant value system, is clearly dependent upon the lower class individual's access to means of material production. In situations where such access is denied or limited then communal and reciprocal based relationships will be employed within the residual forms of production and exchange in which such practices are paramount. This entails reinterpretation of the dominant ideology within a lower class, subordinate, meaning system which provides a moral framework promoting accommodative responses to inequality and marginality.

Socio-economic position and immediate circumstances may influence the lower class individual to draw upon the dominant meaning system of the ex-planter ideology, in contrast to the subordinate value system of plebeian culture. Within Lower Bay, lower class interpretations of the dominant meaning system are of two types, which Parkin (*op.cit.*) refers to as 'deferential' and 'aspirational'.

The deferential interpretation involves acceptance of the dominant value system and symbolic order as natural or of 'God's will' seen as a sort of organic order in which each individual has a place and a part to play. This interpretation tends to be that of the lower classes who have had little, if any, contact with the world outside plebeian Bequia and experience the influence and judgements of the dominant classes in face-to-face relationships.

The aspirational response is one which the mobile, upward or downward, lower classes tend to adopt, such as seamen and entrepreneurs. It rejects the deferential view of inherited social position, endorsing the class system as 'open' in which dedication, hard work and endeavour can lead to movement up the social ladder (see Chapter 7 below for specific examples).

Respect and shame maintain the distribution of power, not only between classes, but between men and women. Upwardly mobile lower class men, who have the material means to aspire to and conform, to certain degrees, with the dominant ideology of self-sufficiency, individualism and nuclear conjugal households, are able to consolidate their position in the social hierarchy by flaunting their respect and protecting their women through confinement to the domestic domain. As such, lower class men are exploiting ideas about respect and shame, which, at this level, govern relations of power among *men*, to demonstrate their socio-economic status and aspiration to planter class meaning systems through oppression of their female partners.

Recent changes in production relations (as we saw in Chapter 3, and which is developed below in Chapter 7) have created wage labour opportunities for women. Furthermore, the increasing marginalisation of many lower class men as a result of the demise of the merchant shipping labour market, has meant that fewer men are able to fulfil their obligations of material support to non-resident female concubines and offspring. A woman living without a co-residential male partner or male household members able to offer the material and financial support necessary to maintain the household, will undertake some sort of extra-domestic work such as part-time or seasonal wage labour, and/or rely upon the material benefits of sexual relations with men with whom she has no stable or permanent conjugal relationship. According to dominant values she will be considered as having no respect and not exhibiting her sense of shame. This conflict between subordinate normative practices and the dominant ideology, expressed in the changing sexual division of labour, leads to social tension between those lower class households who are able, materially and symbolically, to demonstrate respect and shame, and those who are not. In other words, respect and shame, as ideology, display hegemonic characteristics which produce divisions and conflicts within and between the lower classes. Upwardly mobile members of the lower classes are able to aspire to dominant values and, in doing so, create a sense of failure and frustration amongst those with little or no access to material means.

However, few, if any, of the lower classes are able to break free of their material and symbolic dependence on the ex-planter class and foreign capital. Wage labour opportunities are limited and, by nature of their relationship to movements of international capital, are unstable and insecure. Similarly, lower class entrepreneurial activities are confined to small scale enterprises on the periphery of the tourist and real estate industries. The lower classes are unable to articulate their experiences of marginality and dependence because of the dominance of ex-planter ideology: the suppression of effective opposition to such dominance being directly related to lower class impoverishment of both the means of material production and the means of production of discourse. The inter-relationship between access to the means of production of discourse and subordinate class position is highlighted by plebeian systems of classification and evaluation of persons, which is considered in some detail in the following section.

Plebeian classificatory systems

A characteristic of all societies is the categorisation of individuals and groups according to their place in society and the wider world in relation to other individuals and groups. In Bequia this takes the form of a number of diverse and complex symbolic classificatory structures by which individuals regard themselves, and are viewed by others, as representatives of distinct categories of person.

Lower class Lower Bay people employ a trichotomous classificatory and evaluative system for categorising themselves and others according to their place within (i) the 'world', (ii) Bequia, and (iii) Lower Bay community.[4] The classificatory system highlights the way in which polarity and opposition find expression in the process of social categorisation, and draws attention to the relationship between ex-planter ideological dominance, through suppression of discourse, and lower class identity.

Place within the world

As a person in the world a Lower Bay individual is considered and categorised as the equal of all others in the community: reflecting a sense of community solidarity in relation to the world outside Lower Bay. Diagram 6a represents the classificatory hierarchy whereby persons are categorised according to their position in the world *vis-à-vis* Lower Bay. This hierarchy reflects the perceived position of Lower Bay in the international division of labour and, as such, is evaluative of socio-economic and cultural affinity shaped historically: the closer a category falls to Lower Bay folk the greater the perceived degree of affinity and the lesser the perception of opposition.

Residence, whether temporary or permanent, in a foreign country or other island settlement, does not negate a person's community identity: his/her claim to being a Lowbay person remains largely unaffected. Indeed, there are aspirations amongst many in the community towards living and working abroad (see below) considered to be one of the only avenues open for unemployed and under-employed persons to improve their life chances:

> It ain't mean dat as a Lowbay man, I done go lose any respeck by leaving de island. Nah, man, if de opportunity done come I got for be foolish not to take it. I always gonna be a Lowbay man wherever I done be living or working. De roots of dis tree is put down right here and dat where dey staying ...

Inherent in the classification of persons in the outside world is a notion of degree of similarity of historical experience, expressed in

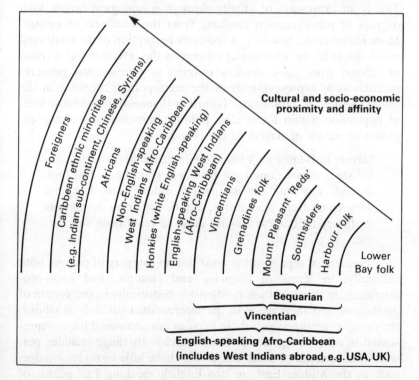

Diagram 6a Categories of person in the 'outside' world

terms of cultural origins, and reflecting local perceptions of others' relationships to the local and international system of production historically. Hence Africans, despite the current rise in black consciousness and 'back to Africa' ideologies (cf. Rastafarianism in many Afro-Caribbean societies) are considered socially and culturally distant to Lower Bay folk. The following statement is typical of lower class perception:

> We in Bequia is much closer to Bajans (Barbadians) and Trinidadians dan we is to Africans. True, we done come from Africa but dat long time pass. De black people in dese islands done experience things and things in de same way as we. We all done come through slavery and now we making life for we selve. Dis is why we is all more close to honkie (English-speaking Caucasians) cos all honkies done come from de English, and we is all more English dan we is African. You ain't want for listen to what dem foolish Rasta done tell you. Africa is pass, today we is Bequarian.

This is an expression of affinity through genealogical origin: high degrees of miscegenation resulting from the smallness of estates. More importantly, however, it indicates perception of the continued involvement of the ex-colonial powers in the international division of labour: from slave masters through to tourists and property speculators as representatives of the metropolitan economy in the island's system of production. It further demonstrates the low level of opposition within lower class political consciousness of the exploitative nature of slavery in the island:

> Slavery in Bequia ain't been like in dem other islands, nah. De slave owner done treat he slaves good here. Just look around: you ain't see we people widout land. Dis land done come from plantations, dey be gift from de masters in slavery time. Dese English done be reasonable and fair, true.

'Foreigners' represent the most distant category of person, both culturally, in terms of language and customs, and socio-economically, in terms of their relationship historically to the system of production and their place in the international division of labour, the category embracing all those persons not accounted for or represented in other categories in the hierarchy. Its range includes persons from societies of which Bequarians have little or no knowledge, such as the Middle East, to non-English speaking Europeans, of whom they have direct knowledge and experience as a result of tourism. In discussing French and Swedish tourists, one rum shop owner in the village told me:

> Dey ain't never gonna make it here in Bequia, speaking dem funny language and carrying demselve dat way ... Like all dem people from other country, dey have dey own way for living and it ain't nuttin for do wid we people at all ....

The extent to which notions of cultural affinity and origins mediate perceptions of outsiders' involvement in the system of production historically is reflected in the classification and evaluation of Caribbean ethnic minorities. In the case of sub-continent Indians who make up one of the largest ethnic minorities in the region (as a result of post-Emancipation indentureship, especially in St Vincent, Trinidad and Guyana) Bequarians demonstrate a degree of hostility and suspicion. Little reference is made to the common experience of sub-continent Asians as an exploited labour force: categorisation being strongly influenced by lower class evaluation of customs and language, although this is regularly qualified by reference to patterns of work amongst minorities:

> Man, I ain't know of one black person who ever done get near to an Indian. Dey for keeping demselve far apart from de rest of de world. Dere ain't no freedom wid dese peoples, dey making arrangements for who marry who, dey for having dey own place for pray, dey own kind of food ... And dey for making money ... dey all looking for dealin's and business. You ain't find a Indian working for National Bulk or Navius. Dey for staying where people for buy things offa dey.

In regard to categories of person designated as closer to Lower Bay folk it is notions of cultural affinity, common historical experience and, nearer the base of the hierarchy, residence, that determine the separation of categories.

The categorisation of 'outsiders' as depicted in Diagram 6a is, however, rarely as rigid as the hierarchy suggests. Each category is a generic term which can be and is subdivided and/or given hierarchical significance according to an individual's or group's knowledge and experience of the particular category of outsider. For example, some families in Lower Bay have strong kinship and/or network ties with individuals and groups in the Lower Grenadine islands and, in certain contexts, will display more affinity with such categories of person than with other Bequarians. This distinction is, however, contextual and specific to certain ideas about family, kinship and networks: most Lower Bay people showed an inherent sense of mistrust of people from the Lower Grenadines. As one woman told me when I suggested that I might go to the island of Canouan for a few days visit:

> You go straight to my mother sister house when you done get off de boat. You ain't want lissen to nuttin dem Canouan people done tell you. Dem people is worthless, dem a steal and cheat you if you ain't for cautious all de time.

Categorisation of persons in the outside world is, then, clearly contextually specific, based upon familiarity and knowledge of outsiders, and flexible to the changing reality of social relations and interaction. This is excellently illustrated by the particular terms of address that community members employed with regard to me. At first most of the children in Lower Bay referred to me as the 'honky' and older people as 'de English man'. Towards the end of my first period of fieldwork close respondents simply called me Neil or jokingly the 'white Rasta' and most others in the community referred to me as 'the red', the term for indigenous lower class Bequarian white people from Mount Pleasant.[5] During an argument between young men from Lower Bay and others from the harbour, towards the end of my second period of fieldwork, one Lower Bay man responding to the claim made by one of the harbour men that I was '... just a damned honky Englishman' stated:

> My man (i.e. me) a Bequarian now – he done move like a Bequia man, and de people of Lowbay done take he for being Bequarian. Sometimes it like he alway done live in Lowbay de way he just seem to fit in. Man, he closer to de people of Lowbay dan any of you damned harbour folk.

Categorisation in this case was clearly influenced by familiarity but was also contextually specific, a boundary-making tool: in situations where only Lower Bay people were present there was never any reference to my being a 'Lowbay man', the term being used in the above case to signify symbolically perceived differences between Lower Bay and other island settlements.

Despite this flexibility in the classificatory hierarchy it was, nevertheless, held by most of the lower classes in Lower Bay, as a symbolic scheme for establishing the place of a Lower Bay person in the wider world. Such a classificatory system is part of a specific type of discourse: in this case a 'way of talking' about the world in relation to the community of Lower Bay, drawing on a classification which constitutes the world according to proximity and affinity with the Lower Bay way of life. This allows lower class people in Lower Bay to communicate these ideas about the world with others whose experience and, consequently, whose way of constituting the world, is similar. Hence, in the case of the argument between Lower Bay men and harbour men, referred to above, during which I was categorised differently by the respective groups, the central focal points of reference for the two groups were at variance with each other: the groups were constituting their immediate worlds from different foci (Lower Bay and the harbour respectively). I would speculate that, in a different context, referring to a sphere outside the immediate locus of the two communities, the men, in similar class positions, would constitute the world in similar ways, adopting the classificatory system laid out in Diagram 6a, (p.181).

What is significant here is that systems of categorisation are far from being fully coherent: meaning in any classificatory system cannot be found in the isolated components that make up the categories, but in the way in which the constitutive categories are combined in the classificatory system. It is the relationships between the units in the system that is significant. In the system described here it is specifically the binary opposition between groups of related categories of person that allows insight into the underlying structure of symbolic thought (see Diagram 6b). The oppositions distinguish categories which stand for solidarity (+) in the context employed, and those which signify hierarchy and domination and therefore distance, avoidance and potential conflict (−). Applying these oppositions to the classificatory system highlights and provides details of the historical formulation of the system through suppression of discourses by dominant classes.

The fundamental binary opposition in the classification is based around perceptions of 'Englishness', i.e. categories of persons considered 'English' and 'not English'. This dichotomy illustrates the relationship between dominant and subordinated discourses. The way a Lower Bay plebeian 'talks' about being more English than African, for example indicates the suppression over time of lower class discourse: the reinterpretation of the experiences of lower class ancestors under slavery through subordination of their African heritage to that of the 'reasonable and fair English slave masters'. (The key to understanding the suppression of discourse and the ideological dominance of the ex-planter class lies in a variant form of the classificatory hierarchy described on pp.188−192).

The 'English' categories include all those persons in the hierar-

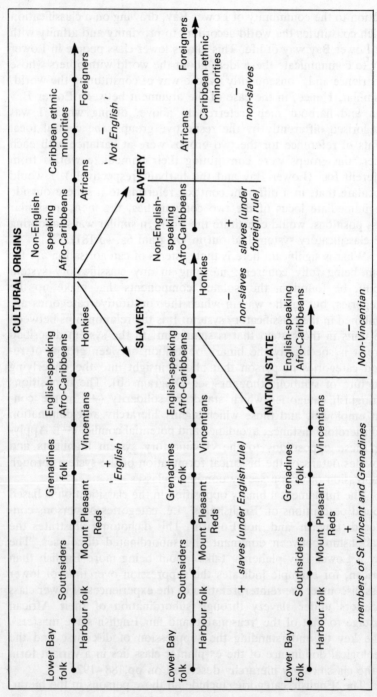

Diagram 6b Binary oppositions in the classification of persons in the 'outside' world

chy from Lower Bay to honky, and describes notions of cultural properness as well as affinity. In this sense 'honkies' refers to all white English-speaking Caucasians because 'dey all done come from de English'. The values, norms and ideologies contained in 'English', and hence planter, culture are seen as germane for lower class Lower Bay people. Consequently, 'Englishness' is a more significant category than, for example, 'West Indian', which includes people whose cultures lie outside the sphere of Englishness, such as French, Dutch and Spanish Afro-Caribbeans, or 'African', which refers to people on the continent of Africa, perceived as having no relationship with English culture.

A further opposition based on those who are seen to have experienced slavery and those who have not, excludes honkies who are categorised as non-slaves/masters. The remaining categories, structured hierarchically, constitute a classificatory system which revolves around experience of slavery under British colonial rule. Within the group of categories excluded under the concept of 'Englishness', the slave/non-slave dichotomy distinguishes those categories of person with experience of slavery under foreign rule, the non English-speaking Afro-Caribbeans, from all others.

The opposition between citizenship and non-citizenship (alien) of the state of St Vincent and the Grenadines constitutes a further dichotomy which effects exclusion of English-speaking Afro-Caribbeans from the classificatory system. The classification categories which remain, that of Lower Bay person ·······→ Vincentian, are then mutually exclusive, based on perceptions of nationality. As we have seen, there is a strong sense of nationalism pervading Bequia society, as being Bequarian, whereby Vincentians are perceived in negative terms. Expressions and convictions such as those below illustrate such negative perceptions:

> We people of Bequia ain't like dem Vincees, nah. We da work true, always looking to make we lives easier by trying some different kind of work. Dem Vincees especk too much of de government.
>
> Man, dey most lazy and cheating people in de world. You cannah trust a Vincee, nah.
>
> Dere two types of Vincentian. Country people and Kingstown people. And both of dem is worthless. Country people still living like from years ago, and Kingstown people are all thieves.
>
> A Vincee is a Vincee ... de government ain't doing nuttin for we people here on Bequia. People from St Vincent dey

is just de same. Dey ain't got no respeck when dey come to Bequia, and when we does go over dere dey especk we be grateful for de things dey do for we, but all de time dey hoping for some money from we ...

Such perception, however, does not preclude association with Vincentians within a conception of nation state: thus, a negative meaning remains meaningful for the agents employing the classification. Categorisation of persons within the state is dealt with in more detail below for it relates to perception of the position of a Lower Bay person in Bequia, but the reader's attention is drawn here to instances of existential acknowledgement by Bequia people of their association with St Vincent, e.g. in their voting behaviour they acknowledge citizenship, albeit in terms opposed to continued membership of the state.

The extent to which categorisation of person is derived from the ex-planter ideology through their control of the means of production of discourse is borne out in the contradiction between what plebeian Lower Bay people 'do' (actions) and the way they 'talk' of such actions (discourse). By classifying themselves as English, lower class people are forced, on the surface, to subscribe to the norms contained within the planter (dominant) value system in order to maintain their perceived status position within the classificatory hierarchy they employ for distinguishing themselves from the world outside. The discourse through which they 'talk' of their lives, constitute the world around them, and convey this meaning to others, is pervaded by the ideals and norms derived from the planter ideology. Clearly, the normative system of the lower classes is sharply at odds with the dominant value system through which they articulate their beliefs. Lower class living conditions, mating patterns, household form, leisure activities of men, etc., contradict the dominant moral framework. Lower class discourse is, therefore, an expression of a culture which is a negotiated form of the ex-planter ideology.

I gained valuable insight into this contradiction between expectations and norms in lower class culture, as a result of uncovering a variant form of the classificatory system locating persons in the world. When the concept 'pre-history', i.e. the world before slavery, is introduced to the classification, a number of categories shift in the hierarchy (see Diagram 6c). The key to my recognising this shift (categories restructured according to an alternative binary opposition) came initially in discussions about Rastafarianism. Although there are few practising Rastafarians in Bequia, the islanders are

Lower Bay lower class culture 189

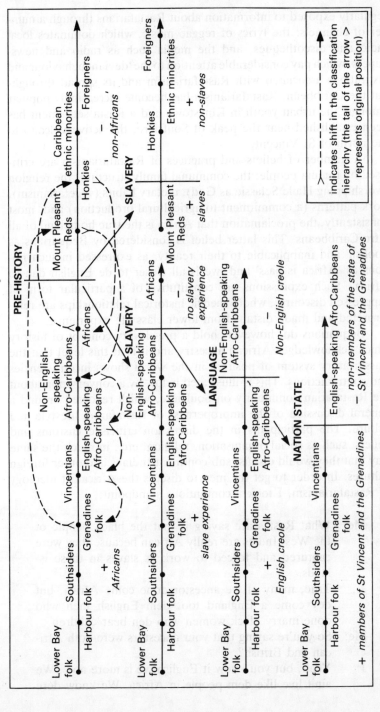

Diagram 6c The classification restructured

regularly exposed to information about Rastafarians through a number of channels: the lyrics of reggae music, which dominates local radio and discotheques, and the media such as radio and newspapers, which pay considerable attention to the 'deviant behaviour and institutions associated with Rastafarianism and its spread throughout the Caribbean. Rastafarianism has become increasingly popular amongst the urban youth in Kingstown and a Rasta settlement has been established near the peak of Soufrière, the active volcano to the north of St Vincent.

A number of beliefs and practices of Rastafarianism are criticised by Bequia people: the communal family structure, the religion (worshipping Haile Selassie as God), dietary habits (vegetarianism), work patterns (a commitment to agricultural production) and, most consistently, the proclamation that Africa is the true homeland of all Afro-Caribbeans. This latter belief is considered by Bequarians as 'foolish' and inapplicable to their reality, as expressed in such notions as 'Africa is pass' and 'we is all closer to de English dan to Africa'. Such expressions are constitutive of a particular form of suppressed discourse, where specific historical relationships are reinterpreted and made distant from lower class life experience.

Bequarians do, however, hold a pre-slavery concept of history which acknowledges African ancestry and it is at this level that the classificatory system of position in the world shows inconsistencies and contradictions. This is illustrated below by a conversation about the Rastafarian community on Soufrière, which revolved around a general discussion of the improperness of Rastafarian lifestyle and culture. The participants in the discussion criticised customs and beliefs, such as social organisation, religion, etc., in much the same way that they would dismiss sub-continent Indians and other foreign cultures. In order to get the men to discuss the Africanist ideology of Rastafarianism, I took a contentious standpoint:

Me: What Rastas are saying is that the black people of the West Indies are really African because they were captured and forced to work as slaves in these islands.

J: True, many of we ancestor done come Africa, but dey come a England too, dem English men who done marry black women who den bear children.

Me: So you're saying that your ancestors were both African and British?

J: Yeah, but you know it English we is more now. We ain't live like dem people in Africa. We know dere one God ... It take de English people who done bring we churches and school for show people dese thing.

Me: Okay, but Rastas are saying that, if the British hadn't gone to Africa to take slaves, your black ancestors would have had land and a way of life there.

P: Okay, man, we all done see dese things just like you saying. What J done say is just how it is today here in Bequia. We living a proper life wid respeck, like people like you from England. We is proud of what we is and we ain't for wanting no Rasta trying for change things. Man, we haf plenty problem wid dem old head who believing in jumbie (spirits) and all.

Me: Are you saying that obeah is wrong? Is it because it comes from Africa?

P: Look, man, I done know you ain't really for dem Rasta, so why you keep at dis Africa thing?

Me: I'm just trying to understand the difference between Rasta beliefs and those that you in Bequia have.

P: Man, you alway aksing endless question about de strangest of thing. Look, if we go back in time afore de English, den any man or woman in Bequia gonna tell you dat dere was Africans. We know slavery done take many black people outa Africa. We ain't ashame of dis thing. We done work and be holding we head high for generations ...

J: P right, man. You look at dem Mount Pleasant people, dey think cos dey red, dey better dan we. Dey ain't got no respeck trying for make we all think dey really English. Dey ain't esperience things de way we black people done ...

Applying the ideas and conceptions inherent in these expressions (and a number of others that I gathered which relate to concepts of pre-slavery history) to the classificatory system in Diagram 6b, p.186 a quite contrasting set of oppositions emerge which require a restructuring of the hierarchy. The opposition based around pre-history combines categories around notions of African and non-African (rather than English and non-English) and moves the categories 'Mount Pleasant reds' and 'honkies' to more distant positions in the hierarchy, excluded from 'African'. This is set out clearly in Diagram 6c, p.189, under 'Pre-history'. The opposition based around slavery then excludes Africans as not having experienced slavery under British colonial control, with 'language' becoming the crucial determinant, based around opposition between English and non-English creole. The classification breaks down under these oppositions to allow recognition of African origin within the state of St Vincent and the Grenadines: the hierarchy Lower Bay person -----> Vincentians having no place for recognition of Mount Pleasant people. This suggests that the classificatory system based around, at its central opposition 'Englishness' is the product of two, or possibly more, discourses, one of which, where Africanism is a crucial determinant, has been suppressed.

Suppression of discourse over time is further evident in relation to representation of French presence in the island since the eighteenth century (see Chapter 1). The Catholic church in Bequia, known locally as 'de French church', is the only recognition of French influence that I encountered: French missionaries worked in the Grenadines throughout the nineteenth century following settlement of French planters in St Vincent and other islands. One of the most powerful planter families in Bequia, the Lafayettes, were the first plantation owners on the island, yet neither they nor other Bequarians seem to recognise their French origin. Having adopted the mantle of 'Englishness' in language, customs, values, etc., the descendants of the Lafayettes, many of whom are lower class because of miscegenation, classify themselves and are classified by others as 'closer to de English'. I would postulate, in the absence of any detailed ethnographic material, that a classificatory system pertaining to pre-slavery history in which French planters were taken into account, would result in opposition based around 'being French' for those for example who carry the surname Lafayette.

Within the classificatory system of Lower Bay folk -----> Vicentians, a further classificatory system is employed which confers ideas about cultural worth and social standing, and reflects the changing reality of production relations in the region. This system is, in effect, an evaluation of persons within the wider category of nationality (as members of the state of St Vincent and the Grenadines) in terms of social relations of production, trade and work. The classification:

```
townsfolk ------> villagers/fishermen ------> country folk
```

is hierarchical, the directions of the arrows indicate decreasing worth and properness. To be 'from de country' or a 'country man' implies a crudeness or backwardness, and is a term commonly used to categorise Vincentians not from coastal villages or the capital, Kingstown (see Case 7a, p.215), but can be used to describe Bequarians who live on sloping hillsides away from immediate access to the sea, notably Mount Pleasant folk. It suggests a level of ignorance of worldly affairs, illiteracy and/or lacking in enterprise. Whilst people who live in towns, harbours or trading centres are often mistrusted, especially Kingstown people, there is, however, an inherent sense of achievement within this category. It is in the towns that 'proper' jobs and the associated status are to be found: clerks, businessmen, teachers, bankers, etc. in full time waged employment.

Lower Bay, within this classification, is seen as midway along the hierarchy (what Gudeman, 1976:65 terms 'a graduated scale of civilisation'). Lower Bay's economic relationship with the sea (fishing, seamanship and, recently, yachts-tourism) is the determining factor in this categorisation: rural communities (country people) dependent on the land are placed at the bottom of this hierarchy, urban populations, by nature of their patterns of work, are at the top. But this scale is more than an evaluation of levels of social advancement, or civilisation, it is based on ideas relating to the division of labour: cultural values associated with work and time use as we have seen.

Place within Bequia

One classification of persons within Bequia takes place along the hierarchy indicated above which locates persons along a scale of properness of production relations: urban (wage labour) -----> rural (backward agricultural work). Intrinsically linked with this classification is that according to settlement of residence, as set out in Chapter 2 above. All Bequarians hold an acute sense of membership of settlement or community which pervades their perceptions of others. Identity and association with groups and community in Bequia is complex. Gibson (1981) observes the tendency of people from Port Elizabeth and Hamilton ('harbour folk') to identify with one another in contexts relating to the people of Southside and Mount Pleasant. Similarly the inhabitants of Southside settlements exhibit a solidarity in relation to the remainder of the island. Lower Bay members, however, despite kinship and some wider network bonds with harbour and Southside folk, exhibit a distinct perception of their community which often excludes Bequarians from outside the community, including those who have entered through marriage, migration, etc.

Classification of Bequarians outside Lower Bay community according to properness (worth) and settlement of residence is along the hierarchy of Lower Bay persons -----> Mount Pleasant 'reds', such that Lower Bay persons perceive themselves as closer to harbour folk than to Southsiders, Mount Pleasant representing the most distant category. We have seen that cultural affinity and notions of common historical experience determine the hierarchy of categorisation (Diagram 6a, p.181), but in differentiation of affinity to Bequarians outside Lower Bay, production relations (work) evaluated according to worth and properness dominate perceptions of others.

Harbour folk, because of their similar experiences of slavery, resulting in far less miscegenation than in Southside, for example, and because of their involvement in merchant shipping, are seen by Lower Bay people as 'closer' than other Bequarians although such affinity is commonly expressed in negative terms. The predominance of National Bulk seamen, until recently at least, and families engaged, if somewhat marginally, in the tourist sector is the most common basis for criticism of the properness of harbour folk:

> Dem harbour men come back from sailing and ack like dey ready for buying up de whole of Bequia ... dey cannah wait for showing off dey new clothes and radios and spending money in de rum shop. It like dey ain't haf no respeck ...
>
> Dem young boys always hanging round honkies offa de yachts. Dey ain't got no shame for what dey'll do for American dollars.'

Whilst criticisms of harbour people tended to stem from their failure to comply with notions of respectability in terms of their use of time and thriftiness, Lower Bay folk emphasised a more deeprooted sense of separateness in relation to Southsiders, especially Paget Farm people. Evaluation of Southsiders, involving an implicit recognition of production relations such as non-involvement in wage labour (notably merchant shipping) and cultural origins (lighterskinned because of greater degrees of miscegenation during slavery), concentrated on 'worthlessness':

> Dem people of Southside is always causing trouble. Dey fighting and cussing and lying down drunk. An' thiefing is dey way of life.

Despite the suspicion and distrust shown by Lower Bay plebeians towards Southsiders, especially Paget Farm folk, it is towards Mount Pleasant that the greatest degree of hostility is shown in Bequia. The racist ideology of Mount Pleasant villagers, expressed through their non-integration in Bequia life has been largely responsible for the attitudes of distrust and emphasis on social avoidance accorded to Mount Pleasant folk by virtually all lower class Bequarians. Membership of the Seventh Day Adventist Church, which is essentially limited to the light-skinned members of planter families and to Mount Pleasant people,[6] is one of the many criteria upon which anti-sentiments for indigenous whites in Bequia is based, in Lower Bay as in the rest of the island's black communities. Ideas relating to work, however, are prominent in the conception of Mount Pleasant:

> Man, dey ain't for try help no-one outside dey village. You cannah aks a Mount Pleasant fisherman for nuttin but you see how quick dey come for help wid fix dey nets and thing. Dey think dey better dan we at everything ...
>
> And de way dey for make dollar – you cannah trust dem nah. De taxi price alway one or two dollar more dan you especk ... and dey shop selling clothes and thing real expensive. It alright for rip off de rich tourist, but ordinary Bequarian, dey should be more fair wid we ...

Ideas relating to Bequia's settlements/communities, and the sense of solidarity shown by Lower Bay plebeians, is a reflection of the changing reality of production relations which permeates notions of cultural properness and common historical experience.

Differentiation and categorisation of persons within Bequia society is complex and contextual. Two categories employed in specific situations to mark off differences between Bequia indigenes, and, in turn, to denote separation within community of residence, are skin colour and 'wealth', the latter embodying ideas relating to class identity.

(a) Skin colour:
Classification into categories of skin colour is based essentially on the dichotomy of 'dark' – 'clear', 'clear' referring to light skin colour. All Bequarians outside Mount Pleasant vary in skin colour from negro black to very light brown as a consequence of mis-

cegenation, but only rarely do people differentiate themselves according to skin colour in more explicit terms than dark or clear.[7] Black is rarely used in reference to skin colour, being held as a term of insult which, together with its derived expression 'nigger' denotes improper or worthless behaviour. Skin colour categorisation denotes far more than physical characteristics: as a legacy from slavery, skin colour reflects positions of power and influence, aside of course from Mount Pleasant people. Light-skinnedness is a valued characteristic, darkness is not. To be light-skinned or clear is considered an advantage in employment, social acceptance and status abroad, being linked to conceptions of the wider world where lightness of skin colour allows social mobility and denotes social status. Parents of light-skinned children, irrespective of their own skin colour, will strive to ensure that such children do not enter into conjugal unions with dark-skinned partners, as the following excerpt from a case study illustrates.

Darrel Jacobson is a 30-year-old black-skinned man from Hamilton, who has had regular employment with National Bulk Carriers. He attended school with many of the young men from Lower Bay and has remained a close member of their peer group. He spends much of his time ashore drinking and fishing with the younger men in Lower Bay. From 1979 he had been 'visiting' ('courting') the sister of one of his close peers in Lower Bay. In his own words he describes the attitude of the girl's mother towards him:

> Man, it ain't matter for she almost dark like me, nah. She still hold wid dis idea dat I ain't de right colour for go mixing wid she darter. Ever since we done get together she fixing for upset thing between we. I ain't even get in de garden afore she start cussing and shouting. It ain't easy for keep up dis relation when I can't for even get into de house cos of de mother. But dat how thing is in Bequia, dem crazy ole people thinking it everything for have clear skin. I man de same inside dis colour ...

(b) Wealth:
Like colour, differentiation of individuals according to their wealth is both descriptive and evaluative (see above p.172ff. for an elaboration of this theme). 'Being rich' and 'being poor' are evaluative terms that denote perceptions of a person's actions and properness: the position a person has in the division of labour thus is a crucial determinant of his/her identity.

Even though there is relative homogeneity in the distribution of economic resources and wealth in Lower Bay, compared with the harbour and Mount Pleasant, there exist (as Chapter 3 has shown) material differences between households based upon ownership of means of production (land and technology) and access to wage labour. Material wealth, with the exception of that of the planter class, is seen as the result of endeavour, good fortune or as an act of God or the spirits. The inverse applies to poverty, which is seen in terms of misfortune, or laziness, the latter being punishable by God for its association with the devil or bad spirits. Ownership of large tracts of ex-plantation lands which are under-exploited or divided solely for sale to outsiders (non-Bequarians) is considered unjust or exploitative, in terms of denying indigenous people the chance to own their own plots of land, and to be independent or self-sufficient.

Individuals do not differentiate themselves in class terms.[8] Instead, descriptive and evaluative notions of colour (dark/clear) and wealth (rich/poor) constitute a classificatory system, unlike that referring to cultural proximity, whereby Lower Bay individuals differentiate themselves both from other Bequarians and from each other.

Place within the Lower Bay community

Within the community, categorisation of people in terms of skin colour and wealth are operative together with a classificatory system based around kin/network and age/sex categories which defines membership of social groups according to relations of obligation and deference. The symbolic representation of divisions in the community can thus be seen to be directly related to, on one level, socio-economic position (although not expressed in class terms) and, on the other, to responsibilities between groups expressed in terms of status and properness.

Kin/network categories and age/sex categories have previously been discussed in some detail, and the responsibilities and obligations that such statuses require have been well-documented. However, although I have introduced the reader to some of the main terms of address used to denote kin relationships and age/sex differentiation, a fuller analysis of actual usage of such terminology and titles will throw light on the ways in which divisions in the community are symbolically represented and plebeian social practices are given value and existential recognition by the actors themselves.

Because of the comparative lack of precision in the patterning of kinship relations, terms familiar to Western societies are used in ways which differ from their accepted usage in such societies. *Kinship terms* are most frequently used in addressing persons of ascending generations: Mama, Papa, are the most common kinship terms in popular usage for they denote kinship relationships with the greatest degree of specificity in an imprecise pattern. Most other kinship terms, such as Grandma, Grandpa, Aunt (taunty) and Uncle, have ambivalent and contextually specific usages, which relate to community/place of residence as well as direct kin relationships.

Older persons in the community acquire titles and names which denote and reflect seniority and deference i.e. *terms of respect*. The term 'Mistress' together with the surname is employed in addressing the senior female member of any household, who must also have achieved adult status. If the woman stands in a socially recognised kin relationship to the addressor the correct term for that relationship is often employed, e.g. Nana Joan, Taunty Mary. A further exception to the normative use of 'Mistress' occurs when the relationship is one between two senior women, who use Christian names. The derived form of 'Mistress' is 'Miss', a term which does not contain the idea of marital status; it denotes a relationship of deference and respect but differs from Mistress in two ways:

(i) it can be used to denote the non-seniority of a woman in her household of residence; or
(ii) it can refer to personal affinity with a senior woman, achieved through physical proximity. For instance in households bordering each other, younger members often referred to the senior female in the next house as 'Miss'. The term also denotes close ties between households in which male members belong to the same network.

In addressing older men in the community 'Mister' was rarely used, being essentially a term of address defining 'outsiderness' amongst adult men. 'Uncle' and the Christian name does not denote a kin relationship but one of respect and deference, and refers to membership of the community. An adult Bequarian of either sex from outside the community, not part of the personal network of a Lowbay man, will address a man by the term 'Mister' followed by surname, whereas a child in the community, whether related by kinship or not, will call the same man 'Uncle' plus Christian name. This is a clear example of terminology reflecting status in terms of being a Lower Bay person.

The titles so far discussed are applied to persons standing in a specific relationship to the addressor: one of seniority and/or direct kinship, of ascending generations. A less specific title, in common use within the community and denoting seniority is 'old head'. It is an ambivalent term which, on the one hand, can be used to denote knowledge, wisdom and experience – i.e. a term of deference and respect – or it can mean quite the opposite: ignorance, traditionalism, out-dated ideas or resistance to change. Two brief examples serve to illustrate this ambivalence.

In enquiring about changes in fishing techniques I was told by one of the fishermen with whom I worked:

> You should aks one of dem old head – dey know how to fish. We young men ain't got skill or knowledge like dem ... dey know where to catch fish and when, just by checking on de moon and de sea, and dey ain't offen wrong.

A group of young men operating a 'sea taxi' service from Lower Bay to the harbour, during the tourist season were discussing ways of attracting more tourists to the village:

> People ain't gonna come to Lowbay when dem old head keep throwning rubbish on de beach and road. Tourist ain't wanna see it when dey holiday. But you can't tell dem old head nuttin, dey can't see what good for Bequia.

Surnames and nicknames are further classificatory devices and terms which refer to the position of a person in the community. Due to the low rate of legal marriage, the instability of conjugal unions and the practice of child shifting, a person may have a choice of up to four surnames: the matronym of his/her biological mother, the matronym of his/her social mother, the patronym of his/her biological father, or the patronym of the partner (husband or common law) of his/her mother.

Despite the availability of a number of surnames from which an individual may choose, the most commonly used is that of the biological mother, which is the one in which the child is normally registered. This is because, with most children born out of wedlock, motherhood is the only definite biological relationship. If a child lives with his/her social mother from birth, or prior to registration in the Registry, and continues to live there during childhood, it is normal practice for the social mother's surname to be taken, although, because of kin relationships between biological and social mothers, this is often the same. Whereas the patronym is rarely used it may be employed in certain contexts, according to the status of the 'father', especially if it involves invoking obligations with network members of the father, e.g. 'You ain't know my name Walters – my father's done plenty work for you ...'. Most individuals then, recognise two surnames, interchanging them according to their usefulness. The surname represents a means of classification of individuals according to descent, status and marital standing of parents, whether social, biological or through concubinage.

Christian names, because of the almost infinite possibilities, and the fact that they are rarely used unless preceded by a further classificatory term, or in official contexts like population censuses, birth certificates, passports and in dealings with state officials/employers, are not classificatory other than to give uniqueness to individuals. Duplication of Christian names amongst consociates[9] in the community is strictly avoided.

Nicknames, however, are classificatory and individuating devices within the community and amongst men they often take precedence over Christian names as terms of address; they define the individual as a member of the community. Almost every male member of the community is endowed with a nickname, usage being normatively controlled. With the exception of close network members residing outside the community, it is only between men of equivalent status within the community that nicknames are employed, unless they are nicknames signifying disrespect (see below). For persons born into the community, nicknames are often bestowed according to some personal quality which marks the person off within the eyes of the community; they are usually descriptive of

Table 6a: A selection of Lower Bay nicknames portraying personal qualities

Physical appearance	Eccentricity of behaviour	Prominent persons
Giant	Blazer (temper)	Sobers
Biggie	Jumbie ('spirit')	Joe Louis
Little Head	Prince (aloof)	Zulu
Little Man	Speedman	Kung (Fu)
Fat	Master	Cass (Clay)
Crab	Bookie (always reading)	Coco
Reds		
Gums		
Teeth		
Teddy Bear		

physical appearance, eccentricity of behaviour or, more recently, of similarities with prominent persons, such as cinema, folklore or sports personalities.

Members of age group networks often have nicknames that are familiarised versions of their Christian names. Usage of these familiar names is also limited to community members of equivalent status, although kin especially siblings and other kin of similar age, will use them affectionately. Examples of such 'familiarised' nicknames include: Mackie (Maxwell), Charlo (Charles), If (Clifton), Clydee (Clyde), and Sylvo (Sylvester). Nicknames which originate prior to, or during a boy's attachment to his first age peer group and over which he has little control, will stick with him for as long as he remains in the community.

Immigrants to the community will be ascribed nicknames denoting their 'outsiderness' unless they have previously established ties with the community. Their nicknames describe partial and incomplete membership in the community and tend to be defamatory or derived from surnames and, as such, are less individuating. Examples include: Wiley (from Williams), Jayman (from Jameson), T'iefman (for a man from Southside, denoting Lower Bay distrust and dislike of Southsiders), and Rasta. The latter referred to a man from Hamilton who had no Rastafarian beliefs but who, since migrating to Lower Bay village through marriage, had failed to participate fully in community life, such as fishing, boat racing, rum shop activities, Friendly Society, etc. The nickname served to describe the man's lack of 'community spirit' in a way that Lower Bay people perceived of Rastafarians.

Nicknames derived from some aspect of moral character are usually disrespectful and the result of perceived deviance from proper behaviour, such as cheating, sexual promiscuity, dishonesty, disrespect to others, failure to fulfil obligations, masturbation, homosexuality, etc. These do not replace the descriptive nicknames of early age, but tend to qualify them, being used as alternatives to the former when intended to 'put somebody in he place'. They thus reflect on the status/respect of the individual's household and close kin. The more explicit nicknames, referring to sexual deviance, can not be cited here as they include reference to incest, size of genitalia, etc. More easily described examples of disrespectful nicknames include: Busy (derived from 'busy bottom' and denoting sexual promiscuity in a particular woman), Claat (referring to blood clot/ menstruation and given to a man who apparently engaged in sexual intercourse with a menstruating woman – considered taboo in plebeian culture), Pot-head (a man whose greed and voracious appetite earned him the title, derived from the local term 'eat the pot' meaning take the remainder of the meal), Foot-man (who was always walking to other island settlements, considered improper for failing to 'mind he own affairs near to home'), and Moucham (Mouth champ – considered to talk too much).

Nicknames and 'distorted' kinship terms, e.g. Uncle plus Christian name, are not used to address the most powerful and aloof members of the community (the ex-planter families), which indicates the latters' non-membership of the plebeian community and reflects the 'social distance' adopted by such individuals (see Case 5d, p.155). Indeed, the use of nicknames, kinship titles and age-specific terminology is restricted to the lower classes, reflecting lower class perception of their distinct cultural identity. Lower class deviation from the prescribed kinship values contained in the dominant ideology of the ex-planter class, viz. that the nuclear family should be the central unit from which to describe and recognise kinship, is given effective recognition and institutionalisation in plebeian culture by using compound and distorted kinship terminology. 'Uncle Mel' is not a specific kinship title but denotes respect and deference together with membership of the plebeian community.

The use of nicknames, by evaluating people and events in plebeian terms of values, expresses a degree of autonomy from the ex-planter class and the wider island society. Ex-planter members of the community are excluded from the frame of reference circumscribed by nickname terminology, as are outsiders. Local knowledge is the basis upon which evaluation of an individual's behaviour and thoughts is conducted and through which nicknames develop, which, by definition, requires membership of and participation in plebeian life. Nicknames further reflect the acceptability of and widespread reliance on personal networks from which most outsiders and *all* dominant classes are excluded. Pitt-Rivers (1977:90) observes an analagous use of nicknames in a Spanish pueblo, where he regards the nickname as an institution for expressing the social and cultural distance of the plebeian community from the Spanish middle classes and the state.

Terms of address in lower class culture not only reflect divisions in the community based upon class, age, sex and kinship, but serve as instruments for asserting plebeian cultural separateness from the dominant classes. In this way, terminology allows insight into the 'two cultures' thesis: the lower classes employing linguistic terms used by the dominant classes and altering their meaning and context to fit the realities of their life situation.

Uncovering an authentic Lower Bay plebeian culture

This chapter has traced the processes through which ex-planter ideology dominates and subordinates the Lower Bay plebeian culture. Such dominance has taken place, and is maintained, through suppression of discourse associated with the ex-planter class position. Consequently the lower classes are unable to express or formulate their experiences of the world in terms distinct from, or in opposition to, those contained in the dominant ideology. The hegemonic processes through which such inculcation of ideology and suppression of discourse occur is not simply a dissemination downwards of a single world view. Hegemony, as ideological transmission is, as I stated at the outset of this chapter, complex and best recognised as:

> ... an ongoing and problematic historical process, conditioned by given structures inherited from the past ... in which diverse social practices and elements of consciousness are ordered in a fashion compatible with the perpetuation of existing relations of production. (Gray, 1976:5)

The suppression of plebeian discourse is essential for the maintenance of a social order in Bequia based upon inequality and hierarchical class relations. The hegemonic structuring of ideological consciousness and suppression of discourse transforms and incorporates subordinate values and meanings, so as to prevent the full working through of their implications for change. Many aspects of lower class behaviour and consciousness are reproduced as a 'negotiated version' of the dominant ideology.

The lower classes, because of their subordinate position materially, i.e. in the production process, and intellectually, through planter control of the means of production of discourse, adopt a conception which is not their own, but 'borrowed' from the dominant classes. This was well illustrated in plebeian pre-occupation with respect and shame and the structure of lower class classificatory systems. Lower class perceptions of the world and their life style is embryonic. Despite the verbal expression of values and ideas in terms of the hegemonic ideology, many lower class practices display elements of a distinct plebeian culture and class consciousness. The terms of the ex-planter class's social and cultural imagery were often reproduced by spokespersons from the lower classes, but co-existed with modes of conduct and belief sharply divergent from those of the ex-planter class, viz. household forms, mating patterns, sex roles, time use, leisure pursuits, and co-operation.

The deep-rooted social practices of solidarity and mutual aid, through networks, have not been eroded by the dominant values, and rhetoric, of self help and individualism. Because of marginality no lower class individual can feel confident enough of his/her material position to reject totally plebeian community based organisations. Consequently plebeian, solidaristic values and practices co-exist with aspirations expressed in the language of hegemonic individualism, leaving a certain ambivalence in the ideology of the lower classes.

This ambivalence is highlighted by the position of upwardly mobile lower classes, such as entrepreneurs and merchant seamen. These groups are able to aspire towards the dominant values of independence and self-sufficiency, reflected in the nuclear family structure of their households and their control over women. Such values, however, co-exist with the pursuit of recognition for worthfulness and respectability in plebeian networks and participation in plebeian community practices. The tensions that arise within the lower classes as a result of the flaunting of material and symbolic superiority by the upper sections of the lower classes has potential for change in social relations in Bequia (see Chapter 7 below). Nevertheless, the majority of the lower classes demonstrate a class pride and solidarity which was evident at the time of the St Vincent Grenadines by-election in 1980, which is documented in detail below.

Such solidarity adds further weight to the assertion that there exists a plebeian culture in Lower Bay, and, indeed, in the other Bequia settlements and communities, which is authentic but which can only be rendered intelligible with reference to the dominant ideology. Plebeian culture, under conditions of suppression, cannot be articulated from within by the lower classes because they are denied the necessary access to means of discourse. Consequently the aspirations and values and meanings of the lower classes are often expressed in the language they have adopted from the planter class; lower class institutions, modes of behaviour and conception being contained within a larger locus dominated by the hegemonic ex-planter class. Many of the expressed values of the lower class, such as individualism, are mediated by the world view of the planters and translated to the conditions of marginality and poverty experienced by the lower classes. The plebeian lower class culture, with its normatively controlled, yet apparently deviant, household and family form, its values and norms relating to work and time use, and its community based mutual support groups and networks, represents a *distinct culture* expressed in terms of 'excuses' for deviance from the ex-planter controlled ideology, which subsumes and suppresses it.

Notes

1 Abercrombie and Turner (1982:398) elaborate further on the relationship between the dominant ideology thesis and 'two cultures' thesis.
2 See Gudeman, 1976:79–80 for a comparative account of honour and shame in a Panamanian lower class community.
3 This man was responsible for the joinery and 'finishing' on the schooner 'Walter Pearl' built for Bob Dylan in 1979.
4 Gudeman (1976) observed a similar classificatory system in lower class Panama. His analysis proved enlightening for my understanding of Lower Bay plebeian classification, and my framework of analysis in this section owes much to his work.
5 The term 'red' originated when the first white indentured servants were introduced to Barbadian plantations. The exposure to the sun led black slaves to call the whites 'red legs', see Jill Sheppard, 1974 (and Chapter 3 above).
6 Recently some of the more prominent black families in and around the harbour have also joined the Seventh Day Adventist Church; Lower Bay has no Adventists.
7 'High brown' is a term sometimes used to refer to a skin colour between 'clear' and 'dark'.
8 The term 'class' in plebeian language refers to style and flamboyance and concerns physical appearance. An expression illustrating its plebeian usage:

> See my man, he ha' real class. See de way he carry heself an' de clothes he wear.

9 Geertz (1975) uses the term to refer to persons who share 'a community of time and space'.

CHAPTER 7
Tourism and real estate: forces of change in Lower Bay

The increasing dominance of foreign capital in the Bequia economy is characteristic of many of the Caribbean islands. The recent boom in long haul air travel from Europe and North America has been accompanied by rising numbers of tourist operators, property speculators, financiers and entrepreneurs in the region.

A few centres in the Caribbean have had well-established tourist industries for many decades, such as Montego Bay, Jamaica, Havana, Cuba, the Bahamas and Barbados. But since the mid 1950s tourism has become increasingly dominant in the economies of all the islands in the region. The larger islands, like Jamaica and Trinidad, have developed regionalised tourist economies: agriculture, manufacturing and other industries remaining the most significant economic activities at the national level. In the smaller islands, like Antigua, Montserrat, the US and British Virgin Islands, and the Cayman Islands, however, tourism and real estate are so paramount economically that they are virtually the only industries; and in Guadaloupe, Martinique, St Lucia and other islands, including St Vincent and the Grenadines tourism has recently replaced agricultural exports as the major earner of foreign exchange.

In Bequia, where agriculture has been of little economic significance outside domestic production since the nineteenth century, the consequences of tourism for economic and social relations, aspirations and perceptions have been far-reaching and diverse. It is with these effects, essentially upon the lower classes in Lower Bay, with which I am concerned here.

The rapid decline in merchant shipping wage labour opportunities in the late 1970s forced many lower class men back into work in the residual forms of production. Lower class activity on the periphery of the tourist/real estate sector reflects their inability to survive solely through production in the traditional sector and highlights their position of marginality and dependence. The complexity of the interrelationship between plebeian residence patterns, division of labour, social organisation and meaning systems under changing economic conditions is drawn out in this chapter, which uses extensive empirical material to articulate and consolidate the concerns that have been paramount thus far.

The State and tourism

Since the period 1958-1962 when the St Vincent government agreed to and encouraged the sale of large tracts of private and government owned land in Bequia and Union Island, the sale of the entire islands of Mustique and Petit St Vincent, and the leasing of all state-owned land in Canouan and Palm Island,[1] little attention has been given to maximising net returns from tourism and real estate. Furthermore, no effort has been made to ensure that returns from these foreign-owned industries are distributed in any way that corresponds with stated objectives regarding increased national income. Instead the emphasis has been on increasing gross returns through higher foreign exchange earnings and increasing the numbers of tourists and non-national residents.

In attracting foreign investment in real estate and tourism to the Grenadines, the St Vincent government has offered lucrative financial incentives to investors, notably the Pioneer Industries Ordinance and the Hotel Aids Ordinance. The latter allows duty-free importation of raw materials and equipment for any 'original investment' in hotels for a minimum period of ten years (in the case of Mustique this was extended to 35 years). Further incentives under the Hotel Aids Ordinance include exemption from the land tax, inheritance tax and capital levies; income tax holidays for hotel owners and their employees (ranging from ten to 35 years); and repatriation of profits.

The Pioneer Industries Ordinance provides duty-free importation of materials and equipment for new industries in the state (again for a minimum of ten years), plus exemption from all state taxes for a conditional period ranging from five to 35 years after which time reduced rates operate. In real estate Pioneer Status incentives are great and government control over the financial and policy-making concerns of the companies is minimal. When government encouragement for the sale of land was at its peak between 1958 and 1962, there was no state limit placed on the amount of land that could be purchased or leased.

All financial incentives include 'conditions of investment' clauses which require developers to undertake infrastructural development in the interest of tourism (see Bryden 1973:150, for instance) in exchange for exemption from taxes and customs duties. The conditions have varied between leases and contracts but all include the provision of roads and the settlement of all land leased or purchased. The state provides no services for real estate or tourist businesses, investors being responsible for the provision of fresh water, sewerage facilities, and all services including transportation, communication, other than telephones and electricity which are owned and operated by St Vincent companies, and supplies. The government does, however, guarantee water supplies to hotels and real estate companies in the event of shortages, a guarantee not extended to indigenes.

Encouragement for the permanent settlement of non-nationals in the state constituted a further incentive for investors by increased diversification of investment potential, allowing for adaptation of existing capital investment in the peripheral and service sectors to a more affluent clientele. But enforcement of the conditions attached to the leasing and selling of land to large companies has been minimal, especially with regard to infrastructural development; smaller plots of land sold to foreigners and indigenes during the 1950s and 1960s escaped government controls. In 1972, under the coalition government, legislature was passed whereby land of two acres or more sold to nationals and non-nationals had to be developed for business or commercial agriculture within two years of purchase. Lands of less than two acres, purchased for the construction of private dwellings, had to be 'settled' within two years. This included provision of water, sewerage facilities, electricity and a track to the main building on the land suitable for vehicles to pass. The Act covered all transactions prior to 1972, but by this time vast areas of Bequia had already been secured and in many cases conditions relating to land transactions which took place prior to the Act have not been enforced. Government policies towards the conditions stipulated in the legislature have been inconsistent. Whilst some foreign investors have been forced to terminate projects because of rigidly imposed conditions of settlement and development,[2] many have escaped controls. For example, a large tract of land sold in 1972 for the construction of a stone quarry in Mount Pleasant was still lying idle in 1981.

Effects of state policies felt locally

Reliance upon foreign skills and finance in tourism and real estate has meant that neither a strong nationally owned or controlled independent private sector nor a vigorous national entrepreneurial class has developed in the state, although in Bequia the ex-planter/merchant classes have maintained a degree of political-economic control over the new service and peripheral tourist industries and have benefited from Pioneer status and other incentives. For example, the Taylor family secured Pioneer status for their trucking and building supplies companies which they set up in the late 1960s, and imported vehicles and raw materials duty free. Just prior to the termination of their Pioneer status the company imported vast quantities of duty free Cuban cement, which, to the anger of many small businesses and householders in Bequia, was being sold in 1981 at the prices demanded in St Vincent, despite the lower costs to the Taylor family.

National and local dependence on foreign labour and capital has been manifested through a number of structural changes in Bequia society:

(i) Foreign ownership and control of major tourist enterprises and island businesses: much of the capital generated in the island has been exported (see Table 7a) leading to minimal capital reinvestment, thus inhibiting economic development.

(ii) The majority of employees in managerial, administrative and supervisory posts in hotels and real estate are non-nationals. After initial high levels of local male employment in construction, employment opportunities have declined rapidly and are subject to seasonality and demand. A high proportion of hotel and housing development employees are in unskilled jobs, and wages are minimal, because of lack of opportunities for waged work in other sectors of the economy. The salary differentials and the low proportion of indigenes in managerial and administrative posts means the proportion of the wage bill going to non-nationals is disporportionate to their representation in the employment structure of the tourist and housing sectors: a striking example of inequality that is created and maintained by foreign dominance.

(iii) Foreign ownership of, and demand for, land for holiday homes, hotels and businesses have caused land prices to soar: a $3\frac{1}{2}$ acre plot of flat and gently sloping land in Friendship which was sold to an American in 1969 for $8,000 EC ($3,100 US) was up for sale in 1981 for $25,000 US. This has meant that very few Bequarians can afford to purchase even the most marginal of land, and family land is being sold to foreigners, reducing access even through inheritance. Land speculation has had and continues to have the triple effect of preventing acquisition of land for public purposes, limiting wider ownership amongst lower

Table 7a: Tourist-oriented enterprises in Bequia (1981)

Type of enterprise	No. on Bequia	Ownership			No. of enterprises employing local labour				No. closed seasonally
		foreign	local	joint foreign & local	1–10	10–20	20+	expatriate in management	
Hotel	5	4	1	–	–	2	3	4	4
Guest house	3	–	3	–	1	2	–	–	–
Rented houses	27	8	19	–	N/A	N/A	N/A	N/A	–
Rented apartments[1]	14	4	9	1	N/A	N/A	N/A	N/A	–
Restaurants/Snack Bars	12	5	6	1	10	2	–	3	2
Souvenir/Clothes shops	10	4	6	–	10	–	–	2	–
Charter yachts[2]	15	14	–	1	3	–	–	14	U/A
Boat hire	3	1	2	–	2	–	–	1	U/A
Water sports	2	1	1	–	2	–	–	1	1
Retail shops catering essentially for tourists foreigners	4	1	2	1	4	–	–	2	–
Real estate/Property developers	2	2	–	–	2	–	2	–	2

'foreign' – does not include Vincentians with close ties in Bequia.
U/A = unavailable. N/A = not applicable
Data collected April 1980 – May 1981 based upon observation, interviews and reference to Dept. of Tourism

Tourism and real estate 211

Type of enterprise	Date of opening				No. under construction or in process of opening			
	pre-1960	1960-9	1970-9	1980s	Total	Foreign owned	Locally owned	Foreign and local joint action
Hotel	1	2	2	–	1	1	–	–
Guest house	1	1	1	–	3	–	1	2
Rented houses	–	U/A	U/A	6	2	–	2	–
Rented apartments[1]	–	U/A	U/A	2	8	–	6	2
Restaurants/ Snack Bars	–	2	6	4	1	–	–	1
Souvenir/ Clothes shops	–	2	8	–	–	–	–	–
Charter yachts[2]	–	3	9	3	N/A	N/A	N/A	N/A
Boat hire	–	–	2	1	2	–	2	–
Water sports	–	–	–	2	–	–	–	–
Retail shops catering essentially for tourists/ foreigners	–	1	3	–	3	1	1	1
Real estate/ Property developers	–	–	2	–	–	–	–	–

(1) Does not include resident non-nationals who rent their houses when not in Bequia. This figure also excludes locals who rent rooms.
(2) This is an underestimate as many yachts are based in Young Island, St Vincent but pick up their charterers in Bequia.

class Bequarians and displacing the best agricultural land to expatriates.

(iv) The state has accepted no responsibility for housing development for nationals, nor for infrastructural and utilities provision in the Grenadines. In accordance with the conditions of leasing and sale, investors are required to provide specified infrastructure, utilities and buildings, while essential services for nationals, such as roads, sewerage and water supplies are neglected and left to community-based 'self-help' projects or indigenous entrepreneurs.

The absence of any housing scheme for nationals in the Grenadines is compounded, not only by the emphasis placed on foreign investors and indigenous entrepreneurs, but also by the formal political structure of the state. In 1981 the Representative of the Grenadines held a seat on the Legislative Council but, because he was neither the Leader of the Opposition nor held a Cabinet position in the House of Assembly, where policy decisions are made, he had no voice in the day-to-day affairs of and policies relating to the Grenadines. Cabinet ministers, concerned with their own constituencies, have implemented housing, roads and water/sewerage projects in St Vincent, but they neglect the Grenadines until a crisis or election occurs (see below).

In an interview with a Housing Development Officer for St Vincent, in April 1981, I was informed that the emphasis on private housing development and other essential services and utilities in Bequia was necessary because of transportation costs. He estimated that 40 per cent of the cost of building a house in Bequia came from the transportation of materials from St Vincent; private building supplies and construction companies being exempt from many of the costs under the incentives schemes.

(v) Rising land prices in Bequia have been accompanied by inflation in foodstuffs, clothing, fishing equipment, building materials and other essential equipment, machinery and supplies. There has been little or no investment, either state or foreign, in traditional economic activities such as agriculture, fishing or small businesses and industries, aside from tourist oriented ones, which constitute the forms of production upon which the lower classes depend during periods of unemployment or under-employment.

This lack of capital investment is in line with the Caribbean Hotel Association directive:

> In the Caribbean in 1980, tourism is the largest GNP and, apart from the few countries with material resources, it is our largest export commodity ... We must seek to encourage development of our agricultural, farming and fishing activities but *remain opposed to the lifting of imported items that visitors have the right to expect* (Tony Mack, President of CHA, 1980, my emphasis).

The effects of state policies on social structure and lower class culture in Lower Bay is considered in the remainder of the chapter by focusing on stratification, employment patterns, and concludes with an analysis of the complex relationship between social and material change and lower class meaning systems.

Tourism in Lower Bay

Lower Bay is still very much on the periphery of the tourist industry in Bequia: hotels and guest houses are absent although a small number of houses for rental to tourists are available. A beach bar, built in 1975, has rooms to let, essentially catering for young 'drifter tourists' (Cohen, 1972:169)[3], and is popular amongst yachtspeople in search of live entertainment. Hawkers selling coral jewellery, coconuts, etc., are ever present on the beach during the tourist months; houses of absent seamen are offered for rent on a short-term basis; young men provide water taxi services in fishing boats; and local entrepreneurs have plans to build guesthouses. Men and women have found seasonal and temporary wage labour outside the community in hotels, expatriate houses, restaurants and charter yachts, and fishermen have secured new markets for their catches, to hotels, restaurants and yachts. The cumulative effects of these developments, set within the context of state policies, have been to increase stratification and polarisation within the community.

Stratification

Tourism and real estate development have led to increased stratification at community level, and have polarised interests as a result of conflicting perceptions of the role of foreign investment in the island. Attitudes to foreign commercial activity are ambivalent in Lower Bay. Tourism and its associated developments in real estate, services, and market and infrastructural growth, are seen by Bequarians as potentially capable of producing social and economic transformation: employment opportunities being the most commonly perceived benefits to be accrued locally. Sustained government and multinational propaganda channelled through the local media such as radio and newspapers, and the absence of any state intervention in social development, appear to be the forces behind much of the lower class belief in the value of tourism.

Most members of the community are, however, becoming increasingly aware of the exploitation inherent in the tourist and housing development industries and their failure to fulfil the promise of economic growth and expansion. Many of the lower classes are critical of the refusal of foreign investors to reinvest the capital generated through real estate and tourist enterprises in Bequia, recognising that most of the profits made in and around the island are to foreign business people:

> Dem rich honkies done take all dey money back home for make more. Before dey start for come back here a man could get $1.00 US for $1.75 EC. Now it nearly twice dat. And dey de only people de bank prepare for give loans to ... Dey ain't for give nuttin back to de island or de people of Bequia. It just de same as robbery ...

Such expressed anger is becoming common amongst the poorest members of the community and is compatible with the facts of the situation.

Conversations relating to foreign control over employment opportunities and grievances about joblessness were commonplace in rum shops during the tourist season. Resentment ran high and represented a publicly expressed perception of lack of government control over foreign business on the island. It is here that divisions in the community become clearer. The unemployed men and women of all ages (although most often expressed by the younger members) considered tourism to have an important role to play in the future development of the community and of Bequia as a whole, but were critical of foreign dominance in the industry. However, for the small numbers of individuals with sufficient resources to establish tourist-oriented businesses, such as rented houses, bars, etc., foreign ownership was not perceived critically. They considered foreign expertise as crucial for the development and planning of tourism and for generating continued interest by Americans and

Europeans in holidays and investments in the island. They saw those who were critical of expatriate entrepreneurs to be a threat to the potential for sustained economic growth.

Many disputes arose over conflicting ideas about the ways in which people in the community should present themselves towards not only expatriates but to tourists. Those in the community with investment in tourism were openly critical of their employees and neighbours for failing to recognise that the expectations of foreigners were different to those of Bequarians. The most common areas of criticism about employees concerned slowness of service, (in bars, as cleaners, etc.), failure to use terms like 'please', 'thank you', 'sir', and 'madam', and reluctance to give preference to tourists over locals. Case 7a, highlights many of these issues.

Case 7a A dispute between the owner of a tourist enterprise and one of his employees

C Smith was, during the first period of my fieldwork in 1980, living in a house owned by Simon Walters' (part owner of the 'Reef' bar) mother's sister who emigrated to the USA in the 1950s. The house had been left idle and was in a poor state of repair when C Smith separated from his wife in 1979. Simon, a long standing friend of C's, suggested that he move into the house. It was agreed between the two that C would do the necessary repairs and be responsible for the upkeep of the house in return for staying there rent free. (Simon had been given responsibility for the house by his aunt when she visited Bequia some years earlier but, because of commitments to the Reef, had found no time to renovate the building). When I returned to Bequia for my second field trip in 1981, the house was far more inhabitable than it had been for many years and as I was in need of accommodation, Simon and C suggested I move into the house and pay a nominal rent for a room of my own.

At the time C worked as a full time maintenance man in Spring Hotel and, during the peak tourist season, as cook in the Reef for nightly functions, like 'jump up' (fête). C had helped in the construction of the Reef in 1975 and continued to do limited building and repair work in the community since; his work on the Reef had earned him a reputation as a fine mason and carpenter.

One night in early February 1981, when the Reef was holding a large fête, featuring a local reggae and calypso band, attended by large numbers of tourists (mostly yacht people), C was cooking roast fish to order, when a number of tourists came and asked for six meals. At the time of asking, he was busy preparing food for a couple from Hamilton and explained to the tourists that they would have to wait. About ten minutes later they returned to ask where their fish was and he again emphasised that they would have to wait because he had only just finished cooking the locals' meals. Simon happened to be passing while this latter conversation was in progress and told C to hurry up with the people's food. When the tourists had gone, Simon rebuked C for not 'talking more correctly to English-speaking tourists'. A violent argument ensued which resulted in Simon sacking C on the spot, and getting one of the women from the bar to carry on with the cooking. The dispute continued over the next few days, both men criticising the other in rum shops and amongst friends and neighbours. Nothing was resolved and the pair maintained a 'pact of silence' between them until early March when Simon's aunt died in the USA and left the house where C and I lived to Simon. The day that Simon received the letter from her solicitors in the USA, he came to the house and, in a very abrupt manner, told C he must vacate the house immediately. As I was effectively C's guest in the house I also felt obliged to leave and found accommodation through Len Lafayette (see Case 5d, p.155). Simon's resentment of C's behaviour was so great that he informed Spring hotel that C had been stealing money and food from them, and from the Reef, and C was immediately sacked from Spring. I never found any evidence to ratify these claims of theft, and the police were never involved.

With no family in Bequia, nowhere to live, and no form of employment, C returned to St Vincent to look for work. In May, having been unsuccessful on the mainland, he returned to Lower Bay where he was given a room in the house owned by the mother of his former apprentice at Spring. He was offered some small repair jobs and hoped to be employed as mason in the construction of a guest house once the land had been cleared (see Case 7b, p.218).

At the time of my departure from Bequia the conflict between Simon and C had not been resolved and the pair maintained their relationship of distance from each other. Simon told me just before I left:

> He a worthless Vincentian, nuttin but a country man. Dey all de same. You done help dem, give dey work, house and all dey do is done rob you. If C done work on de guest house, I ain't even for lift a hand in building it.

This one short example illustrates the disfunctions and conflicts that can arise in a situation where economic relationships are changing far more rapidly than attitudes. Simon, whose family is relatively powerful in the village, saw tourism as his future security and was intolerant of anyone who failed to develop the same enthusiasm as he; but, more importantly, it demonstrates that those people most actively involved in tourism are also the most powerful economically and socially, the consequences of which, as in this example, can be far-reaching.

Furthermore, this particular case illustrates the underlying tensions with regard to monopoly over tourist enterprises. In a very competitive market, local élites endeavour to protect their tourist interests against both foreign capital and enterprising, opportunist, locals. Simon's reaction to this dispute may appear extreme, but in the context of foreign domination he was effectively demonstrating that he could maintain standards of service equal to foreign-owned restaurants and that he would tolerate neither improper behaviour from his employees nor lower class attempts to compete with him for local control over tourist business.

Land is by far the single most significant resource which, because of differential ownership and access, has caused increased stratification in the community, and polarisation between the lower classes dependent upon work in the traditional sector and the land-owning classes. Descendants of planters who own(ed) large tracts of former and peripheral plantation lands have increased their economic and political power in the community since the advent of tourism and real estate property development in Bequia. Land owners have found a demand for all land, including previously unmarketable land, from foreigners wishing to retire to Bequia and with the capital to invest in land clearance in the most inaccessible areas of the community. In the early 1970s an American built houses in the caves and on the cliffs at Moonhole, an inaccessible cove, southwest of Lower Bay. Len Lafayette owns much of the land at Belle's Point, which he inherited from his father, a prominent planter, in the 1940s. Despite the inaccessibility of the land and its steeply sloping, densely wooded nature, Lafayette has sold three large plots since the mid 1970s, which remain unsettled.[4] This land at Belle's Point has been available for many years, as Lafayette told me, at relatively low cost compared with the prices charged for land at Lower Bay Gutter in the 1960s and 1970s, but the costs of land clearance and provision of access infrastructure were prohibitive, despite the extreme land shortages in the village during the early 1960s. This highlights levels of inequality both locally and internationally; today the cost of land settlement is not the only prohibitive factor, the land prices alone prevent access for lower class Bequarians, while resident and non-resident non-nationals are purchasing large tracts for future development. Rising land prices have also led to further fragmentation of land as smallholder and single plot house owners sell part of their land for up to 40 times what they paid for their whole plots in the 1960s. The only members of the lower classes who have been able to accrue sufficient savings to buy land in the community since the early 1970s are regularly employed seamen, which the following brief case illustrates.

When Samuel Walters (see Case 4a, p.117) bought land in Lower Bay Gutter in 1964 from Gerald James he paid $180 EC for 5,000 sq. ft. In 1978 Samuel sold 3,000 sq. ft. of this land to a young recently married seaman from Lower Bay village for $3,200 EC. Samuel chose to sell the land because, as he said:

> Man, de prices so high for land now, I just lose my job wid Barbados Shipping, I just done hafi do it. My sons, dey complaining dat dey want for get de land when I done dead, but I gotta haf some way for living til de day come ...

Many other tracts of unsettled or under-utilised land are now being developed for building tourist accommodation and/or bars. Those with access to land are thus able to utilise it to maintain their positions of dominance at the expense of lower class Lower Bay people. Lafayette, the owner of land at Belle's Point, has recently completed a beach front holiday-let house (see Case 7d, p.233) and is currently constructing a second; three brothers, sons of Charles Walters, the seine owner who operates in Canouan, who purchased land from Powell in 1973, have built a beach bar and dance hall; and a retired teacher who inherited land in 1980 has recently started work on the construction of a guest house and bar in the village, a case which illustrates many of the issues that arise out of utilisation of land for tourist development and articulates theoretical concerns.

Case 7b Construction of a guest house in Lower Bay village (1981)

Stephen Walters is the 50-year-old grandson of the late Clifton William Walters, the owner of Diamond (Lower Bay) estate. Stephen's father owns a small provisions shop in the village, which his wife, Stephen's mother, runs with the help of Stephen's younger son and only daughter. Stephen uses the back of the shop as a small rum shop and for storage of his outboard motor. In 1952, Stephen, who had graduated from the Bequia primary school, went to St Vincent to take a one year teaching certificate. He taught in Bequia for four years until 1957, when he found employment aboard a locally owned inter-island trading schooner. In 1960 he gave up 'sailing' to work on the Bequia District Council (Roads and Works Department), became secretary for the Bequia Fisherman's Co-operative, and fished regularly in one of the seines. Following the collapse of the fishing co-operative, and what Stephen calls his 'realisation of the corruption in the District Council' and the low level of wages, he took up employment with National Bulk Carriers in 1968, with whom he worked until 1973. Since then he has lived off his rum shop and fishing, making regular trips to Canouan to fish with C. Walters, his father's brother.

Stephen is married with three co-resident sons and a daughter, between the ages of 14 and 20. A younger son lives with his wife's sister in Lower Bay Gutter, born in 1975, when as Stephen puts it:

> We was having a hard time wid money. I ain't working except de shop and fishing, and things weren't easy, so de wife sister she done take he, and he stay dere since ...

Stephen has turned to tourism as a result of the recent decline in fish stocks around Bequia, and competition from the 'Reef' limiting his rum shop trade:

> My only chance for get back de way I done live before things done change around here is for making dollar outa tourists.

This shift in economic activity illustrates the dominance of the CMP over the residual forms of economic activity: Stephen effectively shifting from petty-commodity and traditional entrepreneurial production into activity in the modern sector as a result of increased opportunities for making a living in the CMP. This transition was made possible because of his access to land that he inherited from his mother's sister who died in Grenada in 1979, land which he has decided to utilise for the construction of a guest house and a bar. Without sufficient capital for such an investment, Stephen applied in 1981 to the Caribbean Development Bank for a grant; his application was backed by a US businessman who regularly takes his vacation in Bequia.

In 1979, just after Stephen had inherited the land, the American, who had befriended Stephen on his previous holiday offered to put up some of the capital to finance the construction of the guest house in exchange for part ownership, and to act as financial guarantor in the application to CDB for a development grant. Such collaboration between foreign capitalists and local entrepreneurs is a reflection of the decline in indigenous, independent entrepreneurial activity: the dependence of local capital on foreign backing and political support.

Stephen, because of his previous position in the island and community hierarchy, strongly supports the role of foreign capital and expertise in the future of Bequia. He repeatedly pointed out to me the help and support that he and other small entrepreneurs had received from foreigners:

> Dis island ain't for make progress and thing without de help of foreign people. Dey come for help wid building road and school and it only fair dat dey make profit from dey business. You ain't especk people for do thing for nuttin. But I ain't for letting all de money leave Bequia and dis mean we need control in de Grenadines, just like Kid done stand for.

As we have seen in previous chapters, those Bequarians with a vested interest in tourism are strongly in favour of a dominant role for foreign capital and expertise in the island. Stephen's position in the system of production is one of small entrepreneur with access to residual forms of production, but he is unable to establish himself in the modern sector without financial and technical assistance. The support he has received from outsiders includes a retired British architect, who owns a small charter yacht business based in Bequia, who helped him draw up the building plans for his guest house and to locate a suitable site for a well.

Despite assistance from foreign bankers and resident nonnationals, Stephen's guest house project encountered problems which delayed its construction. When the land had been cleared and the well dug (by his sons and a few close friends) in January 1981, he attempted to attract local labour for the construction of the building. In line with recent changes in attitudes towards work, the young men in the community refused to work on the traditional basis of labour/debt, supplemented with rum and meals, and, as we saw in Chapter 4, demanded wages for their labour. After a long period during which Stephen tried to locate labour on a reciprocal basis by invoking previous labour debts and appealing to close kin and friends, he persuaded the men to accept a part wage/part payment-in-kind agreement for their labour.

> If I just wait around for de small amount of help I gonna get from me friend I ain't never gonna finish de building. But dose young men dey think I got plenty of dollar for pay dem. It just ain't true.

Land ownership has indirectly proved lucrative as a result of increased tourist activity in Bequia. During the peak period of hotel and housing construction, building companies, facing an acute shortage of sand and prohibited from taking sand from the beaches around the harbour, turned to Lower Bay and Hope Bay, the only beaches accessible by road for trucks. Two of the descendants of planters, Lafayette and Powell, own much of the land bordering the beach at Lower Bay, and during the sand shortages of the 1960s charged companies, according to the volume of sand they removed, for access to the beach across their land. This led to additional sand loss from the beach due to erosion, causing difficulties for local fishermen in launching their boats. As erosion continued during the 1970s and was exaggerated by Hurricane Allen in 1980 whole sections of the beach became impassable because of fallen trees. The fishermen moved their boats to more suitable launching areas along the beach, but the fishermen, like the owners of the beach bar, were critical of Powell and Lafayette:

> ... dey ain't think of the problem dey creating for de future of de village.

When the owners of the Reef gathered together a work force to clear the beach of trees, Powell threatened to call the police, accusing them of trespass and damage to her property. When I left the island in 1981 some of the sand had returned to the beach, but the area remained difficult to pass by foot and the dispute between locals and Powell remained unresolved.

As large land owners reap lucrative benefits from tourism and other foreign investment in Bequia, the landless and smallholders experience increasing problems of access to land for housing and domestic agricultural production. Inflated land prices mean the lower classes are unable to compete for scarce land. Household sizes amongst the lower classes have grown and young men and women, unable to leave their parental home, are dissatisfied and critical of government failure to control sales and prices of land.

Inequality within the community is consequently exaggerated by the nature of changing production relations, linked internationally to the tourist sector. Such inequality experienced by the impoverished lower classes has been a factor in the recent increased crime rates and tension between the powerful and the poorer members of the community, and between community members and tourists/ expatriates. Dissatisfaction and frustration at the increasingly marginal material position faced by many unemployed and underemployed individuals are often directed at those persons in the community who are gaining as a result of ownership or access to resources, sometimes overshadowing the exploitative role of foreign investors (for example, see Case 3g, p.97 and 7b, p.218). This increased conflict between rich and poor in the community is typical of the complexity of and ambivalence in attitudes towards tourism and land speculation by foreigners, and illustrates the contradictions within plebeian culture in Lower Bay today.

A further polarisation in the community which stems directly from increased tourist activity is what may be termed 'generational', between old and young. Young men engaged in tourist 'promotion', for example those operating the water taxi service and owners of bars/holiday homes, are critical of older peoples' attitudes towards the local environment. Despite a 'Keep Bequia Tidy' campaign by the government, many older people still dump their rubbish on the sides of the road or throw it out to sea. Those with an interest in attracting more tourists to the community regard such practices as 'ignorant' and typical of 'old heads' in the community who fail to recognise the value of aesthetic beauty to increased tourist activity in the community. These sorts of divisions within the community divert attention away from the role of tourists/expatriates in environmental issues. The dumping of waste from yachts and cruise liners increases the risk of infectious bacteria in the sea (such as staphylococcus); tourist ignorance about water conservation threatens island water supplies during the dry months; and inadequate or inappropriate sewerage in hotels and modern houses constitute a health hazard. In much the same way as polarisation between rich and poor diminishes lower class criticism of foreign land speculators and business people, so the criticisms of the older peoples' attitude towards the environment diminishes community criticism of pollution caused directly by foreign exploitation of natural resources and indifference to ecological concerns.

Stratification and polarisation within the community is further enhanced by access to employment: inequality being *created* by limited employment opportunities.

Employment structure and patterns of work

Forster's (1964) dichotomous classification of 'direct' and 'indirect' employment serves as a useful introduction to an analysis of the effects of tourism and expatriate housing on the employment structure of Lower Bay and highlights inequality created by foreign capital.

Direct employment refers to that form of employment in which the employee/practitioner comes into face-to-face contact with tourists/expatriates, and includes hotels and restaurant employment, as barmen/women, waitresses, entertainers (musicians, singers, etc.); servants in permanently resident non-nationals' houses, and tourist houses; shop sales assistants; and yacht crews. Many of these jobs have provided opportunities for women to work in wage labour for the first time in Bequia. These forms of employment, despite the low level of wages (women working as waitresses in hotels earned $5.00 EC [£0.80 sterling in 1981] for a 10 hour day), and the insecurity of the job due to seasonality and demand, are attractive to men and women from the lower classes because of the relatively good working conditions, indirect remunerations (trips), and the possibility of permanent associations with tourists/expatriates (see below on tourist patronage). 'Face-to-face' work within the tourist sector also includes entrepreneurial activities such as hawking, taxi driving, etc.

Indirect employment is that in which the worker performs 'backstage' (see Goffman, 1959) and incorporates customary as well as new forms of work that service or support the tourist and real estate industry without direct face-to-face contact between worker and foreigner. These include agriculture (e.g. sale of fruits to hotels, restaurants), fishing (supply of fish to hotels, yachts, restaurants, etc.), and 'backstage' wage labour employment in hotels, restaurants and expatriate/tourist houses (kitchen staff, chefs, cleaners, chambermaids, etc.). Increased demand for, and the provision of, new services — notably supplies, transport and communications — has stimulated employment openings, although many of the jobs are filled by the kin of the powerful classes in Bequia, the former landowner/merchant and entrepreneurs, who own and control many of these new services.

Some forms of indirect employment, such as food, alcohol and tobacco smuggling are illegal. Although these activities took place before the arrival of foreigners in Bequia they have recently proliferated and diversified in response to increased demand. Increased illegal activity has resulted in more rigid controls and policing: bars are regularly checked for liquor license validity, a small patrol boat checks Bequia waters for smugglers, and the police patrol the beaches, especially during the peak tourist season, looking for marijuana hawkers.

A third category of employment stimulated by foreign investment is what de Kadt (1979) calls investment related employment, referring to short term waged work in the construction of houses, hotels and tourist/public infrastructure, such as roads, hospitals, etc., and in services and supply outlets during such construction. The construction of the hotel at Spring illustrates this form of employment (see Chapter 2). Some men have been successful in securing full time work as maintenance staff following the boom in construction, but many are forced to rely on temporary contracts as painters, decorators, masons, carpenters, etc. with hotel/property developers or individual non-national residents. Some men in Lower Bay supplement their incomes with this sort of employment. For example, shipwrights unable to work because of inflation in boat building costs now work as carpenters and joiners when work is available.

Tourism and real estate, like other sectors of the capitalist mode of production dependent upon international capital, draw labour periodically from co-existent residual forms of production.[5] Few individuals in Lower Bay have secured full time, permanent and stable employment in this sector. Added to the seasonal and/or temporary nature of much employment, there is a high turnover of staff, especially in the face-to-face forms of tourist employment. In 1981 the rates of pay offered in most tourist establishments for bar work, waitressing, etc. was $5.00 EC (80p) a day which, when considered in the context of restaurant prices ($2.50 EC for a small beer) is an obvious source of dissatisfaction amongst workers. The power that employers have over their employees was illustrated in Case 7a, p.215. The fragile position of marginal men and women in the tourist sector is reflected in the high turnover of staff in tourist enterprises. Employers, secure in the knowledge that surplus labour from the lower classes is readily available, are quick to dismiss staff for 'being too familiar wid tourists', 'not showing respeck and manners', and for 'taking nah pride in dey job'. Staff in restaurants, hotels and domestic employment often express grievances about the subservient role they are expected to adopt in working with foreigners: 'Dey think we is still slaves?' A restaurant owner in the harbour told me that he needed three waitresses and one barman for the restaurant to run smoothly and that, between October 1980 and May 1981 he had employed six different waitresses and three barmen:

> You just can't keep staff ... I either having for sack dem cos dey ain't doing dey job proper, or dey up and leave cos dey ain't happy wid de work.

Workers' dissatisfaction with conditions of work within the tourist sector is becomingly increasingly common in Lower Bay. The extent of resignations (desertions) from wage labour posts is dependent upon the degree of viability that remains in the pre- and non-capitalist forms of production. For many lower class individuals peasant and petty-commodity production is insufficient to meet material needs and they are forced to tolerate the exploitative relationships inherent in tourist-related wage labour. Others, however, as already noted, reject symbolically as well as materially the customary work patterns in residual forms of production (see Cases 3g, p.97 and 7b, p.218) in favour of wage labour and other economic activities in the tourist sector. This contradiction needs further discussion.

Personal worth is dependent upon recognition by others of the appropriateness or properness of a particular work activity, measured by moral and material criteria. Following the rise of wage labour opportunities in merchant shipping and recent changes in production associated with tourism and real estate development, individuals and groups in Lower Bay have begun to challenge traditional practices and values relating to work. The rejection of reciprocal labour exchange and petty-commodity fishing and peasant production (as shown in Chapter 3) reflects changing attitudes towards non-salaried customary work patterns and an increasing acceptance by some of the lower classes of their position in the CMP and its logic.

Increased value is now placed on salaried and other tourist sector work, despite the perceived exploitation, because it enables the individual and household to exercise more control over time use and financial running of the domestic unit. This has been accompanied by a moving away from community based communal production: for, as one young man put it:

> ... you done get pay for what you do, and nobody aks for favour. Man, you work in Lower Bay for nuttin but sweat and rum.

Employment in the tourist/real estate sector allows for planning of time and expenditure, which is not possible in traditional work activities and further allows for a separation between time in work and time in leisure.

Employment opportunities for women in the tourist/expatriate housing sector have had significant cultural and structural effects in the plebeian community. Women now have the opportunity for part-time or seasonal wage labour. With the increased marginality of men following the economic demise of the mid-1970s women have made conscious efforts to become (at least partially) materially independent of men indicated by the rising number of matrifocal households. In the past, women had responded to male marginality in the system of production by emigration or migration to wage labour opportunities in and around the Caribbean, but the recent introduction of female occupations in the modern sector has challenged the traditional plebeian cultural ideas relating to the sexual division of labour locally. The confinement of 'women's work' to the domestic sphere, in the household and agriculture, meant that engagement in such activities was not given social or existential recognition as 'proper work' in Lower Bay culture. The same activities performed outside the domestic sphere such as maids in hotels and non-nationals' houses, in which a wage is received, are evaluated differently. Formerly such work would have been defined culturally as improper: a woman working outside the domestic sphere, albeit rare, would have been regarded as having no respect and failing to exhibit her sense of shame. Such sex specific cultural ideas regarding the sexual division of labour are still held by a number of people in the community, notably older members, ex-planters and amongst conjugal households in which the senior male is in wage labour employment, but are being radically questioned by younger men and women in the face of changing material conditions.

As work changes, economic necessity compels other adaptive changes, one of which has been in plebeian ideas and attitudes towards young men's participation in the informal sector of the expanding tourist industry, notably hawking and tourist patronage. Beach hawking is generally recognisd as improper for a number of reasons. This interview with a rum shop owner suggests why this is so:

> Some of dat craft work real good, you know, macramé and dose coral bracelets and all ... But all de time dey making problem for de tourists for buy things. Nah, dey done spend de whole day on de beach, even when dere ain't no person around. Dey ain't for even wanna work. If dey want sell things dey should done put dem in de shops, or de restaurants. Plenty people are gone see dem and dey wouldnah feel harrass like now ...

The involvement of young men in such activities is considered improper for a number of complex reasons, some of which have been discussed in Chapter 6. Responsibility to the community is the most consistently cited criticism of such young men. Refusal to recognise obligations to household and community, the incorrect use of time and space (for example imposition on the privacy of tourists), lack of involvement in community-based groups/institutions or in formal employment, and the illegality of some of the activities are individually and collectively considered as 'worthless': lacking in properness and likely to bring loss of respect to the young men, their households and the community. Whilst waged employment and 'respectful' entrepreneurial activities are recognised as viable, proper and necessary alternatives to work in the traditional sector such as hawking, contravenes plebeian cultural values. Forms of work in the tourist sector, in which lower class values and norms relating to proper person and community worth are displayed, are given local approval.

A group of three young men from the village started operating a water taxi service from Lower Bay beach to the harbour during the 1980–81 tourist season. They were all unemployed at the time, although they collectively owned a small tramil net which they set on days that the climatic conditions permitted. Their remittances from the catches were small, as one of them told me:

> Some days we can make maybe $10 EC each, but dat only when we take a lobster. Most days we ain't making enough for more dan a beer each. So we done get dis idea for start taking tourists back to de harbour, cos plenty of dey be aksing at de Reef for taxi and dey haf for wait an hour sometime for one to come. Simon (part owner of the Reef) done lend we he outboard cos he done reckon dat more people gone come to de Reef if dey know it easy for get back to de harbour. Now some days, after we done pay for de gas (petrol) we making $20 EC each ... (my brackets)

Many people in the community agreed that the taxi enterprise was a valuable contribution to the community by attracting visitors, but the most commonly expressed attitude was that the men maintained their sense of properness and community worth:

> You know dose guys doing alright, and I hope dey done carry on making dollar. Dey ain't like dem youths who done sit around de beach all day; dey know dat dey ain't for make dollar from tourist all de year, so dey keeping up wid de setting of dey net. It ain't easy for anyone a find work in Bequia and dey showing dat it possible for make money if you done really care. Man, dey even help wid de seine some morning after dey done bring in dey tramil.

Working in different co-existent modes and forms of production is considered enterprising and related explicitly to cultural ideas of 'proper person', time use, community identity and work. Such cases are regularly cited, especially by older men and women, in order to show their disapproval of beach hawking. A further tourist oriented activity which has led to conflict and disapproval in the community is tourist patronage.

Patronage

'Tourist patronage' is a phenomenon that has been on the increase in Lower Bay and other parts of the island, notably the harbour, since the early 1970s. It refers to a relationship between an indigene (usually lower class) and a foreigner (tourist or resident non-national, although it occurs far more with the former) in which the indigene offers a service, such as friendship, local information, entertainment, etc., in exchange for information about the tourist's native country, sexual favours, material rewards, such as meals, accommodation, etc., and, most importantly, the opportunity to leave Bequia. This is a fairly common feature of social life in many developing countries, but in Bequia, as I shall show below, tourist patronage has taken on a very specific function in lower class culture.

Patronage is varied in Bequia and can be broadly classified into dominant and non-dominant forms. The dominant form of tourist patronage involves youths and young men, essentially the unemployed who are disillusioned with and frustrated by life in Bequia. The non-dominant forms of patronage include women and older men in direct and indirect tourist employment, and small entrepreneurs who are able to accrue material and/or symbolic benefits from establishing personal relationships with foreigners.

In the dominant form of patronage, tourists represent to young men what Cohen (1971:224) terms '... a window to the wide world outside their small community'. Cohen is referring to the relationships between Arab youths and tourists in a Jewish-Arab Israeli city, the marginality (economically and culturally) of the youths being a major factor in their attempts to secure instrumental exchanges and 'friendships' with visiting Europeans and North Americans. Lower Bay youths, unable to secure employment aboard merchant shipping companies or opportunities for emigration, yet exposed daily to stories of 'far off places' from older men who have been, or remain, employed with international shipping companies, are eager for knowledge of North America and Europe. The most sought-after information pertains to employment prospects, educational opportunities and the music business. Not all tourists/expatriates are of equal interest or attraction to Lower Bay youths, the most popular foreigner being the young drifter, in Lower Bay for adventure and local 'culture'. Because of the relatively non-commercialised nature of the community, and the availability of cheap accommodation, Lower Bay is becoming increasingly popular with drifters who gather at the beach bar and the beach and go spear fishing and coral diving with local youths. The beach bar caters essentially for these tourists, providing cheap accommodation and meals, and playing reggae, North American and European popular music. It is at the beach bar or on the beach that Lower Bay youths make their initial contacts with drifter tourists, introductory conversations revolving around whether the tourists are looking for accommodation and information or assistance on the best areas for diving and fishing. In return, Lower Bay youths expect 'friendship' from which they ultimately hope to be offered the chance to accompany visitors back to their home country. Cohen (*op.cit.*) observed a similar practice in the city he studied, where white tourist girls represent opportunities, which are essentially symbolic, for Arab boys to escape from their bleak economic and social predicament by being offered air tickets to Sweden, Denmark or Canada from where most of the girls come. Tourist girls are also the main attraction for Lower Bay youths and young men as, in accepting the hospitality and company of the men, which is not shown by local girls because of cultural constraints, the foreign girls and women represent an opportunity for men to display their manliness and mettle, and a chance, albeit remote, for the men to visit a foreign country and, if possible, to settle there. Exchanging addresses when the girl leaves Bequia symbolises the perceived continuation of the relationship. The fact that very few men have actually emigrated through this means does not deter others from the idea of becoming sexually involved with white tourist women, for the fact that there have been cases of successful extension of the relationship leading to emigration is held as a justification for continuing the practice.

Lower class young men, with little hope of access to land until middle or old age, are frustrated by their continued dependence upon their parents for accommodation. As one such man, Ormond, (see Case 7c, p.230) expressed it:

> It just great for stay wid dem Italian people when dey renting house in de village. Man, you ain't for know de kind of problem I get from life in I parent home ...

With few wage labour opportunities, little or no fishing equipment or boats, dissatisfaction with customary forms of work and aspirations to travel through merchant shipping destroyed by the recent decline in demand for Bequia seamen, young men are disillusioned with life in Bequia and consider their situation as resolvable only through leaving the island with the help of non-nationals. Cohen (1971:232) notes a similar role for white girls in the Arab-Jewish community of his study:

> ... by the very fact that they derive from *outside the system* (they) perform an ameliorating role *within* the system: they provide these boys with a hope of escape from their situation, a strongly felt opportunity to flee from their present reality and to resolve miraculously their manifold problems. (my brackets, original emphasis).

The lack of successful cases of emigration from Lower Bay does not deter men from adhering to their beliefs in the possibility; continued attempts at securing a passage out of the island, via a white girl, can lead to disillusionment and frustration amongst some of the men which is often manifested in intra-household and intra-community conflict. The case below illustrates one young man's continued attempts at emigration by his relationships with tourists and highlights some of the disputes and tensions which such relationships can cause.

Case 7c   A Lower Bay youth's relationships with Italian drifter tourists

Patricia and Jonni, a young Italian couple in their early twenties, came to Bequia from Barbados in January 1979 as part of an 'island hopping' holiday. They are typical of many of the drifter tourists who visit Bequia, looking for adventure and local culture on as little money as possible. During their initial stay of three months they rented a house in Lower Bay belonging to an absent seaman which was rented out and maintained by his sister while he was away. During their stay in Bequia, Patricia and Jonni befriended a number of young men from the community, with whom they went fishing, diving, etc. and in return they provided meals and, occasionally, a place to stay for the young men.

Since their first visit they have returned to Bequia twice, both times staying in Lower Bay for much of their holiday. On both these latter visits they have been accompanied by a numbr of friends, to whom they have extolled the virtues and beauty of the island during their periods back in Italy. Ormond, an 18-year-old youth from the village, took on the role of 'client' on both these latter visits, being responsible for organising their fishing and diving trips and teaching them how to make coral jewellery. In return he was given a bed in the house they rented, free meals, drinks and cigarettes, and Italian T-shirts. On both of their visits, Ormond has formed sexual relationships with girls who have accompanied the couple. Ormond sees these relationships in expedient terms:

> If a girl done love you, she gonna do everything she can for get you to be near her. For dese Italian girls wid rich family, it possible dat dey gonna get enough money for give I a ticket to Europe ... Man, I just waiting ...

This 'waiting' and 'looking for love' has, however, led to a number of disputes and increased conflict and tension within the community. Arguments and fights have occurred between Ormond and other youths and young men in the community, whom he has accused of sleeping with the girls. On one occasion in 1981 Ormond was forbidden to stay in the house after he had invited some of his friends from the community to have a party while the Italians were at a 'jump up' in the harbour. He and one of the Italian women slept on the beach a number of times subsequently and were seen by fishermen in the early mornings, including his father.

Ormond's father later told me of the acute sense of embarrassment that his son's actions had caused him as, being the head of the household, he would be seen as responsible for his son's action:

> De way he done carry on is just worthless. He ain't got not respeck, and he making so I done lose my own respeck in de village ...

Ormond, in defending his actions, talked about the relief from the tensions and overcrowding in his household when he was able to stay with the Italians, about the relative value of 'good times' with tourists compared with fishing or looking for work and, above all, the possibilities of leaving Bequia:

> Dem girl done give I dey address in Italy, and tell I dat dey gone for look for job for I and try for send me de money for go and see dem. Man, I met an American guy last year who done tell me dat he gone bring me de money for ticket back wid he next time he come. Dese people are my friend, and I know one day I gone leave Bequia.

Youth involvement in the friendship/patronage relationships with drifter tourists is made possible by, and consolidated through, their recent involvement in the formal and informal tourist sector. Diagram 7a demonstrates the relationship between youth activity in tourism and patronage.

Increased interaction with tourists and expatriates through employment in the modern sector, the informal economy and patronage serves to diversify the life experiences of Bequia youths and symbolically to eI...ance their life changes, but brings them into conflict with older members of the community, owners and controllers of the tourist/housing companies and enterprises and, recently, the police.

In contrast to the youths, slightly older lower class men tend to seek friendship and patronage from more 'educated' and 'sincere' (folk expression) tourists, although a degree of compatability, such as musical interests, desire to 'explore', dive, fish, etc., between tourist and indigene is required for the relationship to be effective at an instrumental and personal level for both parties. These tourists tend to be older and less 'adventurous' than those befriended by youths, but the aims of such relationships are essentially the same: material returns and the possibility of escaping from Bequia, and, in the case of female tourists, sex, are expected.

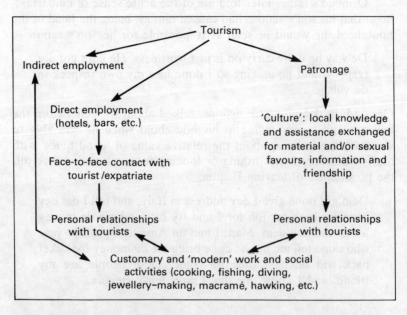

Diagram 7a Lower Bay youths' involvement in the tourist sector: work and patronage

Case 7d An American family's patron-client relationship with a Lower Bay man

Tom, an American lumber company director, and his wife, both in their late 30s, and their two children, have holidayed in Bequia every January for the past three years (1979–1981) renting the Lafayette tourist house in the village. Tom is an ex-college friend of an American woman who lived in Lower Bay for nine months in 1978–79, with a Lower Bay man, (S), having come to the island to work as a volunteer teacher. From his first visit Tom was befriended by S and a number of other young men. A patron-client relationship developed between one of S's friends, an unemployed man in his late 20s named Ch. Ch takes Tom (and sometimes his children and wife) out fishing in S's speed boat, on trips to nearby islands, runs them back and forth to the harbour for supplies, presents, etc., and generally looks after them. In exchange, Ch eats, drinks and smokes for nothing while they are in Bequia, makes some money on 'taxi-ing' and, most importantly, sees the friendship as providing an opportunity to get out of the island, repeatedly talking about working with Tom in upstate New York on the lumber team. Tom, although sensitive to Ch's feelings, told me in confidence that there was no way that Ch could work with his team of cutters as 'they'd eat him for breakfast, being a nigger just wouldn't go down up there ...' But the relationship continues, in a sort of commensalism: Tom gets a good holiday and his family feels they are being accepted by the locals, while Ch gets a break from subsistence and work-searching by living free during their holiday and lives in the hope that next time they come they will take him back with them.

Young men in such patron-client relationships justify their involvement with tourists in terms of the inadequacy of Bequia as it is to provide them with a reasonable standard of living, reflecting Lower Bay lower class youth and young men's increased awareness of their marginality and dependence. The lack of opportunities for self-improvement was repeatedly stressed by young men discussing their patron-friendship relationships with tourists or expatriates. The possibility of achieving an education in North America or Europe was, along with employment, the major aspiration for Lower Bay men, as Ch (above) said:

> De only way outa Bequia dese days is wid de help of some foreigner who done care about de situation. Plenty of people who done come to Lower Bay say dey gonna try for help we get to school or work in dem big country ... You think I want for stay here rest of I life?

Another essential difference between the more mature young men's relationships with foreigners and those of the youths in the community is the former's quest for information and skills that might improve their life chances in Bequia. The sorts of information and skills included clerical work and book-keeping, the law relating to small businesses and property, architectural and construction information, and the music scene in the USA and Europe.

As I have pointed out, it is not only youths and young men who are involved in tourist patronage in Lower Bay. Within the non-dominant forms of patronage older men, tourist entrepreneurs, women in tourist employment and taxi drivers are amongst the indigenous people who benefit from establishing personal relationships with tourists and expatriates. Entrepreneurs setting up tourist businesses look to expatriates and tourists for information and/or financial assistance (see Case 7b, p.218). Taxi drivers tend to establish close relationships with resident non-nationals and regular visitors to the island, gaining a virtual monopoly of service from particular individuals. One taxi driver from Mount Pleasant, for example, always took Tom and his family (see Case 7d, p.233) when they required a taxi. Taxi drivers express no desire to leave Bequia with the assistance of foreigners, but expect returns like drinks, meals, sex, etc., and value the opportunity for a stable, albeit temporary, source of income from a guaranteed clientele.

Women, by virtue of their place within the 'direct' employment sphere of the tourist/expatriate housing economy have been successful in forming patronage and friendship relationships with foreigners. One such woman, the mother of a deaf child, established a close relationship with a Canadian ENT specialist who regularly holidays in Bequia and owns a holiday home in Spring. During the periods she worked for him she ate at the house and did her laundry there, for 'he done haf no problem wid water, him only using de house a few weeks of de year'). After returning to Canada from a holiday in 1980, the doctor was able to raise money through a Third World charity to fly the woman and her child to Canada, where the child underwent surgery and was fitted with a hearing aid which partially restored her hearing. While there, the woman stayed at the doctor's house and was required to make no contribution to her's or the child's living expenses. This was an exceptional case: for many in the community successful manipulation of patrons to this degree is little more than a day dream or a euphoric fantasy.

Few women achieve such a return from relationhips with foreigners, but nevertheless value the material and social rewards, such as gratuities, free meals, access to utilities and scarce resources, etc., that are made possible through such relationships. As with youths and young men the unlikelihood of being able to secure an air ticket to North America or Europe does not deter women from holding on to the belief that one day they will succeed in leaving Bequia.

Conflicting perceptions within the lower classes of the role of the state in tourism and associated industries, like housing, came to the fore during the by-election of 1980, in which the central political issue was that of local control of foreign investment.

The St Vincent Grenadines by-election of 1980: the issue of local control over foreign investment in Bequia

The by-election for the St Vincent Grenadines seat held on 23 June 1980 (see Appendix IV for events leading to the need for a by-election) illustrates many aspects of the relationship between government-supported foreign investment and commercial activity, and changes in lower class social relationships and attitudes towards the economic transformations that have accompanied such activity.

'Kid' Andrews, who represented the New Democratic Party (NDP) in the by-election, stood on a secessionist platform: calling for the independence of the St Vincent Grenadines. The only other candidate was from the ruling St Vincent Labour Party which was strongly opposed to any form of secession or self-determination for the Grenadines.

In Lower Bay, where political affiliations have been divided between the St Vincent Labour Party and Andrews (in whatever party he has stood) since the 1960s the issue of secession became a pre-by-election concern of many groups and individuals. Most unemployed men and women adopted a very pro-secessionist stance, on the basis that the St Vincent government and foreign capitalists were appropriating much of the capital generated by tourism and real estate development without Bequarians receiving a 'fair deal'. The most prominent concerns of these people, supported by some older fishermen, women and entrepreneurs, like Stephen and Simon Walters, were:

(i) employment going to non-nationals in key administrative and managerial positions, and to the 'beard and bikini brigade'[6] on charter yachts;
(ii) failure to control transfer of capital abroad;

(iii) land monopolisation and associated land price increases effectively excluding all but the wealthier Bequarians from access to productive or 'household' land;
(iv) inadequate government concern for the development of Bequia, specifically infrastructure and services such as roads, health and education, despite the flow of taxes to the state;
(v) insufficient credit or training facilities for local entrepreneurs and fishermen;
(vi) the high cost of importing raw materials, via St Vincent, and the abuse of Pioneer Status by powerful groups in Bequia.

Implicit in all these concerns was the virtual absence of any effective means, channels or structures for self-determination by people in Bequia. In looking at attitudes and responses to secession amongst the Lower Bay electorate the role of tourism and property development in the Bequia economy, whilst being the major issue, was not the only one. Other issues which arose, and which are discussed in the context of conflicting interests, are merchant shipping employment, markets and prices for local products and the future of traditional economic activities. As such, the by-election provided illuminating insight into the nature of class interests in Lower Bay.

Attitudes towards secession amongst the Lower Bay electorate can be broadly classified as class specific. The relatively small opposition to the movement came essentially from those with a perceived vested interest in Bequia remaining a member of the state of St Vincent and the Grenadines. Regular seamen and their families feared that a Grenadines administration would be unable to maintain the limited employment that US merchant shipping companies offered to Bequia men. Their fears represent an accurate perception of the situation based on local and national politics. The main agents for US companies operating in and drawing labour from the region were prominent politicians and businessmen in Kingstown.

Seine owners also expressed reluctance towards a separate Grenadines administration. There was a certain amount of disparity in the ways in which seine owners formulated their arguments towards the continued existence of the state (as Case 7e, p.237 illustrates) but they predominantly focused upon markets and poaching as the major problems for an independent Grenadines:

Man, you know how dem French boats from Martinique

done take much of de fish from around Bequia. Now dat St Vincent done get dat patrol boat offa Britain, dey at least trying for make sure dat de other Grenadines ain't fished out by foreign boats. De Grenadines ain't gonna be able for afford things like patrol boat if dey on dey own economy ...

... dere always bin problem for Bequia fishermen a finding somewhere for sell dey catches. Years pass we done have to sail to St Vincent and some of de Mount Pleasant men done go as far as Grenada for find a sale at good price. Now it easier cos de government done give de French traders in Canouan and Union help for build air strips and cooling machines. Dem people (the French) done be happy de way things is for dem down dere – dey ain't paying much tax and dere ain't no problem a find fish and fly it out. Man, we done know dat Andrews looking for tax dese people and if dey go we just gonna hafi rely on dem small sloops a carry fish up to Martinique, cos de people of Bequia ain't gonna be able for afford planes and things ...

The contradiction within this sort of perception are obvious and fairly representative of this class in Bequia, who fear a loss of political power in an independent Grenadines, where their alliance with foreign capital may be made weaker should there be any tightening of the laws governing investment, land fragmentation and pricing, and Pioneer Status. Despite the NDP's pro-foreign capital stance, ex-planters felt their position was secure within the present political economy.

Whilst the perception of the situation by the seamen and their families reflected the reality of the employment structure in merchant shipping, the resistance by seine owners to the proposed changes in the political structure of Bequia were contradictory and ambivalent, reflecting their position of power in the island under state control from Kingstown. The following case illustrates the ambivalence of seine owners towards secession and highlights the position of other classes.

Case 7e A pre-by-election argument in a rum shop

This case is an excerpt from an argument that arose in the 'Reef' on the evening before the by-election. All the men involved are known to the reader, with the exception of Justin, a 52-year-old fisherman whose livelihood depends almost solely upon work in the traditional economy through a range of fishing activities.

Simon: Man, you know we done need tourist, and dis government ain't doing nuttin for encourage tourism in de island. If we was providing service for yachts de harbour gonna be full of yacht all year. We should be looking for setting up proper laundry services, having water for sell to de yachts ... It de future of Bequia we talking on here y'know.

Stephen: True, I ain't see no other way for getting job and money in de island widout tourist. Andrews, he done know dis and he gonna make sure dat de tourist dollar done stay in Bequia instead of in de hand of Vincee politicians.

Charles: Man, you canna see dat it gonna lead to enless
(Walters) problems if de Grenadines is on dey own? Everything gonna cost more, we gonna hafi pay more tax cos dese islands real small. We ain't haf no factory, no bananas for export, no real big hotel ... We just gonna end up for worse off dan now ... How we gonna stop poaching of fish? It hard now and we got police boat for check on dem Martinique and American trawlers.

Simon: Oh, Charlo, man! You ain't believe dem things? You done know dat Cato for let de American tuna boats into de Grenadines, just like for a few dollar he ain't even notice de Martinique boats. And what we gonna need factory or banana for when we got plenty fish and tourist spending money?

Charles: What you gonna do for exporting fish widout St Vincent for help?

Justin: Come on, what you saying? You know it de French in Union and Canouan who done control de trade now, in all de islands except Bequia. Here it nearly all for belong to Prince, wid he boats. You think he paying taxes on all de fish he export? Nah! He friend of Taylor and dat mean plenty extra dollar for he. What we want is a fair way of selling fish at fair prices. And dat only gonna happen if we get rid of dem f——in' Vincees.

Charles: I ain't for see where you coming from Justin. De government done fix de fish price. Dey ain't nuttin for do wid what Martinique paying de traders.

Justin: Yeah, but you think it fair dat we paid $2.00 EC a pound here in Bequia and Prince and dem sellin' for $7–8 EC in Martinique?

Charles: But you ain't gonna stop things like dat – by splitting off from St Vincent. People always looking for make extra dollar. And what gonna happen if we done split? Bequia gonna become de capital of de Grenadines and soon de people of Union and Canouan calling for independence ...

Monty: Man, we is independent already in de Grenadines. It ain't for make no difference wedder we vote for it or not. Look at de roads, and de police station, and de hospital ... de government ain't do nuttin to de island essept just afore de elections. Dat independence! And I ain't for gif a f—— if we done have it through a by-election cos it ain't for make no difference.

Stephen: Yeah, but just cos de government not doing anything for Bequia ain't mean we ain't for be better widout dem. Dey taking de taxes from seamen and yacht and all ... and giving back nuttin!

Simon: Stephen right, y'know. De government looking for we dollar but not for spend in de Grenadines. Dey letting de rich honky dollar speak louder dan de Grenadines people. Look at Spring. You know why we ain't got food for all de island growing up dere? Cos de honky want de place for look pretty and unspoil – so dey pay Cato and he people and dey leave it like a jungle. So dey can go home in America and Europe and tell dey friend how pretty Bequia look, and how cheap it is for dem to buy land here.

Richard: (taxi-driver) Simon right. We should nah hafi line up and fight at de market for get food when all dat plantation land real good for grow vegetable. I say if de government ain't for heeding what

Andrews saying den we just gotta look after weselves, by force if dat what necessary.

This excerpt draws out many of the issues around which the community became polarised over the by-election central issues of secession. The conservative nature of seine owner opposition is excellently illustrated by C. Walters' stance: he considered his position of privilege and dominance within the traditional sector of production to be secure under the administration of the St Vincent Labour Party. His opposition was consequently based upon how secession would affect *other* classes in Bequia, effectively appealing to the lower classes and new entrepreneurs to continue to support membership of the state of St Vincent for their own interests.

Monty's apathetic attitude (We is independent anyway and voting ain't for change a thing') is typical of many of the youths and young men who, although opposed to foreign dominance in the islands and the continued under-development that results from ruling class alliance with international capital, felt that formal secession would be ineffective in providing an adequate means of livelihood for the majority of the lower class population. Youth's preoccupation with escaping from the materially marginal situation through the patronage system is a direct result of the growth of tourism. In this respect, tourism in Bequia has become a force rendering this section of the population less likely to seek solutions to their frustration through political action. Instead they fantasise about tourists who, as such, represent a politically conservative force.

The responses of small entrepreneurs (what I have termed the traditional petty bourgeoisie in Chapter 3 above) to secession is a reflection of the ideology of this class which has, at the economic level, characteristics of both ex-planter and lower classes. It demonstrates anti-capitalist ideals in a status quo fashion: against the rich and powerful foreign capitalist and local ex-planter class but strongly in favour of private property ownership. It makes, as typified by Richard in Case 7e, above, sharp demands against monopolies since its existence is threatened by monopolisation of land and markets. The class calls for change, without the political-economic base changing, exemplified in ideas about 'fair competition' and a share in the distribution of power (e.g. land distribution, guaranteed markets, reduced import charges for small enterprises, etc.). Small entrepreneurs demonstrated aspiration to becoming richer and more influential by upward individual movement through bettering themselves within the existing structure: effectively calling for a replacement of the ex-planter and foreign capitalist classes by the entrepreneurial petty bourgeois class.

Around the call for secession the traditional petty bourgeoisie aligned itself strongly with the majority of the other lower classes. This was noticeable over the issue of the sustained underdevelopment of fertile former plantation lands to the north of the island. Attitudes expressed towards the lack of infrastructural and agricultural development in and around Spring accurately reflect the exploitative role of hotel and real estate companies in Bequia. The reluctance of these multi-nationals to engage in or give support to any proliferation of industry or agriculture on the lands they acquired during the 1960s is, as Simon and Richard above pointed out, intended to maintain the wild, rural image of this part of the island so as to attract further non-nationals to purchase land and houses on the forested hillsides. Brochures directed towards tourists and prospective holiday home buyers glorify the unspoilt scenery:

... Bequia may seem like a step into the past ...
... unspoiled natural beauty above and below the water
... a combination of sloth and flamboyance characterises
Bequia ...

Bequarians are resentful of outsiders' and resident foreigners' description of the island as 'primitive' and 'quaint', as I realised early on in my fieldwork (see Case 2a, p. 34). In the context of perceived exploitation, dependence and inequality, tourist and real estate brochures and other mass media advertisments which celebrate the lack of development and change on the island are bitterly criticised. The by-election, which was easily won by the NDP, served to bring the majority of the lower classes together in a stance against foreign dominance and governmental neglect which they recognised as responsible for their increasing marginalisation and impoverishment.

To conclude this chapter I provide a concise analysis of the influence of tourism and real estate development on selected aspects of plebeian ideology and work patterns. I concentrate on the response of the most disadvantaged of the lower classes to recent changes in production and ownership patterns, to show the adaptability of lower classes in conditions of economic deprivation.

Making sense of foreign domination: meaning in plebeian culture

Tourism and real estate development heralded an initial promise of employment, housing, welfare and infrastructural growth, which was welcomed by the bulk of the population. The lower classes, at the onset of tourism and non-national settlement, showed enthusiasm for the influx of foreigners and overseas capital. However, the consolidation of foreign interests in the island served to reinforce the position of the powerful classes, created limited opportunities for the indigenous small entrepreneurial class, and pushed the bulk of the population into increasingly marginal positions of impoverishment and dependency. As such, tourism and property development highlighted injustices and inequalities at community, island and international level, leading to increased feelings of helplessness, frustration and resentment amongst many of the poorest members of Bequia society.

The desperate shortage of land and housing, the inflation of prices for food and other basic necessities, and the decline in and seasonality of wage labour opportunities, following the initial boom in construction, have forced many to rely upon the fall-back systems of the household and personal networks centred around traditional economic activities in residual forms of production and social organisation.

Certain groups within the subordinate classes, notably the most disadvantaged, have been able to utilise these fall-back systems, under conditions of extreme hardship, to eke out an existence by participating in tourist related activities. Women, for instance, because of matrifocal arrangements, have been able to take advantage of limited and unstable opportunities in waged employment (as barmaids, domestics, etc.) and small scale enterprises (laundry services etc.). These represent strategies by lower class women, under conditions of increasing lower class male unemployment, to maximise their chances of survival and means of subsistence. The rising instances of households without adult male concubines reflects the changing consciousness of lower class women, which can be attributed, at least partly, to the continued dominance of foreign commercial activity on the island.

Young men, who find themselves increasingly dependent upon their households for shelter as land prices soar, have been rendered a politically conservative force in the island. They have rejected any notion of a political solution to the problem of under-development and impoverishment and have instead turned to hawking, tourist patronage and, occasionally, crime, as a means of survival. These activities, at least the former two, represent hope for young men in a potentially hopeless situation. As well as requiring the support of their households, these men look further to their friends and peers for assistance in the search for jobs and emigration opportunities, intermittently activating network ties for instrumental purposes.

Young men, who have rejected reciprocal arrangements for labour exchange in communal production, and unmarried women have effectively challenged traditional plebeian ideas relating to work and sex roles. By making use of the limited social resources available to them within lower class social organisation, these disadvantaged groups have come into conflict with institutionalised lower class practices and meaning systems. Within the wider Lower Bay community context, tourism and land speculation have produced heightened awareness of the exploitative role of foreign capitalists and local dominant classes, and polarised groups along the lines of class interests. The dynamic social and political conditions created by changes in production relations and meaning systems has provided an insight into the relationship between movements of international capital and lower class life chances in Lower Bay.

Notes

1 See Bryden, 1973:149–151, for details of the agreements relating to Canouan and Palm Island, which were leased to Americans, and of Mustique and Petit St Vincent which were sold.
2 In 1981 the 'Grenadines View', a holiday home complex, stood derelict and half-complete on the hillside overlooking Friendship. The founding US company experienced financial problems during the construction of the complex and, because of government restrictions on two-year completion and settlement of projects, which was in this case enforced, the company abandoned the project despite the possibilities of raising capital in future years.
3 The drifter tourists represent a Western 'counter culture', rejecting the middle class values of the developed societies from which they come. They have, in their own terms, reacted against the mechanistic and material view of the world and want to savour the 'backwardness' of island culture, experiencing life as 'native' as possible. Drifter tourists express a desire to interact with indigenes (notably young men) establishing forms of friendship patronage, experiencing the indigenous culture and way of life, and living as cheaply as possible.
4 The first plot of land he sold was in January 1975, to a Canadian woman, now resident in Lower Bay and acting manageress at the Frangipani Hotel in Belmont. The sale involved 43,392 sq. ft. at a cost of $3,500 EC. He has since sold two larger plots, one to a resident nationalised American (the son of the fishing supplies owner) in 1980 and one to a non-resident American in April 1981.
5 Cohen (1976) notes that the viability of pre-capitalist modes of production is crucial to the continued existence of a reserve army of labour in peripheral capitalist economies. In discussing the African context, he concludes that the ideal arrangement is:

one in which agricultural production remained sufficiently virile to produce an exportable primary product and absorb return migrants, but not so viable that it threatened the supply of cheap unskilled labour. Such a delicate balance was impossible to achieve and may indeed be considered one of the central contradictions of the colonial political economy (Cohen in Gutkind & Wallerstein (eds.), 1976:161).

6   Some drifter tourists have settled in Bequia and other Caribbean islands, becoming loosely involved in entrepreneurial activities related to the tourist industry, like wind-surfing hire, T-shirt production, etc. Others arrive with the sole purpose of securing short term employment aboard private charter yachts as a means of extending their limited budget and/or of travelling around the region. Non-nationals operating charter yachts favour giving employment to young white English-speaking non-nationals (the 'beard and bikini brigade') in preference to Bequarians. According to yacht owners this is in response to the tastes of those who charter the yachts. Charter yacht holidays tend to be arranged by hotels and tourist agents as part of a hotel-based package deal. Preference to foreign labour through the 'beard and bikini brigade' on charter yachts, and to foreigners in key positions in hotels and property companies, produces, as we have seen, resentment and ill-feeling amongst the lower classes in Bequia. Some smaller operators do, however, employ local labour largely due to the demand for lower wages.

Conclusion

Each chapter has concluded with a brief summary articulating the main focus contained therein. Consequently I concentrate below on pulling these main themes together into a final concluding statement. In order to avoid repetition the chapter will be concise and will discuss briefly the implications of the theoretical and empirical findings of the project for an understanding of lower class societies in similar marginal positions to that of Lower Bay.

Since the early stages of plantation based slavery in Bequia, the bulk of the population has been dependent upon, and controlled by, external, metropolitan powers. The history of the island, as we saw in Chapters 1 and 2, has seen the unfolding of hierarchical class relations and increased dependence on movements of international capital. The local planter class, through its alliance with metropolitan capital, has been able to consolidate its position of dominance through control over the means of production and markets. Under slavery the planters monopolised land and established an export-oriented economy: all alternative forms of production were suppressed or subordinated to the slave mode. Forms of production which reduced the need for planters to sustain their slave labour force, e.g. household gardens, small-scale fishing, were encouraged but strictly controlled in order to prevent slaves from developing a material base for production outside the plantation sphere.

Following Emancipation the planters introduced sharecropping in an attempt to limit patterns of resistance by ex-slaves, like the exodus from the estates, and thus maintain their positions of power through control of land. The decline in agricultural exports during the nineteenth century, despite attempts by the planters to maintain their power base in land, led to a shift to maritime production. The planter class monopolised the means of production and markets within the maritime mode, based upon inter-island trade and fishing, whilst retaining ownership of much of the land in the island, upon which the lower classes depended for production of essential foodstuffs. The transition to a maritime economy commercialised the system of production in the island and led, in the twentieth century, to the eventual fragmentation and sale of estates to multinational companies and foreign capitalists for the development of tourist and real estate businesses.

These transformations in production deposited pre-capitalist economic forms, subordinated to the capitalist mode; forms which have remained essential for the material survival of the lower classes and for the reproduction of the capitalist mode locally. It is within these residual forms of production, derived from earlier pre-capitalist modes and stages of capitalist development, that household and extra-domestic networks have remained significant categories for the lower classes.

One of the characteristics of many lower class households is their matrifocal nature, where the cultural mother is economically significant and ideologically and structurally central, representing a positive response by women to men's marginality. Indeed, the relationship between material factors and household form is highlighted by the flexibility of domestic organisation amongst the lower classes. The lower classes are only able to survive periods of economic demise because of institutionalised lower class practices such as child shifting, parental role replacement and partible inheritance. Such household forms and domestic organisations are typical of many Afro-Caribbean lower class societies, as the examples from Trinidad, Barbados and Guyana illustrated. However matrifocality and child shifting are not historically determined by acculturation of African practices through slavery, as many Caribbean sociologists have suggested. They are *lower class* responses to impoverishment and marginality and are widespread amongst societies with no experience of slavery.

Kinship and friendship networks outside the domestic unit constitute a further lower class fall back system in the context of the incomplete incorporation of the Bequia economy into the capitalist mode of production. The instrumental activation of bonds outside the household, essentially by lower class men, reflects the absence of adequate state provision of houses, jobs and other essential services and, as we saw in chapter 5, are essential strategies for survival in times of need.

The advent of National Bulk Carriers highlighted the relationship between traditional, household and community based social and economic organisation, and movements of international capital. Households which benefited from male employment with the company turned away from production in residual forms: gardens were left idle and fishing technology was sold or allowed to deteriorate through under-utilisation. The demise in the merchant shipping labour market in the 1970s which followed the capitalisation of the industry and recruitment of cheaper labour from Central America and the East Indies had serious consequences for those lower class households that had rejected traditional work arrangements. Many were without the necessary means of production and faced great difficulties in opening up overgrown gardens and repairing old and under-maintained fishing boats and equipment. The back-up of kin and friends was effective and essential during this transition.

The National Bulk Carriers case further illustrated the abuse of power by dominant groups in the Bequia economy. State representatives who controlled employment with the NBC 'bought' votes from the lower classes around the habour in exchange for jobs with NBC. Other powerful groups, the planter/merchant class and foreign capitalists, have been able to take advantage of lower class competition for jobs and scarce resources by playing worker off against worker. One powerful family instigated a patronage system, again, in exchange for political support, by offering food and access to plantation land; and the employment market in the CMP locally is structured and controlled by outside interests. The lower classes are powerless in the absence of trades unions and workers' representatives: wages are exploitatively low, bargaining power is minimal (reflected in the high turnover of staff in most enterprises) and working conditions are poor.

The rise of direct foreign economic involvement in the island in the form of tourist and real estate developments has further marginalised the subordinate classes: land prices have soared and access for most is now denied, prices of food, and other basic essentials, have been inflated, and competition and rivalry between individuals and groups in the same class position has been manifest in intra-community disputes. Such polarisation within the lower classes has tended to hinder any chance of them developing a united opposition to the powerful groups and classes, as we saw in Chapter 7.

Tourism and real estate, then, have worsened the socio-economic position of many of the lower classes, but for the first time in the island's history have brought them into direct face-to-face contact with representatives of those metropolitan powers that have under-developed and exploited the island and caused the marginalisation and impoverishment of the bulk of the population. This has created heightened awareness of the exploitative role of foreign capital, although the lower classes, as we saw in Chapters 6 and 7, are unable to articulate this experience collectively into effective political or cultural action. It is in this context that the concept of class, which embraces symbolic as well as social and economic elements, becomes of paramount importance in the analysis: allowing insight into the social mechanisms by which such lower class articulation of experience is inhibited and effective action suppressed.

It is not material position alone which prevents the lower classes from generalising their life experiences and channelling them into action which could effect structural changes in social relations, although material pressures, in the form of the struggle to survive, are obviously significant in reducing their potential for effective action. Abercrombie and Turner (1982) emphasise the material dimension in reference to the seasonal opposition of peasants under feudalism: the conditions of everyday life systematically inhibited active, sustained opposition by peasants to the feudal classes, the periods between harvesting and planting being the only times when material pressures on peasants were sufficiently reduced to allow any opposition.

Subordination in cultural as well as economic terms is crucial in understanding lower class responses to marginality:

> Modes of behaviour do not arise simply and directly from socio-economic experience, but from the interpretation of that experience with the cultural resources that people find historically available to them (Gray, 1976:7).

The cultural resources available to lower class Bequarians have been shaped by planter control of the means of production of discourse. The suppression of plebeian discourse has, by definition, only been possible because of their subordinate class position. For this reason, I have been concerned with the inter-relationship between material and cultural production and the implications of this inter-relationship for change. The experiences and life chances of the lower classes are the outcome of socio-economic subordination, their conception of their class experience having been mediated by the ideologies and discourses available to them shaped historically:

> ... experience is construed experience, and the symbolic forms in terms of which it is construed then determine ... its intrinsic texture (Geertz, 1975:405).

The planter class has maintained its position of power and upheld its legitimacy and the legitimacy of its value system by monopoly of the means of material and cultural production. The dialectical relationship between material and cultural factors in the subordination of the lower classes, and the suppression of effective action from them, is illustrated by the concept of the family. Lower class marginality and dependence means the household is an important fall-back system as are wider relationships with significant kinsfolk and other network members within traditional forms of production. The dominant planter ideology, however, places value on the nuclear family and domesticity. Positive evaluation of the nuclear family is, as we have seen, widely diffused in Lower Bay plebeian culture and, under favourable economic conditions, such as regular income, access to land, etc., there are shifts towards its formation.

This movement towards the consolidation of nuclear families in times of relative economic prosperity, e.g. when merchant shipping jobs were readily available in the 1960s and early 1970s, indicates the aspirational dimension of plebeian culture, currently typified by the upper strata of the lower classes (the marine proletariat and entrepreneurial class in particular) who have sought to emulate the domestic behaviour patterns of the ex-planter class within the limits set by economic circumstances, notably in leisure, residence, marriage and control of women. In discussing the role of the lower class family in social change, Poulantzas notes:

> This (the family) is one of the most tenacious sites of the inculcation of bourgeois ideology ... as a result of the decisive role in resisting a radical transformation of social relations that the family plays (1975:296, my brackets).

For the majority of the lower classes the dominant ideology of nuclear family is at odds with and in contradiction to the realities of plebeian life. Lower class impoverishment and marginality make flexible and adaptable domestic and extra-domestic arrangements essential for survival. Child shifting allows for harmonisation between production and reproduction which, together with social parenthood, reduces the risk of total failure under constraining economic conditions. Such plebeian practices clearly conflict with the nuclear family ideology.

Most lower class men and women are currently unable and unwilling to aspire to the dominant ideology of the family: marriage is not institutionalised amongst those of procreative age; residence patterns, as responses to economic circumstances, are variable and flexible; and lower class women, in responding to male economic marginality, are able to exert control over their lives by production outside the household sphere, notably in the tourist sector.

The involvement of women in production in the tourist sector is a reflection of changes in the normative conception of work. Traditionally plebeian women were expected to restrict their production activities to the domestic sphere, including agricultural work, but under increasing material deprivation female wage labour has been given existential recognition and worth within plebeian ideology. The rejection of reciprocal labour arrangements, derived from residual communal production, by many lower class men is a further indication of changes in plebeian conception of work as a result of the continued penetration of capitalism into the lower class economy.

Such changes in plebeian behaviour and conception represent a partial withdrawal of the supports of the social order and constitute a potential threat to the ideological hegemony of the planter class, wherein lies (partly) its power base. However, as we have seen, the complex interplay between ideological hegemony and subordinate material position has proved sufficient in the past to ensure the co-optation of the Bequia lower classes. It remains to be seen whether continued economic deprivation and increased dependence will result in effective, sustained action by the lower classes leading to a radical transformation of social relations.

Appendices

Appendices

Appendix I

Emigration/migration tables

The information was gathered from a house-to-house survey; it in no way represents the total numbers of migrants: it serves as an indication only of the types of movements. It was not possible to check the data against any government records.

Permanent intra-state migration from Lower Bay 1943–1980
(does not include village to Lower Bay Gutter)

Place migrated to	M/F	Age (years)	Date of migration	Reasons	No. of migrants
St Vincent	F	30s	1943	Married Vincentian, took her 3 children	4
St Vincent	M	30s	1945	Two landless brothers bought land	2
St Vincent	F	20s	1948	Marriage	1
St Vincent	F	16	1951	School leaver in search of teaching work	2
Port Elizabeth	F	?	1958	Marriage	1
Canouan Is.	F	31	1962	Married Canouan man, took her 5 children	6
Friendship	M	35	1963	Inherited land, took wife and 4 children	6

Place migrated to	M/F	Age (years)	Date of migration	Reasons	No. of migrants
Canouan Is.	M	39	1963	Fished in Canouan, married there, bought land	1
St Vincent	M F	18 20	1965	Took up employment after leaving school	2
Friendship	M	55	1965	Bought land from shipping savings	1
Friendship	M	60	1965	Bought land from savings, with wife and children	5
Paget Farm	F	28	1966	Marriage, took 4 of her children (one remained with mother)	5
Friendship	M	34	1967	Bought land to build house	1
St Vincent	M	56	1971	Married Vincentian woman, bought house from sailing savings	1
Union Island	F	25	1972	Married man from Union Island	1
St Vincent	F	19	1973	Married Vincentian	1
Port Elizabeth	F	30	1975	Marriage, took 4 children	5

Place migrated to	M/F	Age (years)	Date of migration	Reasons	No. of migrants
Level (Bequia)	M	30	1975	Bought land and built house, married seaman, took family	5
St Vincent	F	28	1975	Married Vincentian, took 2 children	3
Canouan Is.	M M	35 26	1975	Inherited land, 2 brothers fish in and around Canouan	2
Union Island	M	45	1975	Bought land, took family	5
St Vincent	M	44	1977	Bought land, ex-seaman	1
St Vincent	F	32	1979	Married Vincentian	1

International migration and emigration from Lower Bay (1939–1981)

Country emigrated to	M/F	Date left	Details	No. of migrants
Aruba	M	1939	Construction work, returned 1951	1
Aruba	M	1939	Construction work, returned 1953	1
Aruba	F	1943	Found work through kin relationship to above, married there	1

Appendices

Country emigrated to	M/F	Date left	Details	No. of migrants
USA	M	1952	Emigration scheme – work Returned 1977, died 1979	1
USA	M	1952	Emigration scheme – work	1
Barbados	M	1953	Worked on schooner, 2 brothers bought land Barbados	2
Trinidad	F	1953	Landless sharecropper, left to find work with 2 children	3
Guyana	M	1953	Young man, married Guyanese woman met while seaman	1
Grenada	F	1954	Work in nutmeg factory, married Grenadian	1
Grenada	F	1954	Friend of above woman, also work in nutmeg industry	1
USA	M	1954	Working as seaman on shipping line WI to USA, obtained Green Card	1
England	M F	1955 1956	Emigrated – work, sent for wife 18 months later	2
Barbados	M	1958	Seaman, stayed off and settled in Barbados	1
Grenada	F	1958	Young mother with son, contact through kin, work nutmeg factory	2
Barbados	M	1958	Seaman, married Barbadian woman and settled there	1
England	M	1960	Carpenter and wife emigrated under scheme	2
England	F	1960	Married man from Port Elizabeth and emigrated	1
England	M	1961	Young school leaver joined mother (above)	1
Guyana	M	1961	Seaman, settled in Guyana	1
Grenada	F	1963	Worked factory, married Grenadian, emigrated USA 1968	1

Appendices 257

Country emigrated to	M/F	Date left	Details	No. of migrants
Barbados	M	1963	Seaman, settled there	1
USA	F	1966	Au pair work, left with friends, now a nurse	1
St Thomas (US Virgin Islands)	M	1966	Hotel development employment USA 1970	1
St Thomas	M	1966	Friend of above, stayed St Thomas, electrician	1
England	F	1966	Joined sister, immigration scheme	1
Trinidad	F	1966	Joined mother who had left 1953	1
St John (Virgin Is.)	M M	1967	2 brothers, worked in tourist sector, both now settled there	2
St Thomas	M	1967	Work in developing tourist industry	1
Barbados	F	1967	School leaver, joined father (1963), working	1
England	F	1967	Joined parents (1960) immigration	1
St Thomas	M	1967	Joined friends, work in tourism now in Hawaii	1
Canada	F F F	1968	3 sisters, daughters of ex-planter, education, stayed on, 1 nurse, 2 computer programmers	3
USA	F	1968	4th sister, USA as au pair now naturalised citizen	1
England	M	1968	School leaver, joined parents (1956)	1
England	M	1968	Education, trained as engineer worked Nicaragua until 1976, now USA	1
Guyana	M	1969	Seaman, married and settled	1
USA	M	1970	Seaman (NBC) joined family works as railway man	1

Country emigrated to	M/F	Date left	Details	No. of migrants
England	F	1971	Married a man from Hamilton, emigrated	1
England	F M F	1972	3 siblings, joined mother (1960)	3
USA	F M	1973	Brother and sister (young) joined elder brother (1970)	2
England	M M	1973	2 brothers (sons of ex-planter) education	2
Grenada	F	1975	Joined godmother, working nutmeg industry (school leaver)	1
USA	M	1975	Stayed on illegally after shipping job	1
Grenada	F	1975	Searching for work, kin contacts	1
Italy	M	1978	Seaman, met Italian girl, staying there illegally	1
Trinidad	F	1979	Husband died, returned to Trinidad	1
England	F	1979	Training as nurse, father's family there	1
US Virgin Is.	M	1980	Found work in hotel (staying on visitor's visa)	1
USA	M	1981	Adopted by maternal aunt, living in USA	1

Note: there are many more cases of 'illegal' immigration entering USA and other Caribbean islands on visitor's visas, staying from periods of six months to five years.

Appendix II

Population distribution of the community

Age	Total Community			Lower Bay & Lawlers Hill			Lower Bay Gutter		
	Total	Male	Female	Total	Male	Female	Total	Male	Female
0–4	32	14	18	17	8	9	15	6	9
5–14	87	45	42	50	27	23	37	18	19
15–20	50	26	24	32	16	16	18	10	8
	169	85	84	99	51	48	70	34	36
21–30	48	25	23	34	16	18	14	9	5
31–40	36	17	19	25	12	13	11	5	6
41–50	30	13	17	20	8	12	10	5	5
51–60	20	9	11	13	5	8	7	4	3
61+	30	13	17	25	10	15	5	3	2
	164	77	87	117	51	66	47	26	21
Totals	333	162	171	216	102	114	117	60	57

Source: house-to-house survey, September 1980.

No. of households
Total community 66
Lower Bay Village & Lawlers Hill 49
Lower Bay Gutter 17

Appendix III

Annual cycle of agricultural and fishing activities

Month	Average monthly rainfall (inches) 1968–1980		Agricultural activities	Fishing 'seasons'
Jan	3.66		Green peas harvested.	Whale boats launched.
Feb	2.18			
March	1.77	Dry season, seas calm	Cassava harvesting and grinding. Dried peas collected.	Trolling for migratory fish begins.
April	1.98	↑	(Sheep/goats untethered to feed off pea trees).	Turtle and lobster season closes.
May	3.45		Planting of maize, peas, cassava and cash crops.	Trolling ends. Whale boats beached.
June	5.88			
July	6.46			
August	7.73			
Sept	6.02		Maize harvested.	Lobster and turtle season opens.
Oct	8.62	↓	Cash crops harvested (tomatoes, groundnuts, peppers).	
Nov	8.30	Wet season, high ground seas begin		
Dec	6.16			

Appendix IV

The state of emergency in the St Vincent Grenadines, 1979–1980

On 5 December 1979 the St Vincent Labour Party, under the leadership of Milton Cato, was returned to power in the St Vincent and the Grenadines General Election, winning eleven of the twelve seats in the Assembly. The New Democratic Party won the Grenadines constituency, represented by Cosmos Cozier. 'Kid' Andrews, leader of the NDP, lost in the constituency in which he had stood in St Vincent. Cozier resigned his seat on 6 December 1979 in order that Andrews might contest a Grenadines by-election and be returned to the House of Assembly. Andrews had chosen to fight a seat on the mainland in the hope of increasing the political power and influence of the party.

On the day that Cato was sworn in as Prime Minister of St Vincent, 7 December 1979, there was an attempted coup in Union Island, the police station being seized by a group of Rastafarians. On 8 December 1979, a 48-man military contingent from Barbados (requested by Cato), in association with St Vincent Police, quelled the attempted take-over and 46 people were arrested. The Government had declared a State of Emergency on 7 December, imposing a dusk-to-dawn curfew in the State until 31 December 1979. The State of Emergency, however, remained in effect until 15 May 1980, during which time there was no Representative for the Grenadines in the St Vincent House of Assembly, as the by-election could not be held until the State of Emergency was lifted. On 23 May 1980, the Government announced the date for the Grenadines by-election as 23 June 1980. The NDP, under Andrews, decided to contest the by-election on a secessionist platform, and on 31 May 1980 Andrews held the first of many political rallies in Bequia, delivering a speech entitled 'Set My People Free'. Although only the SVLP decided to stand against Andrews in the be-election, all the other main parties in the State, including the PPP, under the new leadership of Clive Taylor*, and the Marxist parties YULIMO and UPM, opposed any form of secession on the basis of economic inviability and political opportunism. The essence of the 'Grenadines Declaration' made by the NDP was that of self-determination, placing control of foreign investment in the hands of a Grenadines government. Andrews released the complete Declaration on 2 June 1980, full details of which appeared in all the national papers. The text below was printed by YULIMO in their weekly newspaper *Freedom* on 6 June 1980, p.5. The full text of this resolution reads:

> We the people of the Grenadines
>
> CONSCIOUS of the control of our destiny by people who are hostile to our aspirations
>
> SENSITIVE to the relentless exploitation of our resources without benefit to deny us representation
>
> RECOGNISING that the Constitution has been and can be violated to deny us representation
>
> SUFFERING under the deliberate restriction of our progress by forces unrepresentative of the will of our people
>
> ANXIOUS to relieve the people of St Vincent of their reluctant responsibility for the Grenadines
>
> SUPPORTING the declaration of the United Nations on the fundamental right of all subject people to self-determination
>
> CONVINCED that we are fully capable of the management of our own affairs and the development of our resources
>
> DETERMINED to free ourselves from all forms of oppression
>
> DO HEREBY RESOLVE that a referendum be called on Independence for the Grenadines to determine the will of the people of the Grenadines.

The NDP Manifesto under which it contested the General Election, had contained no reference to secession, but the Government's handling of the Union Island affair prompted Andrews to write to the Barbados Prime Minister, Tom Adams, a letter which was reprinted in the *Vincentian* (the national paper) in January 1980:

> For my part neither the violence of the uprising, nor the violence subsequently used in its suppression, provide any solution to the neglect, victimisation or colonial exploitation of the Grenadines by the St Vincent Government. These islands possess a tourism resource greater in some

ways than Barbados and granted the right framework can contribute substantially to the security of the region. (Excerpts from letter, quoted by S. Toddles, March 1980:32)

Andrews was to refer repeatedly to the development of tourism as a basis for the economic prosperity of an independent Grenadines during the lead up to the by-election. The political fervour which accompanied his speeches and declarations in Bequia reflected this concern with Government control of tourist and expatriate business in the islands.

The NDP won the election easily, but by a lower majority than in the General Election. The significance of the events surrounding the attempted coup and leading up to the by-election are discussed in detail in the main script.

---

* Joshua retired from politics on 4 June 1980, and Taylor was appointed leader of the PPP.

Bibliography

Abercrombie, N. and Turner, B. S. (1982) 'The Dominant Ideology Thesis' in Giddens, A. and Held, D. (eds.), pp.396–416
Abstracts of the Census of St Vincent, 1931, Kingstown, St Vincent, The Registry.
Aceves, J. (1971) *Social Change in a Spanish Village*, Cambridge, Mass. Schenkman Publishing Co.
Adams, J. E. (1970) 'Marine Industries of the St Vincent Grenadines, West Indies,' Unpublished Ph.D. thesis, University of Minnesota
— (1971a) 'Historical Geography of Whaling in Bequia', *Journal of Caribbean Studies*, Vol. II, No. 3, October 1971, pp.55–74
— (1971b) 'The Lobster Fishing Industry of Mount Pleasant, Bequia Island, West Indies', *Proceedings of the Gulf and Caribbean Fisheries Institutes*, November 1971, pp.126–133
— (1972) 'Maritime Industry of the St Vincent Grenadines', in *America Neptune*, Vol. XXXII, No. 3, pp.180–194
— (1976) 'Environmental and Cultural Factors in the Decline of Agriculture in a Small West Indian Island'. The University of Wisconsin, Centre for Latin America, *Centre Essay Series*, No. 7, December 1976
Annual Report of the Agricultural Department, Kingstown, St Vincent, Ministry of Trade and Agriculture
Annual Report of the Fisheries Division, 1978, 1979, Kingstown, St Vincent, Ministry of Trade and Agriculture
Annual Report of the Registrar of Co-operative Societies, 1960–64, Kingstown, St Vincent
Anon (1776) *The State of Carriacou and the other Grenadine Islands*, Oxford, Rhodes House Library
Arensberg, C. (1957): 'Discussion' in V. Rubin (ed.) (1960), pp.92–98
Barnes, J. A. (1954) 'Class and Committee in a Norwegian Parish', *Human Relations*, Vol. 7, No. 1, pp.39–58
Bastide, R. (1971) *African Civilisations in the New World*, London, Hurst & Co
Beckles, H. (1986) 'From Land to Sea: Runaway Barbados Slaves and Servants, 1630–1700', in Heuman, G. (ed.) pp.79–94
Berger, P. (1964) *The Human Shape of Work*, New York, Macmillan
Berger, P. and Luckman, T. (1967) *The Social Construction of Reality*, London, Allen Lane, Penguin
Boissevain, J. (1974) *Friends of Friends: Networks, Manipulations and Coalitions*, Oxford, Blackwell
Bottimore, T. B. and Rubel, M. (eds.) (1976) *Karl Marx: Selected Writings*, Harmondsworth, Penguin
Brown, H. H. (1945) *Fisheries of the Windward and Leeward Islands: A Report*, Bridgetown, Barbados, Advocate and Co Ltd

Brown, S. E. (1975) 'Love Unites Them and Hunger Separates Them: Poor Women in the Dominican Republic', in Reiter, R. (ed.) (1975) pp.322-332

Brown, W. H. (1967) 'Marine Fisheries of the British West Indies', ONR Contract Nonr-3656 (83) Project NR 388 067, Department of Geography, University of California, Berkeley

Bryden, J. M. (1973) *Tourism and Development*, Cambridge University Press

Chayanov, A. (1925) *The Theory of Peasant Economy*, Trans. by D. Thrower and R. E. F. Smith, Urwin Press (1966)

Clarke, E. (1966) *My Mother Who Fathered Me*, London, George Allen & Unwin

Cohen, A. P. (1979) 'The Whaling Craft: Traditional Work and Customary Identity in Modern Times', in Wallman (ed.), 1979

Cohen, E. (1971) 'Arab Boys and Tourist Girls in a Mixed Jewish-Arab Community', *International Journal of Comparative Sociology*, Vol. 12, No. 4, pp.217-233

(1972) 'Towards a Sociology of International Tourism', *Social Research* Vol. 39, No. 1, pp.164-182

Cohen, R. (1976) 'From Peasants to Workers in Africa', in Gutkind and Wallerstein (eds.) (1976)

De Kadt, E. (1979) *Tourism - Passport to Development?*, Oxford University Press

Deas, B. (1981) 'Relations of Production in the Scottish Inshore Fishing Industry', *International Journal of Sociology and Social Policy*, Vol. 1, No. 2

Denich, B. (1974) 'Sex and Power in the Balkans', in Rosaldo (ed.) (1974) pp.243-262

Dirks, R. (1972) 'Networks, Groups and Adaptation in an Afro-Caribbean Community', *Man (NS)*, Vol. 7, No. 4, pp.565-585, December 1972

Duncan, E. (1941) *A Brief History of St Vincent*, Kingstown, St Vincent, Government House

Eisenstadt, (1956) *From Generation to Generation*, London, Routledge & Kegan Paul

Electoral Register for the St Vincent Grenadines, (1979) Kingstown, St Vincent

Forster, J. (1964) 'The Sociological Consequences of Tourism', *International Journal of Comparative Sociology*, Vol. 5, No. 2, pp.217-227

Frank, C. (1976) *The History of Begos - the Grenadines from Columbus to Today*, Barbados, Consultant Sales & Marketing, Christchurch

Frazier, E. F. (1939) *The Negro Family in the USA*, University of Chicago Press

(1957) *The Negro in the US*, (revised edition) Toronto, Macmillan

Friedl, E. (1964) *Vasilika: a Village in Modern Greece*, New York, Holt, Rinehard & Winston

Geertz, C. (1975) *The Interpretation of Cultures*, Londo, Hutchinson & Co

Gibson, G. (1981) 'Ranking and Reciprocity in Bequia', Unpublished Ph.D. thesis, University College, Swansea

Giddens, A. and Held, D. (eds.) (1982) *Class, Power and Conflict*, London, Macmillan Books

Goffman, E. (1959) *The Presentation of Self in Everyday Life*, New York,

Doubleday

Gonzalez, N. L. (1970) 'Towards a Definition of Matrifocality', in Whitten & Szwed (eds.) (1970) pp.231–244

Gray, R. Q. (1976) *The Labour Aristocracy in Victorian Edinburgh*, Oxford, Clarendon Press

Greenfield, S. M. (1961) 'Socio-Economic Factors and Family Form', *Social and Economic Studies*, Vol. 10, No. 1, pp. 72–85

Greenfield, S. M. (1966) *English Rustics in Black Skins*, New Haven, Connecticut, College and University Press (sub-titled: *A Study of Modern Family Forms in a Pre-Industrialised Society*)

Gudeman, S. (1976) *Relationships, Residence and the Individual: a Rural Panamanian Community*, London, Routledge & Kegan Paul

Gutman, H. (1977) *The Black Family in Slavery and Freedom, 1750–1925*, New York, Vintage Books

Gutkind, P. C. W. and Wallerstein, I. (eds.) (1976) *The Political Economy of Contemporary Africa*, London, Sage

Handler, J. S. (1974) *The Unappropriated People*, London, Johns Hopkins Press

Harding, P. (1980) 'Behind God's Back', Unpublished Ph.D. thesis, University College, Swansea

Harris, C. C. (1969) *The Family*, London, George, Allen & Unwin

Herskovits, M. J. (1937) *Life in a Haitian Village*, New York, Knopf

(1941) *The Myth of the Negro Past*, New York, Knopf

Herskovits, M. J. and F. S. (1934) *Rebel Destiny: Among the Bush Negroes of Dutch Guiana*, New York, McGraw-Hill

(1964) *Trinidad Village*, New York, Ontagon Books (reprint from 1947)

Heuman, G. (ed.) (1986) *Out of the House of Bondage: runaways, resistance and marronage in Africa and the New World*, London, Frank Cass

Hindess, B. and Hirst, R. (1975) *Pre-Capitalist Modes of Production*, London, Routledge & Kegan Paul

Kobben, A. J. F. (1963) 'Unity and Disunity: Cottica Djuka Society as a Kinship System', in Price, R. (ed.) (1973)

Kunstadter, D. (1963) 'A Survey of the Consanguine or Matrifocal Family', *American Anthropologist*, Vol. 65, 1963, pp.56–66

Lenin, V. I. (1971) [1919] *A Great Beginning: Selected Works Vol. III*, Moscow, Progress Publishers

Levi-Strauss, C. (1972) *Structural Anthropology*, Harmondsworth, England, Penguin University Press

Lowenthal, D. (1972) *West Indian Societies*, London, Oxford University Press

Lukas, A. (1971) 'The Plaint of the Virgin Islands', *New York Times Magazine*, 10 April 1971, p.30 and pp.101–110

Mack, A. 'On the Fourth Caribbean Tourism Conference in Santo Domingo, June 1980', quoted in *Caribbean Life and Times*, Vol. 1, No. 5, 1980, p.61

Marshall, W. K. (1968) 'Notes on Peasant Development in the West Indies since 1838', *Social and Economic Studies*, Vol. 17, No. 3, September 1968

Marx, K. (1845) *The German Ideology*, as quoted in Bottimore and Rubel (eds.) (1976)

Marx, K. and Engels, F. (1968) *Selected Works*, Lawrence & Wishart
Matthews, B. (1953) *The Crisis of the West Indian Family*, Trinidad, Extra-Mural Department, University of West Indies
Meillassoux, C. (1981) *Maidens, Meals and Money*, Cambridge University Press
Mintz, S. (ed.) (1960) *Papers in Caribbean Anthropology*, Nos. 57–64, Yale University, Yale University Publications in Anthropology
Mitchell, J. C. (ed.) (1969) *Social Networks in Urban Situations: Analyses of Personal Relationships in Central African Towns*, Manchester University Press
Morris, V. (1776) *Memoirs*, published and held in Registry, Kingstown, St Vincent
Mukherjee, R. (1957) *The Dynamics of a Rural Society*, Berlin, Akademie-Verlag
Ober, F. A. (1880) *Camps in the Caribbees: The Adventures of a Naturalist in the Lesser Antilles*, Edinburgh, David Douglas
Parkin, F. (1971) *Class, Inequality and Political Order*, London, MacGibbon & Kee
Patchett, K. W. (1959) 'Some Aspects of Divorce and Marriage in the West Indies', *International and Comparative Law Quarterly*, October 1959
Peach, C. (1968) *West Indian Migration to Britain*, London, Oxford University Press
Pitt-Rivers, J. A. (1954) *The People of the Sierra*, Chicago, University of Chicago Press
(1977) *The Fate of Shechem or the Politics of Sex: Essays in the Anthropology of the Mediterranean*, Cambridge University Press
Population Census of the Commonwealth Caribbean (1979) Vol. IX, Jamaica, Census Research Programme, University of West Indies, Mona
Post, K. (1978) *Arise Ye Starvelings: the Jamaican Labour Rebellion of 1938 and its Aftermath*, The Hague, Institute of Social Studies, Martinus Nijhoff
Poulantzas, N. (1973) *Political Power and Social Classes*, London, New Left Books
(1975) *Classes in Contemporary Capitalism*, London, New Left Books
Price, N. (1984) 'Behind the Planter's Back: Work, Change and Ideology in a lower class Afro-Caribbean Community, University of Bristol, unpublished Ph.D. thesis
Price, R. (1966) 'Caribbean Fishing and Fishermen – a Historical Sketch', *American Anthropologist*, Vol. 68, No. 6, December 1966, pp.1363–83
(1973) *Maroon Societies*, New York, Doubleday Anchor Books
Radcliffe-Brown, A. R. (1952) *Structure and Function in Primitive Society*, Illinois, Glencoe Press
Reiter, R. (ed.) (1975) *Toward an Anthropology of Women*, London, Monthly Review Press
Robinson, C. (1969) *The Fighting Maroons of Jamaica*, Collins & Sangster (Jamaica) Ltd.
Rodman, H. (1971) *Lower Class Families*, London, Oxford University Press
Rosaldo, M. (1974) 'A Theoretical Overview', in Rosaldo & Lampere (eds.) pp.17–43

Rosaldo, M. Z. and Lamphere, L. (eds.) (1974) *Woman, Culture and Society*, Stamford, California, Stamford University Press
Rubbo, A. (1975) 'The Spread of Capitalism in Rural Colombia: Effects on Poor Women', in Reiter (ed.) pp.333-357
Rubin, V. (ed.) (1960) '*Caribbean Studies: A Symposium*', Seattle, University of Washington Press
St Vincent Bluebooks, Kingstown, St Vincent, 1831, 1835, 1851, 1854
St Vincent Government Gazette (1876) Kingstown, St Vincent and (1888) 'Land and House Tax Rolls', Kingstown, St Vincent
Schneider, J. (1971) 'Of Vigilance and Virgins: Honour, Shame and Access to Resources in Mediterranean Societies', *Ethnology*, Vol. X, No. 1, January 1971, pp.1-24
Shanin, T. (1966) 'The Peasantry as a Political Factor', *Sociological Review*, Vol. 14, No. 1, pp.5-27
Shephard, C. (1831) *An Historical Account of the Island of St Vincent*, Frank Cass & Co Ltd (reprint 1971)
Sheppard, J. (1974) 'A Historical Sketch of the "Poor Whites" of Barbados: from Indentured Servants to Redlegs', *Journal of Caribbean Studies*, Vol. 14, No. 3, pp.71-94
Smith, M. G. (1953) 'Some Aspects of Social Structure in the British Caribbean about 1820', *Social and Economic Studies*, Vol. 1, No. 4, August 1953, pp.55-80
  (1962) *West Indian Family Structure*, Seattle, University of Washington Press
  (1966) 'Introduction', to Clarke, E. pp.i-xliv
Smith, R. T. (1956) *The Negro Family in British Guiana*, London, Routledge & Kegan Paul
Toddles, S. V. (1980) 'Is There Something to Fear', in *The Bajan*, No. 316, March 1980, Barbados, Carib Publicity Co, p.32
Turton, A. (1986) 'Patrolling the Middle Ground: Methodological Perspectives on "Everyday Peasant Resistance",' *Journal of Peasant Studies*, Vol. 13, No. 2, Jan. 1986 pp.36-48
Van Onselen, C. (1976) *Chibaro: African Mine Labour in Southern Rhodesia*, London, Pluto Press
Wallman, S. (1979) 'Introduction', in Wallman, S. (ed.) (1979)
  (ed.) (1979) *The Social Anthropology of Work*, London, Academic Press
Whitten, N. and Szwed, J. F. (eds.) (1970) *Afro-American Anthropology*, New York, Free Press
Wilson, P. J. (1973) *Crab Antics: the Social Anthropology of English-speaking Negro Societies of the Caribbean*, New York, Yale University Press
Wolf, E. (1957) 'Closed corporate peasant communities in Mesop-America and Central Java', *South-western Journal of Anthropology*, Vol. 13, No. 1
Young, Sir W. (1764) *Considerations which may tend to Promote the Settlement of our New West Indian Colonies*, London
  (1795) *An Account of the Black Charaibs in the Island of St Vincent*, London, Frank Cass & Co, (reprint 1971)

Index

Accommodation: for tourists, 75
Accretion: of household members, 127–8
Admiralty Bay, 17, 30; fishing in, 77
Adoption, 122, 123; and child shifting, 124
Affinal households, 103, 105–6, 108–9, 136; and common law unions, 113
African heritage: and family structure, 132–3, 246
Age: categories, 197; and household head, 110; and small-scale entrepreneurial activities, 89
Agriculture, 89–95, 223; annual cycle, 260; in Bequia, 10–13, 52; community, 24; decline in, 14, 19, 29, 241; plantation, 19; women in, 23, 68, 89, 134
Andrews, 'Kid', NDP leader, 42–4, 235, 261–3

Barbados, 7, 10; household comparison, 135; (International) Shipping, 18; poor whites from, 36
Belmont, 12, 13, 28, 30
Bequia: community, 193; dependence in, 27–49; 'dinghies', 28, 77; 'drought' 19; French in, 7, 192; history of, 6–26; interdependence in, 27–49; the island, 1; settlements on, 27–38; society in, 27; Vincentians role in, 46–7
Binary opposition, 185, 186
Boat building, 1, 14, 15, 17, 28, 31, 38; decline in, 20; at Paget Farm, 33; whale, 16, 32
Boat ownership, 76–7; in Lower Bay, 78–9
Bonded alien labour system, 59–60

Canouan, 37, 184; and fishing, 16, 23, 80, 157; and tourism, 207

Capital, international, 3, 6, 30, 245; dependence on, 24–5, 38; dominance by, 3, 38–49, 179, 206, 220, 241; export of, 209; expropriation, 8, 20
Capital investment: lack of, 212–3, 214
Capitalism, 11, 24, 174
Caribbean: steamships, 18; tourism, 206
Caribs, 21; wars, 7
Carriacou: cotton in, 8; fishing in, 80
Cassava: mill, 55, 93; baking, 93–4; harvest, in Lower Bay, 92–4; ownership of, 92
Casual work, 95, 96
Child-shifting, 4, 120, 122–6, 128–9, 135, 199, 246, 249; and poverty, 123–4
Church: and respect, 167
Class, 11, 247; dominant, 3, 7, 9, 23; and ideology, 161; middle, 51–2; relations, 6; and state, 3, 27; *see also under* Ex-planter class; Lower classes
CMP, capitalist mode of production, 3, 7, 20, 21, 24, 28, 38, 50–1, 70, 98, 99, 219, 225, 247; and employment, 76; instability of, 76
Communal activities, 2, 21–4, 52, 99; decline in, 98, 225; production, 95–8; rejection of, 97–8
Community: child-shifting within, 126; concept of, 1; identity, 31, 181, 193; Lower Bay, 1–4, 31; and shame, 172; stratification in, 213–5, 217
Conjugal: households, 127; instability of, 104, 199; unions, 130
Consanguineal households, 103, 105, 107–9; matrifocal, 109
Cotton, 8, 10, 12; collapse of, 19; Sea Island, 19
Crown lands: sale of, 12–13

269

Culture: of lower classes, 4, 160–205
Curaçao, 17, 41; migration to, 54, 55
Customary work activities, 30, 38, 52, 225; status of, 53

Development cycle: of households, 103–4
Diamond estate, 13, 92, 218
Discourse, 188; and culture, 161–4; suppression of, 162–3, 180, 185, 192, 203–5, 248
Drinking: as social activity, 154; and women, 171
Dyadic relations: networks of, 4, 158

Economic activities, 2, 236; attitudes to foreign, 214; and family structure, 133–6; foreign, 19–20, 247; and household form, 102; and respect, 173
Emancipation, 22, 36, 245; and agriculture, 10–13; and migration, 54
Emigrants: remittances from, 1, 20, 30, 38, 48, 52, 61
Emigration, 10, 17, 70, 226; difficulties of, 230; from Lower Bay, 255–8
Employment: direct, 223; indirect, 223; investment related, 223–4; in merchant shipping, 17, 28, 66; opportunities, 3, 29, 214; and peer groups, 150; private sector, 64–70; public sector, 61–4; seasonal, 1, 30, 48, 61, 67, 69, 224; temporary, 1, 30, 48, 61, 68, 69, 224; in tourism, 209, 214; in whaling, 16
Entrepreneurial activities, 54, 70–89
Estates: fragmentation of, 18, 19, 23
Ethnic minorities, in Caribbean, 183
European: colonialism, 7–10; expansionism, 8
Expatriate: entrepreneurs, 3, 4, 18, 27, 45–6, 215
Ex-planter class, 4, 7, 17, 50; dominance of, 27, 163, 179, 180, 245; and friendship network, 154–5; ideology, 160–3, 188; and kinship terms, 202; and tourism, 208–9
Exploitation: in employment, 67, 99, 214, 247; by foreign investors, 222, 241, 243, 247; and tourism, 214, 225

Exports, from Bequia, 9, 12, 15, 16, 19

Family: biological, 102; concept of, 102–3, 248; flexibility of, 129, 130; and material conditions, 129–30; structure of, 116, 129–36
Family land, 117–19; dispute over, 117–19; inheritance of, 117; sale of, 209
Farine, cassava flour, 92, 94
Favouritism: to siblings, 120–2, 129, 143
Fillet fishing, 14, 80, 81, 86–8
Fishing, 1, 15, 38, 45, 52, 76–89, 223, 245; annual cycle, 260; commercialisation, 16, 22–4; competition in, 80–1; costs of, 87–8; crews, 77, 80–1; ice-storage transports, 16, 73, 88; in Lower Bay, 30–1; markets for, 31, 88; and peer groups, 151, 152–3; petty-commodity, 2, 31, 73–4, 77, 225; prices for, 80; residual production, 29, 44; share in, 76, 80, 82; by slaves, 13; small-scale, 14, 24, 77
Foreign investment, 4; influence of, 67; in tourism and real estate, 207–9, 213–4, 220, 242
Foreigners: dominance by, 241–3; help from, 220
Fostering, 122, 123
Friendship: Bay hotel, 31; estate, 1, 10, 13, 15, 17, 31–2, 58; migration to, 100, 114; sharecropping, 92
Friendship networks, 2, 4, 61, 69, 71, 95, 100, 139, 145–57, 246
Fruit: small-scale production, 71, 91

Gender: and household tasks, 166; and properness, 169–72
Girls: peer groups of, 145–6
Grandparents: and kinship, 141–3
Grenada, 8
Grenadines: 'Declaration', 262; independence of, 235–41, 261–3; *see also under* St Vincent and the Grenadines

Hamilton, 28–30, 114, 193
Hawking, 28, 30, 67, 71, 72, 223, 226–8, 242; and age, 89; of fruit, 71,

91; and respect, 174; and Vincentian competition, 47, 99
Headship: of household, 103–4; age of, 110, 113, 127; and respect, 167–8; responsibilities of, 111; sex of, 108, 109, 110
Holiday: let accommodation, 32, 34, 55, 218; homes, 209
Honour: in plebeian culture, 164–5
Households: agricultural production of, 90; and boat ownership, 77–9; composition, 106–7, 126–9; concept of, 102–3; conjugal, 127; cycle, 126; distribution, 109–10; as fall back system, 100, 248–9; and family, in Lower Bay, 102–38; form, 4; formation, 111–14, 126, 170; and inheritance, 114; and material conditions, 130–6; organisation of, 3–4; and respect, 167, 168–9; sizes, 105; skills, 15; types, 108; as unit of production, 52; *see also* Affinal; Consanguineal; Headship: of household; Matrifocal
Housing, 29; construction, 45–6, 223–4; for nationals, 212; and peer groups, 151; shortage, 242
Hurricanes, 82; Allen, 74, 92, 143, 221; damage by, 92, 95

Ideology, 248; aspirational, 178–9; conflicts in, 179; deferential, 178; dominant, 4, 177, 180, 203–5; in Lower Bay, 4
Illigitimacy: and household formation, 111; and inheritance, 115–16, 117
Immigration: illegal, 57–9; to UK, 17, 56–7; to USA, 17, 56
Industry estate, 18, 29
Industry: in Caribbean, 59
Inequality: lower class response to, 3, 100, 163; perceptions of, 99, 176; and tourism, 221–2, 242
Inflation, 212, 242, 247
Infrastructure: development of, 208; lack of, 212, 241
Inheritance, 114–22; customary, 117; and kinship, 140; partible, 134, 246
Inter-island trading, 14, 16, 19, 22–4, 32, 38, 65, 245; employment in, 64, 158; growth in, 17; vessels for, 23

Intestacy: and inheritance, 117; and kinship, 140

James, Gerald, 218; as cassava mill owner, 92; as pig breeder, 91
Jameson family, 32, 33; William T., 15

Kingstown, St Vincent, 190, 193, 236; fish market, 15, 16, 82, 88
Kinship networks, 2, 4, 61, 69, 71, 100, 103, 139–45, 197, 246; corporate, 140; extra-domestic, 141; and labour exchange, 95; patterns, 139–45; structure, 102; terms, 198–202

La Pompe, 12, 31, 32–3, 65, 142
Labour, 2; exchange, 2, 95–8, 153; international division of, 182; reserve of, 23, 24; and schooners, 14; seamen, 17, 18; sexual division of, 23, 69, 91, 130, 146, 155, 226; Vincentian, 46–7; *see also* Wage labour
Lafayette: family, 15, 32, 33, 192
Lafayette, Len: as cassava mill owner, 92, 93; as land owner, 217–8, 221; migration by, 54–5; and networks; 155–7; as seine owner, 55, 83
Land: and intestacy, 116; as means of production, 100; ownership, 13; price of, 30, 45, 209, 217–8, 221, 247; and property developers, 18, 19; sale of, 19, 45, 116, 245; settlement, 12, 13; shortage, 1, 3, 10, 61, 242; size, of holdings, 19; speculation, 209; and stratification, 217–8; value, 119; *see also* Crown lands; Marginality: of land
Language, 166; and discourse, 161
Laundry work, 74–5
Lawler's Hill, 1, 2, 30, 67, 152, 168; household size, 105
Lobster fishing, 33, 36–7, 77
Lower Bay, 30–1, 67; agriculture in, 90; cassava harvest, 92–4; child shifting in, 126; community, 1, 2, 21; culture, 160–205; economy, 50–101; household and family in, 102–38; international migration, 255–8; and intra state migration, 253–5; membership of, 2; in plebeian

classification, 180–202; political economy, 3; population of, 259; village, 1, 12; wage labour in, 62–3; women in, 68–9
Lower Bay Gutter (Friendship), 1, 2, 30, 67, 91, 171; household size, 105; land in, 217
Lower classes, 50; conflicts in, 179; culture, 4, 160–205; economic activity, 28; frustration by, 99, 179, 221, 242; and marriage, 114; practices, 4; resentment by, 99, 214, 242; response to inequality, 3

Marginality, 3, 4, 20, 23, 24, 52, 59, 61, 98, 204, 242, 248, 249; in agriculture, 90, 95; and child-shifting, 125; for ex-slaves, 12; of land, 11; of men, 129, 226, 246
Maritime activities, 1, 20, 22–4; production, 13–18, 19, 245
Markets: access to, 3, 236; for fish, 77; and merchant class dominance, 88; world, 8
Maroons, 132–3, 136
Marriage, 249; and child-shifting, 124; common law, 112, 113, 130; legal, 112, 114, 129, 134, 135, 136, 199; and peer groups, 150; rates, 114, 115; and respect, 170
Martinique, 16, 20, 37, 73, 88
Material conditions: change in, 226, 248; and culture, 160; and family, 129; and household, 130–6; and networks, 154–5, 158; and sibling relationship, 143, 144
Matrifocality, 4, 59; and child-shifting, 124; of households, 68–9, 74, 102, 103, 104, 129, 133–6, 141, 226, 246; and inheritance, 114
Meaning: and culture, 161–4
Men: in fishing, 89; and friendship networks, 145; in household, 127; marginality, 128, 129, 226, 246; and respect, 170; small-scale production, 71; stereotype for, 147; wage labour for, 67, 69
Merchant (ex-planter) class, 7, 50; dominance by, 23–4, 27; and petty-commodity fishing, 88
Merchant shipping: companies, 17–18; decline in, 20, 29, 70, 206, 246;

employment in, 17, 38, 56, 59, 65, 67, 75, 153, 158, 236
Migration, 3, 17, 30, 38, 54–61, 70, 100, 226; in 1950s, 56; inter-state, 253–5; international, 255–8
Mother, biological: and child-shifting, 123; – child relationship, 140; and worth, 171
Mount Pleasant, 13, 36–7, 65, 207; community, 37, 38, 193; tourism in, 37

NBC, National Bulk Carriers, 17, 18, 28, 37, 38–45, 58, 112, 153, 194, 246, 247; and employment, 39–41, 44, 64, 65, 219
NDP, New Democratic Party, 235, 241, 261, 263
Networks, 204, 249; categories, 195; definition of, 139; and economic change, 158; and employment, 153; exchanges within, 153
Nicknames: use of, 200–1
Nuclear family, 108–9, 136, 204, 249

Occupations: of Lower Bay, 67
Oil refinery construction industry, 17, 54, 55
Outsiders: categories of, 183, 184

Paget Farm estate (Derrick), 9, 10, 12, 13, 15, 31, 65; community, 33–6, 194–5
Parental role replacement, 4, 122, 123–6, 128, 246
Patronage, 247; tourist, 226, 228–35, 240, 242
Peasant production: restrictions, 90; small-scale, 1, 10–13, 51, 89–90, 225; by women, 14
Petty-commodity production, 21–4, 51, 70–89; whaling, 15
Peer groups: boys, 146–51; girls, 145–6; importance of, 149–51, 157; reciprocity in, 152–3
Place: within Bequia, 193–7; in Lower Bay community, 197–202; within world, 180–93
Plantation sugar production, 22; in Bequia, 9; in St Vincent, 9; and slavery, 7–10
Planter class: dominance by, 23–4,

163, 245, 248; and land monopolisation, 11, 13; and land sales, 18, 19; and maritime economy, 14, 17
Plebeian: classificatory systems, 180–202; culture, 163, 241–3, 249; gender roles, 169–70; and work, 173
Polarisation, 247; generational, 222
Population, 1, 3, 9, 11, 43, 100; distribution, of Lower Bay, 259
Port Elizabeth (the harbour), 28, 45, 114, 193; fish market, 77
PPP, People's Political Party, 41–2
Pregnancy: teenage, and respect, 167–8
Primary socialisation, 166–9
Production: and child-shifting, 125; dependence in, 3; means of, 3, 4; modes of, 3, 6–7, 24, 50–2; relations of, 4, 6, 50–1, 179; residual, 6, 52, 61, 99, 176, 206, 219, 224, 246; small-scale, 71; *see also* CMP
Properness, 187, 193, 195–6; and gender, 169–72; *see also* Worth
Property: development, 45–6, 67; speculators, 4
Preovision grounds, 29, 32, 102; return to, 42, 44
Purse seine, 81, 82, 88

Rastafarianism, 182, 188–91, 201
Real estate, 206–44, 246, 247; enterprises, 4; labour in, 64, 69
Reciprocal work, 96–7, 220, 225, 242; decline in, 98, 250
Relationships, 1–2, 6, 7; kinship, and family, 102–3, 139–45; male, 148–51; parent-child, 140; of production, 50; of siblings, 120–2
Residual forms of production, 29, 44, 52, 61, 99, 176, 206, 219, 224, 246
Respect, 163, 166–9; and gender, 169–72; as ideology, 177–80; and shame, 164; and work, 172–7, 226
Rum shops, 58, 72, 171, 219; disputes at, 84, 168–9, 214; ownership of, 72; and peer groups, 154, 157

Sailing, 15, 67; skills, 16
St Vincent and the Grenadines, 1, 7; by-election, 1980, 204, 235–41; citizenship of, 187, 188; emigration from, 56–7; housing in, 212; inheritance laws, 114–16; population, 10–11; seamen in, 14; state of emergency, 1970–80, 261–2; and tourism, 45, 207
Seamanship, 1, 29; Bequia reputation of, 16–17, 39; skills of, 16–17, 23, 45; as work, 30, 64, 66
Schooner: aristocracy, 14, 15, 88; construction, 14, 17, 22–4, 28, 38; trading, 15, 54, 88; wooden, 32
Secession: of Grenadines, 235–41, 261–3
Seine fishing, 14, 16, 23, 77, 80, 81–7, 236–7, 240; costs of, 87–8; dependence on, 85–6; by Lafayette, 55, 83; share dispute, 82–5
Services, 223; provision of, 74–6
Shame, 163, 164–72; as ideology, 177–80
Share system, in fishing, 15, 76, 80, 82–5, 87–8, 153; exploitation in, 99
Sharecropping, 1, 2, 10–13, 19, 20, 21–4, 32, 51, 89–90, 245; and fishing, 14; by women, 14, 91–2, 94
Sibling: bond, 143–5; female groups, 122; relationships, 120–2, 143
Skin, colour of, 29, 30, 31, 43–4; classification, 195–6
Slavery, 8–10, 99, 187, 245; and culture, 162–3; exploitation in, 13, 182; and family structure, 131
Small-scale peasant production, 1, 9, 10, 21–4
Smuggling, 223; and rum shops, 72
Southside, 65, 77, 193–5
Spring estate, 13, 18, 29, 41, 241; land sales at, 45–6
Squatting, 12, 29
Stratification: and land, 217–8; through tourism, 213–5
Structural functionalist theory, 133–4
Subsistence agriculture, 10, 12, 32, 77, 91, 95; and child-shifting, 125; return to, 48–9
Sugar production, 8, 9, 10, 11, 12, 16
Sunny Caribbee complex, Belmont, 30
Surnames: and kinship, 199–200
SVLP, St Vincent Labour Party, 42, 235, 240, 261

Taylor, family, 41–3, 208
Tourism, 4, 17, 28, 64, 183, 206–44, 246, 247; dissatisfaction in, 224–5; effects of, 49, 208–9; employment in, 20, 38, 67, 174; enterprises, in Bequia, 210–11; and land development, 18, 19, 45–6; in Lower Bay, 31, 213–35; men in, 69; monopoly in, 217; and the State, 207–13; women in, 68, 146, 249–50
Trading: inter-island, 14, 16, 22–4; maritime, 14; schooner, 15; small-scale, 71–4
Tramil netting, 80; cost of, 80
Trinidad: household comparison, 135; tourism in, 206; work in, 54, 58

UK: Commonwealth Immigration Scheme, 56; migration to, 56–7
Under-employment, 17, 20, 61
Unemployment, 17, 20, 39, 61; and attitude to tourism, 214; and CMP, 76; male, 146; and patronage, 228
Union, 37; and fishing, 16, 23, 80
USA: illegal entry, 57–9; migration to, 56
Use-values, 77

Vincentians: perception of, 187–8, 216; in public sector employment, 61–4; role in Bequia economy, 46–7, 48
Virgin Islands, US: and bonded alien labour system, 59–60; and network ties, 158; and smuggling, 72

Visiting: relationship, 112, 134

Wage labour, 4, 12, 15, 30, 38–49, 51, 52, 54–70, 175; changes in, 176; decrease in, 20; demand for, 70; opportunities, 20, 23, 242; redundancies, 95
Wage rates, 39, 68–70, 96, 176, 224, 247
Walters family, 28, 200, 235, 240; and family land, 117–19; and networks, 157; Samuel, 218; Stephen, 218–9
Wealth: classification by, 196–7
Whaling, 14, 15–16, 22–4, 28, 33, 64
Women: in agriculture, 89, 91; in conjugal households, 127; employment for, 56, 63, 67–9, 89, 179, 225, 242, 250; and friendship networks, 145–6; groups of, 91–3; independence of, 134–6, 146, 249; migration by, 56; and patronage, 234; and respect, 169–72; and service provision, 74–5; and shame, 165, 170–2; and small-scale production, 71; in tourism, 68, 146, 249–50
Work, 4, 53; and community life, 173–4; patterns of, 222–8; and respect, 167, 172–7; salaried, 175, 176, 225; values, 225
Worth, 164, 192–3, 225, 227, 250; evaluation of, 165; and household, 171; *see also* Properness

Yachts, charter, 45, 220; crews on, 67, 174